the microwave
kitchen handbook

the microwave kitchen handbook

How to get the best out of your
microwave: techniques, tips, guidelines
and 160 step-by-step recipes

carol bowen

southwater

This edition is published by Southwater, an imprint of Anness Publishing Ltd,
108 Great Russell Street, London WC1B 3NA; info@anness.com

www.southwaterbooks.com; www.annesspublishing.com; twitter: @Anness_Books

If you like the images in this book and would like to investigate using them
for publishing, promotions or advertising, please visit our website www.practicalpictures.com
for more information.

A CIP catalogue record for this book is available from the British Library.

Publisher: Joanna Lorenz
Editor: Bridget Jones
Indexer: Hilary Bird
Designer: William Mason

NOTES

For all recipes, quantities are given in both metric and imperial measures and,
where appropriate, in standard cups and spoons. Follow one set of measures,
but not a mixture, because they are not interchangeable.
Standard spoon and cup measures are level.
1 tsp = 5ml, 1 tbsp = 15ml, 1 cup = 250ml/8fl oz.
Australian standard tablespoons are 20ml.
Australian readers should use 3 tsp in place of
1 tbsp for measuring small quantities.
American pints are 16fl oz/2 cups. American readers should use
20fl oz/2.5 cups in place of 1 pint when measuring liquids.
Electric oven temperatures in this book are for conventional ovens.
When using a fan oven, the temperature will probably need to be reduced
by about 10–20°C/20–40°F. Since ovens vary, you should check
with your manufacturer's instruction book for guidance.
Medium (US large) eggs are used unless otherwise stated.

PUBLISHER'S NOTE

CONTENTS

Introduction

Undeniably, speed is the main advantage of microwave cooking; however, it is not this in isolation that has made microwaves the success story they are. Not only do microwaves make light work of cooking many staple dishes and family favourites, but they also cook them to perfection. With a microwave cooker, limp, soggy greens, over-sticky rice, nutritionally poor fruit-based desserts and labour- and time-intensive meat, fish and poultry dishes are things of the past; these emerge from the microwave fresh, colourful, nutritionally rich and, moreover, most appetizing. The time-saving aspect may be great, as when cooking a jacket potato in about 6 minutes, or minimal, for example in the case of rice and pasta, but the additional benefit is being able to cook foods with the minimum attention and to just the right degree, be it *al dente*, tender-crisp, fork-tender or succulently moist.

ADVANTAGES OF MICROWAVE COOKING

Speed
You can reduce normal cooking times by up to 75 per cent by using a microwave oven.

Nutrient Retention
Nutrient loss from food is often associated with other cooking methods. With microwave cooking, since timings are short and so precise, and additional cooking liquid is minimal, there is less likely to be a loss of nutrients during cooking or by seepage as when boiling.

Economy
Since microwave cooking does not involve a lengthy preheating period and cooks for a shorter period of time, this method requires less energy and therefore saves money on energy bills.

Few Cooking Smells
Cooking odours are usually contained within the microwave oven cavity, so kitchen odours are kept to an absolute minimum.

Cool Kitchen
Because of the mechanics of microwave cooking, the microwave oven, dishes and the kitchen all stay cool, while only the food becomes piping hot. Also, in kitchens where there is a problem with ventilation, the microwave is a great improvement on the conventional hob, which creates a lot of steam during boiling or other moist cooking methods.

Less Risk of Burns
Since dishes do not become red hot, but only heat up by the conduction of heat from the food, there is less risk of getting a nasty

burn from dishes or from the oven itself. This makes the microwave one of the safest cooking machines for the very young and for the elderly or infirm to use.

Less Cleaning and Washing Up
It is possible to cook and serve in the same container with microwave cooking, thereby reducing the amount of washing up. Cleaning the cooker is also easier as food does not bake on or splatter as found in conventional ovens and on hobs.

An End to Dried-out Dinners
With a microwave oven, dried-out dinners can become a thing of the past. Individual members of the family can eat when they want and late-comers can have a meal reheated in minutes to just-cooked perfection.

SELECTING FOOD FOR MICROWAVE COOKING

Apart from a few restrictions, virtually any food can be cooked in the microwave, but there are some foods that cook better than others. When planning a meal or choosing a recipe consider the following:

Fish and Shellfish
Whether fresh or frozen, whole or filleted, plain cooked or in a fancy sauce, microwave-cooked fish and shellfish are hard to beat for texture, flavour, appearance and ease of preparation. With little fear of drying out, these delicate foods stay succulently moist. Often, the only additional ingredients required are a tablespoon or two of water, lemon juice or stock, or a little butter, so fish and seafood are favourites with those following a healthy diet regime or watching their weight.

Whole Fish Slit the skin in two or three places on whole fish, such as salmon, trout and mackerel, to prevent it from bursting during cooking. (Boil-in-the-bag prepared fish should also have the pouch pierced.) The narrow end of the tail may need protecting for half the cooking time by shielding with a little foil.

Fillets, Steaks and Portions For best results when cooking fillets, roll them up into an even shape and secure each one with a wooden cocktail stick. Brush with lemon juice or melted butter and cover tightly during cooking. Fish steaks and pieces should be cooked so that the thicker portions are to the outer edge of the dish and the thinner pieces to the centre, where they receive the least microwave energy.

Coated Portions Breadcrumb-coated and battered fish can be cooked in the microwave, but the result will not be as crisp as when cooked conventionally. A microwave browning dish may help appreciably with these products.

Shellfish Prawns, shrimps, lobster and scallops cook superbly, but always start with the minimum time when cooking these items as they cook very quickly; also remember to take the standing time into account as part of the overall cooking process. Mussels and clams can also be steamed and cooked in the microwave with unbelievable ease.

Poultry and Game

Whole birds; quarters; breast, thigh and drumstick portions; stir-fry strips; and medallions of poultry and game can be cooked in the microwave with good results. Those dishes that require little browning, with portions cooked in a sauce, are most successful.

Whole Birds Truss well to hold the wings and legs close to the body to give a neat, compact shape. The narrow wing tips and drumstick bone ends may have to be protected with small pieces of foil for part of the cooking time. Start cooking whole birds breast-side down and turn over halfway through cooking. Place on a special microwaveproof roasting rack or on an upturned saucer so that the bird is lifted above the cooking juices.

With large birds and longer cooking times, browning is usually sufficient, but smaller birds and portions may need a little help. In all cases, whether cooking a whole bird or portions, these can be browned under a preheated hot grill after microwave cooking – the time savings are still considerable and warrant microwave cooking.

When cooking birds that have been stuffed, add an extra 1 minute per 450g/1lb to the times recommended in cooking charts. After cooking, leave to stand, covered in a tent of foil, to make best use of the residual heat; you will also find that the bird is easier to carve.

Small Birds and Portions Small birds, chicken quarters and small poultry joints should be cooked skin-side up, with the thicker parts towards the outside of the dish. Many will brown and crisp more readily if placed in a roasting bag.

If you are unsure of timings, then consider investing in a microwave thermometer, which takes the guesswork out of roasting and cooking times by indicating the internal temperature of the food.

Meat

With careful consideration of the quality and cut, meat cooked in the microwave is a great success. Cheaper, longer-cooking cuts can be microwaved with a measure of success, but the microwave performs better with prime-quality cuts. With the exception of roast pork, do not salt meat before microwave cooking as this draws out the moisture and toughens the meat.

Joints Ideally, choose joints that are symmetrically shaped; in other words, bone and roll joints like legs and shoulders for perfect results.

Minced Meat Minced beef, lamb and pork cook magnificently, whether as burgers or in moist dishes, like chilli con carne or Bolognese sauce. Meatloaves should be made in a ring mould for faster cooking.

Cubed Meat Cubes of meat for dishes such as casseroles, hot pots and curries, should be cut into pieces of the same size to ensure even cooking. Reduce the liquid required for such dishes by up to a third as there is very little evaporation in microwave cooking. Vegetables in casserole-type dishes tend to retain their shape and do not break down to thicken the liquid.

Sausages, Bacon and Kebabs Sausages, bacon and other fatty meats cook quickly with some degree of browning, but cover them with a sheet of absorbent kitchen paper during cooking to prevent fat from splattering on the oven walls. Wooden skewers should be used for kebabs which ideally should be cooked on a microwave roasting rack or placed across a shallow microwaveproof dish for success.

Vegetables

Whether freshly harvested from your garden, bought in the market, plucked from the supermarket shelf or taken from the freezer or store cupboard, the microwave will cook your vegetable selection to perfection. Only the minimum amount of water is used for most vegetables, so results are temptingly colourful and tender-crisp. Season with salt after cooking, as salt sprinkled directly on to vegetables can cause them to dehydrate and toughen.

Whole Vegetables Potatoes, aubergines and tomatoes need pricking before cooking to prevent them from bursting. Jacket potatoes will also have a crisper, drier skin if cooked on a sheet of absorbent kitchen paper. Whole vegetables or items which are not cut into small pieces should be positioned so that thicker parts are towards the outer edge of the dish, where they receive the most energy.

Cut Vegetables Most vegetables should be cut into uniformly sized pieces and placed in a cook bag or covered dish. Stir, shake or rearrange the vegetables halfway through the cooking time to ensure even results.

Fruit

From the basic apple to the exotic mango, fruit can be cooked in the microwave to retain its glorious characteristics. Most fruits can be prepared, sprinkled with sugar and cooked in a roasting bag or dish in the same way as fresh vegetables. Other items can be baked whole, poached in wine, cider or syrup, or stuffed with a sweetened filling.

Whole Fruit These must be scored or pricked if they are not peeled, so that the skin does not burst during cooking. Careful timing is important as fruit cooks surprisingly quickly.

Dried Fruit Dried fruit mixtures can also be cooked quickly to make fruit salads, compôtes and crumbles. Try mixtures of dried apple, pear, mango, peach, apricot and prune, and cook them in fruit juice and water for mouthwatering puddings at any time of the year.

Frozen Fruit The microwave is also useful for preparing fruit for the freezer when there is a glut, good price at the market or windfall of tree fruit. Use the microwave for cooking the fruit or for speedily making the sugar syrup in which to freeze fruit for long-term storage.

Pasta, Rice, Grains and Pulses

Any healthy diet should have its fair share of pasta, rice, grains and pulses; but, so often, it is the lengthy preparation of the latter that prevents us from serving them more often. The microwave makes light work of rehydrating beans and pulses, reducing what was once a long, overnight process of soaking to about 1½ hours.

The time savings with cooking pasta, rice, grains and pulses are virtually negligible but the bonuses are that little or no attention is required during cooking; the results are superb; there is no sticky, tacky saucepan to wash afterwards; no steamy kitchen and boil-over spills; and the food can be cooked ahead and reheated to perfection later.

All About Microwaves

For centuries people have cooked food to make it more palatable, easier to digest and safe to eat. From the smoky fire of prehistoric times through to today's high-tech microwave ovens, the principle of heating food to cook it has remained the same; the difference is in the speed of cooking and the methods employed. Traditional methods of cooking food in the fire, in the gas or electric oven and under or over the charcoal grill use conduction as the prime method of introducing heat, but what are microwaves and how do they cook?

MICROWAVE COOKING MADE SIMPLE

The mechanics of microwave cooking are no more magical than a television or radio. Inside the microwave is a magnetron vacuum tube, the "heart" or "brains" of the microwave, which converts ordinary household electrical energy into high-frequency electro-magnetic waves, called microwaves. The microwaves are then directed into the oven cavity, through a wave guide, and stirred by a fan for even distribution.

MICROWAVES IN ACTION

The waves are either reflected, pass through some materials or are absorbed by other materials. Metals reflect them (so cooking utensils must be non-metallic); glass, pottery, china, paper and most plastics allow them to pass through (so they make ideal cooking utensils); and foods absorb them. The microwaves are absorbed by the moisture in food, causing the food molecules to vibrate rapidly, thus producing heat to cook food.

Imagine the boy scout rubbing two twigs together to light a fire and you have the general idea. However, the speed at which the microwaves cause the molecules to vibrate is millions of times per second, producing remarkably intense heat that cooks super fast.

This is completely different from conventional methods, where heat is passed along a chain from one molecule to the next until the whole becomes hot and cooked. It is especially different in that dishes remain cool, metals cannot be used and timings are fast, calling for different cooking procedures and techniques.

FACTORS WHICH AFFECT MICROWAVE COOKING

Starting Temperature of Food
Foods that are cooked from room temperature will take less time to cook than foods that are frozen or chilled. Cooking times in the recipes that follow are based on starting temperatures at which the foods are normally stored, unless otherwise stated.

Density of Food
The denser the food, the longer it takes to cook. Heavy, dense foods, like potatoes, will take longer to cook than light porous foods, like sponge cakes. For the same reason a solid, dense mass of food, like a whole cauliflower, will take longer to cook than the same food divided into pieces (in the case of cauliflower, cut into small florets) and spread out for cooking.

Composition of Food
Foods which are high in fats and sugars will cook faster than foods high in liquid because fats and sugars absorb microwave energy more readily. They also reach higher temperatures during the cooking process than water-based foods. It therefore takes longer to cook foods that are high in moisture, like vegetables, than it does to cook those with little moisture, such as breads and cakes.

Quantity of Food
As the volume or quantity of food being cooked in the microwave increases, the cooking time increases too. If you double the amount of food you cook, cooking time will increase by about half as much again.

Size and Shape of Food
Smaller pieces of food will cook more quickly than larger pieces and uniformly shaped pieces cook more evenly than irregular-shaped items. Cutting foods into regular pieces, fingers or rounds and slicing meat across the grain prior to cooking will all help to ensure even cooking. With unevenly shaped pieces that cannot be cut, the thinner parts will cook faster than the thicker areas and they should be placed towards the centre of the dish where they can be grouped together to receive less energy. Ideally, portions of food that are of the same size and shape cook most evenly.

It is also important to remember that round and ring shapes cook more evenly than square, oval or rectangular shapes. With the latter, there is a concentration of energy in the corners and at the ends that can cause charring; to avoid this, protect the corners with small pieces of smooth foil to shield them from the microwave energy.

Bones in Meat

Bones in meat conduct heat, therefore meat next to the bone in a joint will cook first. Wherever possible, it is wise to bone and roll meat for even cooking. If this is not possible, remember to shield thin areas of meat next to the bone halfway through the cooking time to prevent overcooking.

Height in the Oven

Areas that are closest to any source of energy cook faster than those further away, and the microwave is no exception to this rule. Depending on its design, your microwave may cook faster near the floor or the roof, where the energy source is located. Rotating, turning over and stirring foods will minimize this effect.

THE MICROWAVE COOKER

All basic models are much the same in design: they consist of a cabinet, magnetron, wave guide, wave stirrer, power supply, power cord and controls. Some have special extra features such as automatic defrost, variable power control, turntable, integral thermometer or temperature probe, browning or crisping elements and stay-hot devices.

The microwaves are safely contained in the cavity by the metal lining inside the base and walls, which reflects the microwaves into the food. All cooker doors and frames are fitted with special seals as an extra safety measure to ensure that the microwaves stay in the cooker. In addition, all microwave cookers have one or more cut-out devices so that the flow of microwaves stops automatically whenever the door is opened or if the door has not been shut properly or is damaged.

Many portable microwave cookers have a turntable, which means that foods, such as fish, do not need turning.

Portable Microwave Cookers

These are undoubtedly the most popular. Almost as light and certainly as portable as a television, they require a 13 or 15 amp plug for use, making such cooking machines popular choices for students, flat-dwellers and the elderly. They are also good for use in a boat, caravan or second home.

A portable microwave may be sited conveniently on a work top, trolley or other firm, stable surface. Some models, with very basic controls, have been developed for the 'simplistic cooking and reheating' market, and are usually short in height, designed to fit under the work surface. Often budget-priced, this type of microwave will accommodate a chicken or a couple of stacked plated meals, but it is not suitable for those who require a flexible oven arrangement or sophisticated cooking.

Double Oven Cooker

A few microwave models are available in the same unit as a conventional cooker, with the microwave acting as a second or double oven. Most models are built-in, but a few free-standing models are available.

Combination Cookers

This is an expanding section of the microwave market and one that is likely to attract second-time buyers. These cookers have the facility to cook by both microwave and conventional means in one single operation and in one unit. The conventional and microwave powers can operate separately, simultaneously or in sequence, as required. Some models also offer further choice, with fan-assisted ovens, grills or automatic cooking sequence controls for microwave, combination and conventional cooking. In the chapters that follow, look out for recipes that can be cooked using combination controls, but follow the timings given in your manufacturer's instruction booklet.

Installing the Microwave

All that is required to install a portable microwave cooker is a fused power socket. Manufacturers also recommend that you place the microwave on a stable surface and have adequate ventilation. It is therefore possible to site the microwave in a multitude of places – the kitchen work surface is typical, but also consider a trolley that can be wheeled between rooms or even out on to the terrace or patio for outdoor dining, providing wonderful flexibility when preparing accompaniments for barbecues.

If you plan to build-in your microwave, then ensure that you buy the correct fixing kit or housing unit, with adequate venting, and always check your microwave handbook for any special instructions.

Cleaning the Microwave

This is something of a bonus! Since the walls in the microwave oven cavity remain cool during cooking, cleaning is often just a quick-wipe operation. Food does not have the opportunity to bake on, so wiping the inside at regular intervals, or when spills occur, with a damp, soapy cloth is sufficient. Remember always to disconnect the oven from the electrical supply before wiping or cleaning. Remove and wash oven trays, shelving and bases according to the manufacturer's instructions.

Wipe the outside surfaces and door regularly, but do not allow water to seep into the vents. If necessary, also clean any air filters or the stirrer fan guard according to the manufacturer's instructions.

Stale cooking smells can be removed by boiling a solution of 1 part lemon juice to 3 parts water in a microwaveproof bowl in the microwave for about 5 minutes on HIGH. Then wipe the oven cavity dry with a clean cloth.

Servicing

Remember to have the microwave checked by a qualified engineer every 12 months, or as recommended by the manufacturer.

NOTE
Do not operate the microwave oven when it is empty. For safety, especially when young children are around, place a cup of water in the cooker when it is not in use. If the cooker is accidentally switched on, the water will absorb the energy, then there is negligible risk of damaging the magnetron, something that can occur if the oven is operated when empty.

A sophisticated microwave cooker with combination cooking facility.

Microwave Dishes and Utensils

Without doubt, the range of dishes and utensils that can be used in the microwave is wider than that for cooking conventionally.

Avoid using metal in any form, including dishes wth metal decoration or trims; porous pottery and mugs or cups with glued-on handles; crystal glass; and polystyrene trays or non-dishwasher-safe plastics.

GLASS, POTTERY AND CHINA

Ovenproof and plain glass, pottery and china are all suitable for microwave cooking. Be sure to check that they do not have any metallic trim, screws or handles and, if using a pottery dish, that it is non-porous.

Clear glass dishes, such as Pyrex, are particularly useful since you can actually see the food being cooked and check its progress during cooking.

Glass measuring jugs are also superb and allow you to measure, mix, cook and, sometimes, serve from the same container. Ovenproof glass and glass-ceramic dishes are invaluable for use in one operation from the freezer to the microwave and vice versa (once the food has cooled completely).

The only type of glass to avoid for microwave cooking is the leaded type most often found as decorative drinking glassware.

PAPER

Paper is a good utensil for low heat and short cooking times, such as thawing, reheating or very short cooking, and for foods with a low fat, sugar or water content. Napkins, absorbent kitchen paper, cups, cartons, paper freezer wrap and the paper pulp board often used for supermarket packaging are all suitable. Absorbent kitchen paper or paper towels are especially useful for cooking fatty foods, since they absorb excess fats and oils and can be used to prevent splattering on the oven walls.

Wax-coated paper cups and plates should be avoided since the high temperature of the food will cause the wax to melt; they can be used for thawing items to be served cold, like frozen cakes and desserts.

PLASTICS

Whether these are dishwasher safe or not provides a useful indication as to whether or not a plastic item is suitable for microwave use. Unless made of a thermoplastic material, plastic dishes and containers should not be used for cooking foods with a high fat or sugar content, since the heat of the food may cause the plastic to melt and lose its shape.

Plastic or clear film for microwave use and items like bags suitable for boil-in-the-bag cooking work well.

Pierce a bag or film before cooking to allow steam to escape or fold back a corner to vent the film and prevent it from ballooning during cooking. Also take extra special care when removing clear film or opening plastic bags in case any trapped steam escapes and burns the hand or forearm.

Roasting bags provide a clean, convenient way of cooking many foods, from vegetables to roasts. Roasts particularly benefit from their use since browning seems to take place more readily in a roasting bag. Either tie loosely with room for steam to escape or snip a couple of holes in the bag to aid the escape of steam and replace the metal ties with elastic, string or a non-metal tie.

Do not attempt to microwave in thin polythene bags as they will not withstand the heat of the food. Thicker storage or freezer bags are acceptable. Use elastic bands, string or non-metal ties to secure the bags loosely before cooking the food.

Melamine is not recommended for microwave cooking as it absorbs enough microwave energy to cause charring.

COTTON AND LINEN

Napkins are ideal for short warming or reheating procedures, such as reheating bread rolls for serving. It is important to use only cotton or linen, as synthetic fibres, or fabrics containing a proportion of them, will be damaged.

WOODEN BOWLS AND BAKEWARE

These are suitable only for short periods of reheating, otherwise the wood or wicker will tend to dry out, crack or char.

SPECIAL MICROWAVE EQUIPMENT

With the increased popularity of microwave cooking, there are many specialist innovations in microwave cookware. Several ranges manufactured from polythene, polystyrene and

A selection of everyday items that are useful for microwave cooking.

thermoplastics are now widely available and come in a comprehensive range of shapes and sizes. If you are an enthusiastic microwave cook then you might consider investing in some of the more useful items such as a microwave baking tray, roasting rack, bun or muffin tray, ring mould and whisk.

If the microwave is your only form of cooker, you may well be interested in some other very special items of cookware, developed to broaden the options when cooking in a microwave. These include a special popcorn cooker, a microwave pressure cooker, special kebab and burger or chop cooker, and a range of microwaveproof saucepans.

Thermometers

Thermometers made specially for microwave ovens are available but can be used in an oven only when specified by the oven's manufacturer. Their main use is for checking the internal temperature of a meat roast to ensure it is cooked to your requirements. They can also be used to check that, after cooking for the recommended time, the internal temperature of ready-made meals is sufficiently high to destroy micro-organisms which may be present and could cause food poisoning. Some newer ovens have an automatic cooking control based on a temperature-sensing probe that can be inserted into the food while in the oven. When the food reaches a precise temperature, the oven turns itself off automatically.

Browning Dishes

Available from most microwave dealers and large kitchenware stores, these duplicate the browning and searing processes of conventional cooking. Especially useful for pre-browning burgers, chops, sausages and steaks, they can also be used to 'fry' eggs and sandwiches, and to brown vegetables.

The browning dish is made of a glass ceramic substance with a special coating that absorbs microwave energy. It is preheated in the microwave until the base coating changes colour, usually for about 8 minutes on HIGH. Always follow specific manufacturer's instructions as dishes, coatings and timings vary.

Examples of special microwave cookware.

The food is then placed on the dish to brown and turned to sear both sides. Preheating times and browning or searing times differ according to the food being cooked and the power output of the oven. Always follow the manufacturer's instructions for best results.

CHECKING SUITABILITY FOR MICROWAVE COOKING

If you intend to cook food in both the microwave and the conventional oven in a continuous operation, be sure to use a dish that is ovenproof as well as microwaveproof. The following is a simple test to check microwave suitability.

Fill a heatproof cup with cold water and stand it in the utensil being checked. Place the utensil in the microwave and microwave on HIGH for 1¼ minutes. If the water is warm in the cup and the utensil is cool, go ahead and use the utensil. If the utensil is warm or even hot and the water is still cool, or barely lukewarm, do not use the utensil for microwave cooking.

THE SHAPE AND SIZE OF DISH TO USE

After checking the material, consider the shape and size of the dish or utensil. Ideally, the more regular the shape the better for microwave cooking. For example, a round shape is much better than an oval; a straight-sided container is better than a curved one as the microwaves can penetrate more evenly; and a large shallow dish is better than a small deep one as the food is spread over a greater surface area and therefore exposed to more microwave energy.

A Few Ideas
The following novel pieces of cookware can be used successfully in the microwave:
• scallop shells
• glass or plastic baby bottles for warming milk and juice
• wooden toothpicks for securing foods and wooden kebab skewers for brochettes and kebabs
• paper bun cases for buns and muffins – support them in teacups or ramekin dishes.

MATERIAL TO AVOID – METALS

Most manufacturers object to the use of metal. Even small amounts in the oven will reflect the microwaves so that they do not penetrate the food to be cooked.

Therefore, avoid metal dishes, baking trays and metal baking tins, foil dishes, cast-iron cookware, plates and china trimmed with a metallic design, metal kebab skewers, any dish with a metal screw or attachment and the paper-coated metal ties often found with freezer and cook bags.

Microwave Techniques

PREPARING INGREDIENTS

When cutting ingredients, prepare even-sized pieces so that they cook at the same rate.

• Slim strips of vegetables, such as carrots, cook more quickly and evenly than large, irregular pieces or different-sized whole vegetables.

• Even cubes or dice cook well. Large vegetables, such as swede, turnip, potato or pumpkin can all be cut into neat cubes to promote quick, even cooking.

• Slicing meat across the grain into thin pieces helps to tenderize it.

SCORING OR PRICKING FOODS

Foods with tight skins or membranes, such as sausages, kidneys, giblets, whole fish, jacket potatoes, egg yolks and apples must be lightly pricked or scored prior to cooking or they are liable to burst or explode. This is because of the tremendous amount of pressure that develops within foods that cook very quickly.

STIRRING

Stirring is important when cooking conventionally, and it is also necessary when cooking by microwave. Conventionally, we stir to redistribute heat from the bottom of the pan to the top, but with a microwave the aim is to redistribute heat and cooked areas from the outside to the centre of a dish for even cooking. Precise stirring instructions will be given in a recipe if it is important; if not, stirring halfway through cooking is usually sufficient.

ROTATING

If your microwave has a turntable, then this cooking technique becomes redundant. In models without a turntable, a quarter or half turn of the dish at regular intervals during the cooking period will ensure even results when food cannot be stirred or turned over.

TURNING OVER

Many large or dense items of food, such as potatoes or chicken drumsticks, should be turned over about halfway through cooking to ensure good results.

COOK'S TIP

A pair of food tongs is useful for turning firm foods, such as chicken portions, chops and sausages, for example.

ARRANGING FOOD

Arranging foods carefully in a dish for microwave cooking can mean that an ingredient is perfectly cooked rather than merely adequately cooked. For success, follow these guidelines.

• Try to cook foods of an even or similar size together and, if possible, arrange them in a ring pattern in a dish, leaving the centre empty.

• If foods are of an irregular shape, like chicken drumsticks or spears of broccoli, then arrange the thicker sections to the outside of the dish in a spoke-like arrangement so that the thick areas will receive the most energy and cook more quickly than the thin areas that are grouped together.

• Arrange whole fish in pairs, head to tail, to form an even area that will cook uniformly. Thin areas cook more quickly than thick or large areas, which are not penetrated as quickly by microwaves.

• When reheating plated meals, ensure food is spread out evenly. Thicker vegetables should be arranged towards the edge to receive the most energy.

• When heating more than one plated meal at a time, special plastic microwave stacking rings can be placed between plates. These rings ensure plates are positioned so that they all receive an equal amount of energy and therefore the meals reheat at the same rate.

• Try to ensure that the depth of food is even; if it is not, stir or rearrange ingredients.

• Foods cooked in a ring pattern or mould make the most of the microwave. Cakes cook particularly well in a ring mould. If you don't have one, then improvise: place a glass tumbler in a round microwaveproof dish, and hold it in place while adding the mixture.

REARRANGING FOODS

Even with a turntable, rearranging foods (usually once) will ensure even results. Move foods from the outside of the dish to the centre and vice versa.

• Rearrange foods cooked in a bag by gently shaking the bag. Remember that scalding-hot steam can escape as the contents of the bag are shuffled, so protect your hand and forearm with a folded dish towel or oven glove.

SHIELDING

As with conventional baking, some parts of foods are more vulnerable to overcooking than others. In such cases, it is acceptable to use small smooth strips of foil to protect thin or vulnerable areas.

This is the only time when metal may be introduced into a typical microwave oven, and it is important to make sure it does not touch the oven walls. Position the foil on the food for about half the cooking time, securing small patches with wooden cocktail sticks, if necessary.

Check the manufacturer's handbook to ensure that this is permissible in your particular model of microwave oven.

• Fish heads and tails should be protected to prevent eyes from bursting and thin areas from overcooking.

• Wing tips on poultry and the thinner tail-ends on ducks should be shielded to prevent them from overcooking and drying out.

• Protruding bones, for example as on a rack of lamb, should be shielded to prevent scorching.

• Narrow ends of joints of meat, such as at the end of a leg of lamb or pork, should be shielded.

COVERING AND WRAPPING

Problems of surfaces drying out, splattering of food on the cavity walls and slower-than-optimum cooking times can all be eliminated by covering or wrapping foods. This locks in moisture, retains juices and speeds up cooking by trapping heat-retaining steam.

• Use double-strength plastic cooking bags, suitable for boiling

(sometimes referred to as "boil-in-the-bag" bags or "cook bags") or roasting bags for vegetables, meat and poultry. Replace metal ties with elastic bands.

• Some bags come with special, microwaveproof plastic clips.

• String can be used to loosely tie bags closed.

COOK'S TIP

Remember to ensure that a cooking bag is not too hot to hold before picking it up; protect your hand with a folded dish towel, if necessary, and be aware that scalding-hot steam may escape from any small opening at the top of the bag as the contents move when lifted or as they are being rearranged.

• Use a tight-fitting purpose-made lid or improvise by using a saucer or plate instead.

• Greaseproof paper may be used to cover small bowls, for example as when cooking steamed puddings. The paper may be secured with a large elastic band.

• Covering bacon with absorbent kitchen paper prevents spattering as well as ensuring that moisture that is given off is absorbed.

• Absorbent kitchen paper is also invaluable for drying herbs.

• When dampened, absorbent kitchen paper can be used for reheating and steaming pancakes and shellfish.

• Cover bowls with a tight membrane of microwave-safe clear film. Puncture the top to allow some steam to escape during cooking.

• Use absorbent kitchen paper as a base on which to stand food.

• Turn back a small area of clear film to provide a vent to prevent a ballooning effect during cooking. Take care when removing clear film, as it will trap a significant amount of scalding-hot steam even when it is vented.

• Absorbent kitchen paper can also be used as a cover for some foods. It is especially good for absorbing excess moisture given off by foods like potatoes and bread.

COOK'S TIP

Even though microwave cooking is a moist method, foods can dry out because of the speed with which moisture evaporates from them. Microwave-safe clear film is often the most practical choice of covering, allowing you to see what's happening in the dish. When folded back at one corner, the contents can be stirred during cooking without discarding the film. Always remove the film starting at the side furthest away from you to avoid scalding your hands or forearms.

REMOVING EXCESS COOKING JUICES

Any juices that seep from food will absorb microwave energy. If these juices are considerable, and the cooking time is longer than about 5 minutes on HIGH, it is advisable to remove some liquid regularly during cooking. Excess juices can prolong the cooking time appreciably. The juices can always be replaced towards the end of the cooking time if the food starts to dry out too much. Examples include cooking a chicken, duck or turkey.

OBSERVING STANDING TIMES

Food continues to cook by conduction after the microwave energy has been turned off. This is not solely a feature of microwave cooking – the same applies to a lesser degree with conventional cooking. With microwave cooking there is greater residual heat, so it is important to err on the side of safety and undercook rather than overcook food. Whereas there is no rescue package for overcooked food, additional cooking time can always be given if the dish is still inadequately cooked after observing the standing time.

BROWNING FOODS

As a result of little applied surface heat during rapid cooking, foods cooked in the microwave do not readily brown. Try the following tips to encourage browning or disguise any pale results.

• Grill foods like gratins and roasts before or after microwave cooking.

• Use a specialist microwave browning dish, especially for foods like chops, steaks, fried eggs, toasted sandwiches, stir-fries and chicken portions.

• Buy or make a browning mix to coat foods – paprika, toasted breadcrumbs, crushed crisps, soy sauce, Worcestershire sauce and soup mixes all work well.

• Due to its high fat content, bacon browns readily, so it can be laid over poultry or roast meat.

• Baked items, such as cakes, biscuits, breads and muffins, can be sprinkled or coated with toasted coconut, chocolate vermicelli, chopped nuts, chopped glacé fruits, poppy seeds, toasted seeds and dark-coloured spices.

• Glaze ham, poultry or game with fruit preserve, particularly redcurrant jelly or citrus marmalade, before cooking to add colour.

• Add icing or frosting to a pale cake or other baked items after cooking.

Herby Baked Tomatoes are cooked in the microwave, then browned under the grill.

The Microwave and Freezer

During its introductory years, the domestic microwave was often referred to as "the unfreezer" due to its ability to defrost food both quickly and efficiently, and this is still one of the major advantages of microwave ownership.

Capitalizing on this effect, almost all microwave manufacturers have introduced a special DEFROST control or button to ensure optimum defrosting microwave action. This control programmes the microwave to introduce just the right amount of energy to defrost food without cooking it. This is done by pulsing the power on and off at regular intervals over a period of time.

When a defrost setting is not built in, it is possible to simulate the action of the setting by turning the microwave on and off manually at regular intervals, allowing rest periods in between; but this is rarely as successful as using a pre-programmed setting and it can be time-consuming.

DEFROSTING TIPS

Refer to your own manufacturer's handbook for a guide to defrosting times, but always err on the side of safety by heating for too short a period, rather than too long, until you can readily judge the defrosting speed of your own particular type of microwave.

• Open all cartons and remove any metal lids, ties or fastenings before defrosting food.

• Defrost foods slowly. Never try to hurry the process as there is the danger of overcooking the food or drying it out unnecessarily.

• Frozen foods wrapped in foil or placed in foil containers should have all foil removed, and they should be placed in a suitable dish for the microwave.

• Turn foods over during defrosting, about halfway through the recommended time.

• If it is not possible to turn food over during defrosting (for example, as with a decorated cake), then rotate the item or container regularly for even defrosting.

• Flex any pouches of food that cannot be broken up or stirred during the defrosting time and rotate on a regular basis.

• Place foods like cakes, bread rolls and pastry items on a double sheet of absorbent kitchen paper to absorb excess moisture that could cause the food to become soggy.

• Blocks of frozen food should be broken up with a fork during defrosting so that frozen chunks receive the maximum amount of microwave energy.

• Separate any blocks of frozen meat items, such as hamburgers, steaks, chops and sausages, as they defrost.

• Remove any giblets from the cavity of a chicken and other poultry or game birds as soon as they have defrosted.

• Remove any juices or drips from frozen foods during the defrosting time with a bulb baster or spoon as these will only continue to absorb microwave energy, leaving less to defrost the main food.

• Items like meat joints, whole birds and whole fish should be defrosted until icy, then left to defrost completely at room temperature before cooking.

• If any parts of the food start to defrost too fast (or even begin to become warm or cook), shield or protect these areas with small strips of smooth foil. These can be attached with wooden cocktail sticks where necessary. Check that this is acceptable for your model of microwave by reading the manufacturer's instructions.

• Always observe standing times as foods will continue to thaw by means of conduction from the small level of internal heat that is produced. Allow foods to defrost until they are just icy.

• Before defrosting, prick, slash or vent membranes and skins. Also, pierce clear film, pouches or similar wrappings in the same way as when cooking food in a skin.

• If you intend to defrost and cook in one operation, then follow all the guidelines on stirring, turning, rotating and rearranging foods, not forgetting to allow standing time before serving.

C O O K ' S   T I P

If a member of your household is not a confident cook, but has to reheat an occasional meal, freeze suitable portions with a label giving brief instructions for defrosting and reheating the food in the microwave.

FREEZER TO MICROWAVE REMINDERS

The microwave and freezer are a terrific twosome to ease the life of the regular home cook, working mother, busy hostess and anyone with a prolific vegetable garden. When freezing home-made food that will later be defrosted or cooked in the microwave, the following hints are worth remembering.

• Freeze food in a microwaveproof container, so it can be defrosted, reheated or cooked straight from the freezer.

• Single portions are very useful in the freezer, allowing any member of the family to quickly and easily defrost and cook an individual meal at any time.

• Before freezing a conventionally made pizza, pie, flan or quiche, cut it into portions so that the required number of servings can be removed from the freezer as required, rather than having to defrost the whole item.

• Complete cooked main courses can be plated on microwaveproof plates and frozen for almost instant dinners. Remember to follow the advice on arranging food for microwave cooking and reheating when preparing complete meals. Adding a sauce of some kind helps to keep the meal succulent and moist during defrosting and reheating.

• When cooking a main course, consider doubling the quantities and freezing the second meal for future use.

• Save time and effort in the future by freezing soups, casseroles and hot pots in freezerproof bags that are also suitable for microwave defrosting. Use large bags and knot the tops firmly to prevent the contents from leaking, and avoid using metal ties. The unopened bags can be placed in the microwave until the contents are slightly defrosted and free of the plastic, then the food is ready to be transferred to a suitable microwaveproof serving dish for the final reheating.

• Consider freezing home-grown or bargain vegetable produce in freezer and microwaveproof boil-in-the-bags. These will serve as freezing, defrosting and cooking containers, without the need to transfer the contents at all before serving.

FREEZING FOOD TO FIT A DISH

1 If you do not want to lose the use of the dish while the food is in the freezer, line it with freezer film or foil, arrange the food in the dish and then freeze.

2 Once frozen, turn the food out of the container, wrap it tightly, label and return to the freezer.

3 To defrost or reheat the food, remove the freezer film or foil and return the food to the original container before placing in the microwave.

COOKING AND FREEZING IN ONE BAG

1 Fruits like apples and pears can be cooked in a roasting bag or boilable bag.

2 When cooked, the fruit can be crushed in the bag to make a purée and sealed while still hot. As the mixture cools it will form a vacuum pack that is ideal for freezing and ready for defrosting or reheating in the microwave.

> ### COOK'S TIP
> ❧
> Make a note of the weight of vegetables or fruit on freezer labels so you can calculate the microwave cooking time easily for the whole bag.

FREEZING AND DEFROSTING BABY FOOD

• Leftovers from suitable meals can easily be puréed and frozen in ice cube trays ready for baby and toddler meals. To defrost and reheat 2 cubes (about 60ml/4 tbsp food), place in a microwaveproof bowl. Place a small glass or cup of water in the microwave at the same time to absorb some energy and prevent the baby food from overheating. Microwave on HIGH for 1–1¼ minutes until thawed and hot, stirring once to break up. Leave to stand and check the temperature before serving.

> ### COOK'S TIP
> ❧
> Once the trays of baby food are frozen, release the hard cubes of purée and store them in an airtight polythene bag. This way you will not have all your ice cube trays in use.

REHEATING FOODS IN THE MICROWAVE

Most foods will reheat successfully in the microwave without loss of quality, flavour and colour, and with maximum nutrient retention compared to alternative reheating methods. For best results follow these guidelines.

• Arrange foods on a plate with the thicker portions to the outer edge where they will receive the most energy.

• When plating meals for reheating, try to arrange the food in an even layer.

• Cover foods with clear film if a lid is not used to retain moisture.

• Observe the standing time to make maximum use of the microwave energy and to prevent the food overcooking.

• When reheating potatoes, pastry items and other moist baked foods, place them on a double sheet of absorbent kitchen paper to absorb the excess moisture and prevent sogginess.

• If possible, stir foods regularly during reheating; if this is not possible, then turn foods over or rearrange them, or at least rotate the dish for even reheating.

Basic Recipes

The microwave is invaluable for cooking a host of dishes, as you will see from the recipes that follow in this book, and it is also indispensable for cooking a range of basic recipes that form the basis for more complicated dishes and meals. The following are a few of the most useful basic recipes.

Giblet Stock for Gravy

1 Place the contents of a bag of giblets from a chicken, turkey or duck in a microwaveproof bowl with 300ml/½ pint/1¼ cups boiling water and a few sliced seasoning vegetables, such as carrots, celery and onion.

2 Microwave on HIGH for 7–10 minutes. Strain and use the gravy as required.

White Pouring Sauce

1 Place 25g/1oz/2 tbsp butter in a microwaveproof jug and microwave on HIGH for 30–60 seconds, until melted.

2 Stir in 25g/1oz/2 tbsp plain flour and 300ml/½ pint/1¼ cups milk. Microwave on HIGH for 3½–4 minutes, stirring or whisking once every minute, until smooth, boiling and thickened. Season to taste and serve. Makes 300ml/½ pint/1¼ cups.

VARIATIONS

One-stage Sauce: Place the flour and butter in a microwaveproof jug, then add the milk and whisk lightly. The ingredients will not combine thoroughly at this stage as the butter does not mix in, but it will break into small pieces. Continue as above.

Caper Sauce: Add 15ml/1 tbsp drained capers and 5ml/1 tsp vinegar from the jar of capers or lemon juice to the cooked sauce. Good with cooked lamb.

Cheese Sauce: Add 50–115g/2–4oz grated cheese, a pinch of dry mustard powder and a pinch of cayenne pepper to the cooked sauce. Whisk or stir well. Serve with vegetables, eggs, fish or pasta.

Parsley Sauce: Add 15–30ml/ 1–2 tbsp chopped fresh parsley and a squeeze of lemon juice (optional) to the cooked sauce and whisk or stir well. Serve with fish, ham or bacon and vegetables.

Scrambled Eggs

1 Place 15g/½oz/1 tbsp butter in a microwaveproof jug or bowl and microwave on HIGH for about 30 seconds to melt.

2 Beat 4 eggs with 30ml/2 tbsp milk and salt and pepper to taste. Add to the butter and microwave on HIGH for 1¼ minutes. Stir or whisk the set pieces of egg from the outside of the bowl or jug to the centre.

3 Microwave on HIGH for a further 1¼–1¾ minutes, stirring or whisking twice. When about three-quarters cooked, there is still a significant amount of runny egg, as shown here. When cooked, the eggs are moist, not completely set. Leave to stand for 1–2 minutes, by which time the eggs will be set ready for serving. Serves 2.

JACKET POTATOES

1 Scrub and prick the potatoes. Place on a double thickness of absorbent kitchen paper. If cooking more than two potatoes, arrange them in a ring pattern.

2 Microwave on HIGH for the time given, turning over halfway through cooking. Leave to stand for 3–4 minutes before serving.

3 The potatoes may be cut in half and the flesh forked up or mashed, then replaced in the shells, topped with cheese or butter and heated for a few seconds in the microwave to melt the butter or cheese before serving.

COOKING TIMES FOR JACKET POTATOES

1 x 175g/6oz	potato	4–6 minutes
2 x 175g/6oz	potatoes	6–8 minutes
3 x 175g/6oz	potatoes	8–12 minutes
4 x 175g/6oz	potatoes	12-15 minutes

CORN-ON-THE-COB

These can either be cooked husked or unhusked.

1 For fresh unhusked corn-on-the-cob, fold back the husk and discard the silk.

2 Replace the husk to cover the corn and arrange the cobs, evenly spaced, on the base of the cooker or turntable. Microwave on HIGH for the time given, rotating and rearranging once halfway through cooking. Leave to stand for 5 minutes before removing the husk and cutting off the woody base with a sharp knife.

3 Alternatively, wrap fresh husked cobs individually in clear film or place in a microwave-proof dish with 60ml/4 tbsp water and cover. Microwave on HIGH for the time given, rotating and rearranging once halfway through cooking. Leave to stand for 3–5 minutes before serving.

COOKING TIMES FOR CORN-ON-THE-COB

Cooking Times for Corn Cobs in Husks

1 x 175–225g/6–8oz cob	3–5 minutes
2 x 175–225g/6–8oz cobs	6–8 minutes
3 x 175–225g/6–8oz cobs	8–10 minutes
4 x 175–225g/6–8oz cobs	10–12 minutes

Cooking Times for Husked Corn Cobs

1 x 175–225g/6–8oz cob	3–4 minutes
2 x 175–225g/6–8oz cobs	5–6 minutes
3 x 175–225g/6–8oz cobs	7–8 minutes
4 x 175–225g/6–8oz cobs	9–10 minutes

HOLLANDAISE SAUCE

1 Place 115g/4oz/8 tbsp butter in a large microwaveproof jug and microwave on HIGH for 1½ minutes until melted. Whisk in 45ml/3 tbsp lemon juice, 2 egg yolks, a pinch of mustard powder and salt and pepper to taste.

2 Microwave on MEDIUM for 1 minute, whisk and serve. This sauce is delicious with poached salmon or cooked asparagus. Serves 4–6.

RED LENTILS

1 Place 225g/8oz/1 cup lentils in a large microwaveproof bowl. Add a little chopped onion, celery and lemon juice, if you like. Cover with 900ml/1½ pints/3¾ cups boiling water or stock and add salt and pepper to taste.

2 Cover, leaving a gap for steam to escape, and microwave on HIGH for 15–25 minutes, stirring once halfway through cooking. Time the cooking according to requirements: if you want the lentils to retain some shape, use the shorter time; if you want soft lentils for a soup or dip, use the longer cooking time. Serves 4.

QUICK SOAKING OF DRIED BEANS

1 To shorten the soaking time for dried beans, place them in a microwaveproof bowl and cover with boiling water.

2 Cover and microwave on HIGH for 5 minutes. Leave to stand for 1½ hours, then drain, rinse and cook the beans.

VEGETABLE RICE

1 Place 225g/8oz/generous 1 cup long grain white rice in a microwaveproof bowl with 550ml/18fl oz/scant 2½ cups boiling water, 5ml/1 tsp salt, and a knob of butter, if you like. Cover loosely with a lid or vented clear film and microwave on HIGH for 3 minutes.

2 Reduce the power setting to MEDIUM and microwave for a further 12 minutes, stirring two or three times.

3 Add 175g/6oz/about 1 cup diced and softened vegetables (for example a single vegetable or selection from peas, beans, peppers, onion and sweetcorn). Stir well to mix, cover and microwave on HIGH for 1½ minutes.

4 Leave to stand, tightly covered, for 5 minutes. Fluff the rice with a fork to separate the grains before serving. Serves 4.

PORRIDGE

1 Traditional and quick-cook varieties of porridge can be prepared quickly and easily in the microwave. To make traditional porridge, place 30g/1¼oz/⅓ cup oatmeal in a microwaveproof bowl with 1.5ml/¼ tsp salt.

2 Stir in 175ml/6 fl oz/¾ cup water or milk, making sure that the oatmeal and liquid are thoroughly mixed.

3 Cover with vented clear film and microwave on LOW for 10–12 minutes, stirring twice. Leave to stand, covered, for 2 minutes before serving.

4 Prepare quick-cook oatmeal as above, but microwave on LOW for 5 minutes. Serves 1.

GARLIC OR HERB BREAD

1 Cut a 115g/4oz short, crusty French stick or Vienna loaf into diagonal slices about 4cm/1½in thick, almost to the base of the loaf but not quite through. Spread garlic or herb butter between the slices and re-form the loaf into a neat shape.

2 Wrap loosely in absorbent kitchen paper and microwave on HIGH for 1½ minutes. Serve at once, while still warm. Serves 4.

Making the Most of Your Microwave

Getting used to the speed of microwave cooking does take time, patience and perseverance, so you are unlikely to become a microwave mastercook overnight. The golden rule is to become a constant clock-watcher until you know your microwave really well. Do not be afraid or intimidated by the microwave – open the door, peer in and poke food as much as you like to see if it is defrosting, cooking or reheating adequately. You will soon be able to cook the recipes in this book successfully, adapt some of your own conventional favourites and halve or double quantities with practised ease.

The following are tips that will provide amusing, useful tricks to make you wonder how you ever managed without a microwave!

PEELING TOMATOES

Place up to 6 tomatoes in a ring on absorbent kitchen paper. Microwave on HIGH for 10–15 seconds. Leave to stand for 15 minutes, then peel the tomatoes.

PEELING PEACHES AND APRICOTS

Place up to 4 peaches in a microwaveproof bowl with very little water. Cover and microwave on HIGH for 1–1½ minutes. Leave the peaches to stand for 5 minutes, then drain and peel them.

TO SOFTEN CHILLED HARD CHEESES

Place about 225g/8oz chilled hard cheese on a microwaveproof serving plate and microwave on LOW for 30–34 seconds, turning over after half the time. Leave to stand for 5 minutes before serving.

TO RIPEN SEMI-SOFT CHEESE

Place about 225g/8oz semi-soft cheese on a microwaveproof serving dish and microwave on LOW for 15–45 seconds depending upon degree of ripeness, checking constantly and turning over after half of the time. Leave to stand for 5 minutes before serving.

SOFTENING BUTTER

Microwave on HIGH for 5–10 seconds, then leave to stand for 5 minutes before using.

BLANCHING ALMONDS

Place 250ml/8fl oz/1 cup water in a jug. Microwave on HIGH for 2½ minutes or until boiling, add the almonds and microwave for 30 seconds. Drain the nuts, then slip off their skins.

TOASTING NUTS

For a golden result, place in a browning dish and microwave on HIGH for 4–5 minutes, stirring each minute. Alternatively, for a lighter result, cook in an ordinary microwaveproof dish.

TOASTING COCONUT

Spread 115g/4oz/1 cup desiccated coconut on a microwaveproof plate. Microwave on HIGH for 5–6 minutes, stirring every 1 minute.

DRYING HERBS AND CITRUS RINDS

Place on a microwaveproof plate and microwave on HIGH until dry. Never leave unattended and check at 1 minute intervals to ensure success.

SQUEEZING CITRUS JUICE

To extract the maximum juice from citrus fruit, prick the skins and microwave on HIGH for 5–10 seconds.

TO DRY BREAD FOR CRUMBS

1 Place a thick slice of bread on a microwaveproof plate and microwave on HIGH for 2½–3½ minutes, until dry.

2 Allow the bread to cool completely before crumbling or grating it for use.

TO MAKE CROÛTONS

1 To make dry, oil-free croûtons, dice 175g/6oz bread into cubes. Place on kitchen paper on a large flat microwaveproof plate and microwave on HIGH for 3–4 minutes, stirring once every minute, until dry.

2 To make butter-crisp croûtons, place 25g/1oz/2 tbsp butter in a microwaveproof dish and microwave on HIGH for 30 seconds to melt.

3 Add 175g/6oz bread cubes and toss to coat them in the melted butter. Microwave on HIGH for 3–4 minutes, stirring every minute, until crisp and brown.

> ### COOK'S TIP
>
> Croûtons can be flavoured in a variety of ways to complement the dishes they garnish. A crushed garlic clove or a little dried oregano can be added to the butter for butter-crisp croûtons. Chopped fresh herbs, such as tarragon or parsley, should be tossed with the cooked croûtons. Grated Parmesan cheese or lemon rind can be added to cooked croûtons.

PROVING YEAST DOUGH

1 To rise bread dough quickly, give a 900g/2lb piece of dough short bursts of microwave energy on HIGH for 5–10 second intervals, observing a 10 minute standing time between each heating period.

2 Repeat until the dough has risen to double its size.

DEFROSTING FROZEN SHORTCRUST OR PUFF PASTRY

Place a 400g/14oz packet of pastry on a microwaveproof plate and microwave on DEFROST for 4–4½ minutes, turning over once during the time. Leave to stand for 5 minutes before using.

To Cook Poppadoms

1 Arrange two or three plain or spiced poppadoms on the base of the cooker or on the turntable so that they do not touch or overlap. Microwave on HIGH for 45–60 seconds until puffy and bubbling. Leave to stand on a wire rack for 15 seconds to crisp.

2 To make poppadom cases or cups (ideal for holding salad) position a poppadom over a small microwaveproof bowl and microwave on HIGH for 20–25 seconds. As it cooks, the poppadom will droop in folds over the bowl to make a cup shape. Leave to stand for about 15 seconds to crisp before removing from the bowl.

To Make Biscuit Cups

Ready-made biscuits, like brandy snaps and florentines, can be heated in the microwave over a microwaveproof bowl to form a cup shape that can later hold mousse, ice cream or fruit salad for an almost instant dessert. Position two biscuits over the top of two microwaveproof bowls and microwave on HIGH for 30–45 seconds, until very warm and pliable. While hot, mould the biscuits around the bowls to form cup shapes. Leave until completely cold and firm before removing from the bowls.

Softening Jams and Spreads

Remove any lids and any metal trims or transfer the jam or spread to a microwaveproof dish. Microwave on HIGH for about 5–10 seconds per 450g/1lb.

Dissolving Gelatine

1 Sprinkle the gelatine over cold water, as usual, and leave to stand until spongy.

2 Microwave on HIGH for 30 seconds until clear and completely dissolved.

Clarifying Crystallized Honey

Remove the lid and any metal trims on the jar. Microwave on HIGH for 1–2 minutes. Stir well.

Dissolving Jelly

1 Break up a 135g/4½oz jelly tablet and place in a microwaveproof bowl or jug with 150ml/¼ pint/⅔ cup water.

2 Microwave the jelly on HIGH for 2 minutes.

3 Stir well to dissolve, then make up with cold water according to the packet instructions.

MELTING CHOCOLATE

Break chocolate into pieces and place in a microwaveproof bowl. Microwave on HIGH, for about 1 minute per 25g/1oz.

SOFTENING ICE CREAM FOR SCOOPING

Microwave about 1 litre/ 1¾ pints/4 cups hard (not soft scoop) ice cream on MEDIUM for 45–90 seconds. Leave to stand for 1–2 minutes before scooping.

FLAMBÉING WITH ALCOHOL

Heat the alcohol, such as brandy, in a microwaveproof and flame-proof jug on HIGH for 15 seconds. It will then ignite more easily ready for pouring over Christmas pudding, pancakes or fresh fruit.

TO REHEAT READY-MADE FRESH BLACK COFFEE

Place 600ml/1 pint/2½ cups cold coffee in a microwaveproof jug and microwave on HIGH for 4½–5 minutes.

TO REHEAT A MUG OF TEA OR COFFEE

Make sure the mug is microwave-proof. Heat on HIGH for 30–60 seconds and stir before tasting. Repeat if necessary, always stirring before tasting as hot spots in the liquid can burn the mouth.

WARMING BABY'S BOTTLE

Invert the teat and microwave 250ml/8fl oz/1 cup prepared milk on HIGH for 1 minute to warm. Shake the bottle gently and test the milk to check the temperature before attempting to feed the baby. If in doubt check your baby milk formula instructions for preparing in the microwave.

TO HEAT MILK FOR DRINKS

Frothy hot milk for café au lait, hot chocolate or other beverages can be heated very quickly. Place 300ml/½ pint/1¼ cups cold milk in a microwaveproof jug and microwave on HIGH for 2–2½ minutes. Whisk well until frothy, if you like, and serve immediately.

TO MAKE MULLED WINE

Mix 750ml/1¼ pints/3 cups red wine, 12 cloves, 2 small cinnamon sticks, the grated rind and juice of 1 orange and 1 lemon, and 30–45ml/2–3 tbsp brown sugar in a microwaveproof bowl or jug. Microwave on HIGH for 5 minutes, or until almost boiling. Add extra sugar to taste, if you like, and serve the wine warm. This quantity serves about six.

Before You Begin

Microwave Powers and Settings

• All the recipes and charts in this book were created and tested using microwave ovens with a maximum power output of 650–700 watts.

• The ovens had variable power and the descriptions used refer to the following power outputs.

HIGH = 650–750 watts or 100%
MEDIUM HIGH = 500–550 watts or 75%
MEDIUM = 400 watts or 55–60%
LOW = 250 watts or 40%
DEFROST = 200 watts or 30%

• The chart below gives the approximate power input in watts at these levels and relative cooking times.

• The microwave ovens used for testing had turntables - if yours does not and tends to have an irregular heating pattern with hot and cold spots, then follow the rules on turning, rotating and rearranging foods.

• Metric measurements may vary from one recipe to another within the book, and it is essential to follow EITHER metric or Imperial. The recipes have been carefully balanced to get the very best results using only one set of measures and cannot be interchanged.

Unless Otherwise Stated

- eggs are size 3
- all spoon quantities are measured level

Foods to Avoid

The following foods do not cook well in the microwave and they are best avoided.

Eggs in Shells
These are liable to explode due to the build-up of pressure within the shell. Eggs can however be baked, scrambled, poached and "fried" in the microwave with superb results.

Popcorn
This can prove to be too dry to attract microwave energy, although some manufacturers have produced microwave popcorn, sold in a special bag with seasonings and flavourings, and this works superbly. A special microwave popcorn machine can also be purchased to cook ordinary popcorn in the microwave.

Batter based and Some Air-incorporated Recipes
Items like Yorkshire pudding, soufflé, pancakes, choux pastry, batter-coated fish and whisked sponge mixtures need conventional cooking to become crisp and firm. The microwave will, however, make the basic sauce for a soufflé and will reheat pancakes perfectly.

Conventional Meringues
These should be cooked in the conventional oven since they do not dry sufficiently and become crisp in the microwave.

Deep-fat Frying
This is not recommended since it requires prolonged heating, it is difficult to control the temperature of the fat and the food may burn.

Liquid in Bottles and Pots
Check that bottles do not have necks that are too narrow to allow sufficient escape since steam as built up pressure may cause them to shatter. Similarly, tall coffee pots, with slim spouts can break or cause coffee to spurt out.

Guide to Comparative Microwave Oven Control Settings

Settings used in these recipes	Setting variations on popular microwave ovens				Approximate % power input	Approximate power outputs in watts	Cooking times in minutes – for times greater than 10 minutes simply add together the figures in the appropriate columns									
	1	keep warm	low	2	25%	150W	4	8	12	16	20	24	28	32	36	40
Defrost	2	simmer	simmer	3	30%	200W	3¼	6¾	10	13¼	16¾	20	26¼	26¼	30	33¼
Low	3	stew	medium/low	4	40%	250W	2½	5	7½	10	12½	15	17½	20	22½	25
	4	defrost	medium	5	50%	300W	2	4	6	8	10	12	14	16	18	20
Medium	5	bake	medium	6	60%	400W	1¾	3¾	5	6¾	8¼	10	12	13¼	15	16½
Medium High	6	roast	high	7–8	75%	500–600W	1¼	2¾	4	5¼	6¾	8	9¼	10¾	12	13¼
High	7	full/high	normal	10	100%	700W	1	2	3	4	5	6	7	8	9	10

SOUPS AND
STARTERS

~

Italian Fish Soup

INGREDIENTS

Serves 4

30ml/2 tbsp olive oil

1 onion, thinly sliced

a few saffron threads

5ml/1 tsp dried thyme

large pinch of cayenne pepper

2 garlic cloves, finely chopped

2 x 400g/14oz cans peeled tomatoes,
    drained and chopped

175ml/6fl oz/³/₄ cup dry white wine

1.85 litres/3¹/₄ pints/8 cups hot fish stock

350g/12oz white, skinless fish fillets, cut
    into pieces

450g/1lb monkfish, membrane removed,
    cut into pieces

450g/1lb mussels in the shell,
    thoroughly scrubbed

225g/8oz small squid, cleaned and cut
    into rings

30ml/2 tbsp chopped fresh parsley

salt and ground black pepper

thickly sliced bread, to serve

1 Place the oil in a large microwaveproof bowl. Stir in the onion, saffron, thyme, cayenne pepper and salt to taste. Microwave on HIGH for 3 minutes, until soft. Add the garlic and microwave on HIGH for 1 minute.

2 Stir in the tomatoes, white wine and fish stock. Cover and microwave on HIGH for 10 minutes, stirring halfway through the cooking time.

3 Add the fish fillet and monkfish pieces to the bowl. Cover and microwave on HIGH for 2 minutes, stirring once.

4 Mix in the mussels and squid. Cover and microwave on HIGH for 2–3 minutes, stirring once, until the mussels open. Stir in the parsley and season with salt and pepper.

5 Ladle into warmed soup bowls and serve immediately, with warm crusty bread.

Creamy Cod Chowder

INGREDIENTS

Serves 4–6

350g/12oz smoked cod fillet
1 small onion, finely chopped
1 bay leaf
4 black peppercorns
900ml/1½ pints/3¾ cups skimmed milk
10ml/2 tsp cornflour
10ml/2 tsp water
200g/7oz canned sweetcorn kernels
15ml/1 tbsp chopped fresh parsley

1 Skin the fish fillet. Hold the tail firmly and cut the fish off its skin using a sharp knife. Cut at an acute angle, taking care not to cut the skin and folding back the fish fillet.

2 Place the fish in a large microwaveproof bowl with the onion, bay leaf and peppercorns. Pour in the milk.

3 Cover and microwave on HIGH for 8–10 minutes, stirring twice, or until the fish is just cooked.

4 Using a slotted spoon, lift out the fish and flake it into large chunks. Remove and discard the bay leaf and peppercorns.

5 Blend the cornflour with the water and add to the milk mixture. Microwave on HIGH for 2–3 minutes, stirring twice, until slightly thickened.

6 Drain the sweetcorn kernels and add to the milk mixture with the flaked fish and parsley.

7 To reheat the chowder, microwave on HIGH for 2–3 minutes until piping hot, stirring twice, but do not boil. Ladle the chowder into four or six soup bowls and serve straight away.

Beef Chilli Soup

This hearty dish, based on a traditional chilli recipe, is excellent with fresh crusty bread as a warming start to any meal.

INGREDIENTS

Serves 4

15ml/1 tbsp oil
1 onion, chopped
175g/6oz/1½ cups minced beef
2 garlic cloves, chopped
1 red chilli, sliced
25g/1oz/2 tbsp plain flour
400g/14oz can chopped tomatoes
600ml/1 pint/2½ cups hot beef stock
222g/8oz/2 cups canned red kidney
   beans, drained
30ml/2 tbsp chopped fresh parsley
salt and ground black pepper

1 Place the oil and onion in a microwaveproof bowl. Microwave on HIGH for 2 minutes, stirring once. Mix in the beef and microwave on HIGH for 4–4½ minutes, stirring twice.

2 Add the garlic, chilli and flour. Microwave on HIGH for 1 minute, stirring once.

3 Add the tomatoes and stock, mixing well. Cover and microwave on HIGH for 8 minutes, stirring twice.

4 Stir in the red kidney beans and season well with salt and pepper. Cover and microwave on HIGH for 10 minutes, stirring halfway through cooking.

5 Add the chopped fresh parsley and check the seasoning, adjusting to taste. Serve the soup with crusty bread.

Chunky Bean and Vegetable Soup

A substantial soup, not unlike minestrone, using a selection of vegetables, with cannellini beans for extra protein and fibre. Serve with a hunk of wholegrain bread.

INGREDIENTS

Serves 4

30ml/2 tbsp olive oil

2 celery sticks, chopped

2 leeks, sliced

3 carrots, sliced

2 garlic cloves, crushed

400g/14oz can chopped tomatoes
    with basil

1.2 litres/2 pints/5 cups hot
    vegetable stock

425g/15oz can cannellini beans (or mixed
    pulses), drained

15ml/1 tbsp pesto sauce

salt and ground black pepper

shavings of Parmesan cheese, to serve

1 Place the olive oil in a large microwaveproof bowl with the celery, leeks, carrots and garlic. Microwave on HIGH for 4 minutes, stirring halfway through cooking, until softened.

2 Stir in the tomatoes and the stock. Cover and microwave on HIGH for 10 minutes, stirring halfway through cooking.

3 Stir in the beans and pesto, with salt and pepper to taste. Microwave on HIGH for a further 3–5 minutes, stirring halfway through cooking. Serve in heated bowls, sprinkled with shavings of Parmesan cheese.

COOK'S TIP

Canned chick-peas give the soup a delicious nutty flavour. Flageolet beans are more delicate and borlotti beans are slightly more substantial.

Chilled Leek and Potato Soup

This creamy, chilled soup is a version of the classic Vichyssoise, originally created by a French chef at the Ritz Carlton Hotel in New York to celebrate the opening of the roof gardens.

INGREDIENTS

Serves 4

25g/1oz/2 tbsp butter
15ml/1 tbsp vegetable oil
1 small onion, chopped
3 leeks, sliced
2 potatoes, diced
600ml/1 pint/2½ cups hot vegetable stock
300ml/½ pint/1¼ cups milk
45ml/3 tbsp single cream
a little extra milk (optional)
salt and ground black pepper
60ml/4 tbsp natural yogurt and chopped
　chives, to garnish

1 Place the butter and oil in a large microwaveproof bowl, then add the onion, leeks and potatoes. Cover and microwave on HIGH for 10 minutes, stirring halfway through cooking. Stir in the stock and milk. Microwave on HIGH for a further 5–8 minutes, until the potatoes are tender.

2 Purée the vegetables and liquid in a blender or food processor until smooth. Return the soup to the bowl, stir in the cream and season well.

3 Leave the soup to cool and then chill it for 3–4 hours, or until really cold. You may need to add a little extra milk to thin the soup down as it will thicken slightly on cooling.

4 Serve the chilled soup in individual bowls, each topped with a tablespoon of natural yogurt and a sprinkling of chopped fresh chives.

Curried Parsnip Soup

The spices impart a delicious, mild curry flavour to sweet parsnips.

INGREDIENTS

Serves 4

25g/1oz/2 tbsp butter
1 garlic clove, crushed
1 onion, chopped
5ml/1 tsp ground cumin
5ml/1 tsp ground coriander
450g/1lb parsnips, (about 4) sliced
10ml/2 tsp medium curry paste
450ml/¾ pint/1⅞ cups hot chicken stock
450ml/¾ pint/1⅞ cups milk
60ml/4 tbsp soured cream
squeeze of lemon juice
salt and ground black pepper
chopped fresh coriander, to garnish
garlic and coriander naan bread, to serve

1 Place the butter in a large microwaveproof bowl with the garlic and onion. Cover the bowl and microwave on HIGH for 2 minutes. Stir in the spices and microwave on HIGH for a further 1 minute.

2 Add the parsnips and stir until well coated with butter. Then stir in the curry paste, followed by the stock. Cover and microwave on HIGH for 10–12 minutes, stirring halfway through cooking, until the parsnips are tender.

3 Purée the soup in a blender or food processor until smooth. Return the soup to the bowl and stir in the milk. Microwave on HIGH for 2–3 minutes, stirring halfway through cooking, then add 30ml/2 tbsp of the soured cream, the lemon juice and seasoning to taste.

4 Stir the fresh coriander into the remaining soured cream and use to top each portion of soup. Serve with naan bread.

Cauliflower and Walnut Cream Soup

Even though cream is not added to this soup, the cauliflower gives it a delicious, rich, creamy texture.

INGREDIENTS

Serves 4

1 medium cauliflower
1 onion, coarsely chopped
450ml/¾ pint/1⅞ cups hot chicken or
    vegetable stock
450ml/¾ pint/1⅞ cups skimmed milk
45ml/3 tbsp walnut pieces
salt and ground black pepper
paprika and chopped walnuts, to garnish

1 Trim the cauliflower of outer leaves and break it into small florets. Place the cauliflower, onion and stock in a large microwave-proof bowl.

2 Cover and microwave on HIGH for 8–10 minutes, stirring halfway through cooking, or until soft. Add the milk and walnuts, then purée in a food processor until smooth.

3 Return the soup to the bowl and season to taste. Microwave on HIGH for 2 minutes to reheat. Serve sprinkled with paprika and chopped walnuts.

VARIATIONS

To make Cauliflower and Almond Cream Soup, use 45ml/3 tbsp ground almonds in place of the walnut pieces.

Curried Carrot and Apple Soup

INGREDIENTS

Serves 4

10ml/2 tsp sunflower oil
15ml/1 tbsp mild curry powder
500g/1¼lb carrots, chopped
1 large onion, chopped
1 cooking apple, cored and chopped
750ml/1¼ pints/3 cups hot chicken stock
salt and ground black pepper
natural low-fat yogurt and carrot curls,
    to garnish

COOK'S TIP

Choose an acidic apple that will soften and fluff up as it cooks. Chop it into fairly small pieces before adding to the bowl.

1 Place the oil in a large microwaveproof bowl. Add the curry powder and microwave on HIGH for 1 minute, stirring halfway through cooking.

2 Add the carrots, onion and apple, stir well, then cover and microwave on HIGH for 8–10 minutes, stirring halfway through cooking, until softened.

3 Spoon the vegetable mixture into a food processor or blender, then add half the stock and process until smooth.

4 Return the soup to the bowl and pour in the remaining stock. Microwave on HIGH for 3–4 minutes, stirring once, to reheat. Adjust the seasoning before serving in bowls, garnished with swirls of yogurt and a few curls of carrot.

Jerusalem Artichoke Soup

Topped with saffron cream, this soup is wonderful on a chilly day.

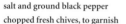

Serves 4

50g/2oz/4 tbsp butter

1 onion, chopped

450g/1lb Jerusalem artichokes, peeled and
    cut into chunks

900ml/1½ pints/3¾ cups hot chicken
    stock

150ml/¼ pint/⅔ cup milk

150ml/¼ pint/⅔ cup double cream

good pinch of saffron powder

salt and ground black pepper

chopped fresh chives, to garnish

1 Place the butter and onion in a large microwaveproof bowl and microwave on HIGH for 2–3 minutes, until soft, stirring once.

2 Add the artichokes to the bowl and stir to coat them in the butter. Cover and microwave on HIGH for 8–10 minutes, stirring halfway through cooking. Pour in the stock and milk, then cover and microwave on HIGH for 5–8 minutes, stirring once. Cool slightly, then process in a blender or food processor until smooth.

3 Strain the soup back into the bowl. Add half the cream, season to taste, and microwave on HIGH for 2–3 minutes to reheat. Lightly whip the remaining cream with the saffron powder. Ladle the soup into warmed soup bowls and put a spoonful of saffron cream in the centre of each. Sprinkle over the chives and serve immediately.

Broccoli and Stilton Soup

A really easy, but rich, soup – choose something simple to follow, such as plainly roasted or grilled meat, poultry or fish.

Serves 4

350g/12oz broccoli

25g/1oz/2 tbsp butter

1 onion, chopped

1 leek, white part only, chopped

1 small potato, cut into chunks

600ml/1 pint/2½ cups hot chicken stock

300ml/½ pint/1¼ cups milk

45ml/3 tbsp double cream

115g/4oz Stilton cheese, rind removed,
    crumbled

salt and ground black pepper

1 Break the broccoli into florets, discarding tough stems. Set aside two small florets for garnishing the soup.

2 Place the butter in a large microwaveproof bowl with the onion and leek. Microwave on HIGH for 3 minutes, until soft. Add the broccoli and potato, then pour in the stock. Cover and microwave on HIGH for 12–15 minutes, stirring twice, until the vegetables are tender.

3 Cool slightly, then purée in a blender or food processor. Strain through a sieve back into the bowl.

4 Add the milk, cream and seasoning to the bowl and microwave on HIGH for 3–4 minutes to reheat. At the last minute, add the cheese and stir until it just melts.

5 Place the reserved broccoli florets in a small microwave-proof bowl, cover and microwave on HIGH for 30 seconds, then cut them vertically into thin slices. Ladle the soup into warmed bowls. Garnish with the broccoli florets and serve with a generous grinding of black pepper.

Artichoke and Mushroom Soup

Delicate Jerusalem artichokes are perfectly matched with mushrooms in this simple soup. Select closed-cap mushrooms for good colour and light flavour.

INGREDIENTS

Serves 4

30–60ml/2–4 tbsp butter

115g/4oz/2 cups mushrooms, sliced

2 onions, chopped

450g/1lb Jerusalem artichokes, peeled
   and sliced

300ml/½ pint/1¼ cups hot vegetable stock

300ml/½ pint/1¼ cups milk

salt and ground black pepper

1 Place the butter and mushrooms in a large microwaveproof bowl. Cover and microwave on HIGH for 2 minutes. Using a slotted spoon, lift out the mushrooms and reserve on a plate. Add the onions and artichokes to the bowl, mixing well. Cover and microwave on HIGH for 8–10 minutes, stirring halfway through cooking.

2 Add the vegetable stock to the bowl and microwave on HIGH for a further 5 minutes, until the artichokes are soft, then season to taste.

3 Purée the soup in a blender or food processor, adding the milk slowly until smooth. Return the soup to the bowl. Stir in the mushrooms and microwave on HIGH for 2–3 minutes to reheat before serving.

Tomato and Red Pepper Soup

A late summer soup that can be served cold. Made using very ripe peppers and tomatoes, it won't be nearly as tasty if made with winter vegetables that have not been ripened in the sun.

INGREDIENTS

Serves 4

5 large tomatoes

30–60ml/2–4 tbsp olive oil

1 onion, chopped

450g/1lb thinly sliced red or
   orange peppers

30ml/2 tbsp tomato purée

a pinch of sugar

475ml/16fl oz/2 cups hot vegetable stock

60ml/4 tbsp soured cream (optional)

salt and ground black pepper

chopped fresh dill, to garnish

1 Skin the tomatoes by plunging them into boiling water for 30 seconds. Chop the flesh and reserve any juice.

2 Place half the oil in a microwaveproof bowl with the onion. Microwave on HIGH for 2 minutes, stirring once. Add the peppers and the remaining oil, mixing well. Cover and microwave on HIGH for 5 minutes, stirring halfway through cooking.

3 Stir in the chopped tomatoes, tomato purée, seasoning, sugar and a few tablespoons of stock. Cover and microwave on HIGH for 4 minutes, stirring halfway through cooking, until the vegetables are tender.

4 Stir in the rest of the stock and purée in a blender or food processor until smooth. Strain the soup to remove the skins and season to taste.

5 Pour into bowls, swirl in the soured cream, if using, and garnish with dill.

Corn Soup

This is a simple-to-make yet very flavoursome soup. It is also sometimes made with soured cream and cream cheese.

INGREDIENTS

Serves 4

30ml/2 tbsp corn oil

1 onion, finely chopped

1 red pepper, seeded and chopped

450g/1lb sweetcorn kernels, thawed
    if frozen

750ml/1¼ pints/3 cups hot chicken stock

250ml/8fl oz/1 cup single cream

salt and ground black pepper

½ red pepper, seeded and cut into small
    dice, to garnish

1 Place the oil, onion and red pepper in a microwaveproof bowl. Cover and microwave on HIGH for 4 minutes, stirring once. Add the sweetcorn and microwave on HIGH for 4 minutes, stirring once during cooking.

2 Carefully tip the contents of the bowl into a food processor or blender. Process until smooth, scraping the mixture down the container occasionally and adding a little of the stock, if necessary.

3 Put the mixture into a microwaveproof bowl and stir in the stock. Season to taste, then microwave on HIGH for 4 minutes, stirring once.

4 Gently stir in the cream. Serve the soup hot or chilled, sprinkled with the diced red pepper. If serving hot, microwave on HIGH for 1–2 minutes after adding the cream, but do not allow the soup to boil.

Courgette Soup

INGREDIENTS

Serves 4

30ml/2 tbsp butter

1 onion, finely chopped

450g/1lb young courgettes, trimmed
    and chopped

750ml/1¼ pints/3 cups hot chicken stock

120ml/4fl oz/½ cup single cream, plus
    extra to serve

salt and ground black pepper

COOK'S TIP

This simple soup is ideal for using up a glut of home-grown courgettes. Be sure to select young vegetables with fine skin as large old courgettes tend to be watery, with a weaker flavour and coarse skin.

1 Place the butter and onion in a large microwaveproof bowl. Cover and microwave on HIGH for 2 minutes, stirring once. Add the courgettes and microwave on HIGH for 6 minutes, stirring once.

2 Pour in the chicken stock, cover and microwave on HIGH for 3 minutes, stirring once.

3 Purée the mixture in a blender or food processor until smooth, then season to taste.

4 Stir the cream into the soup, return it to the bowl and microwave on HIGH for 1 minute to heat through very gently without allowing it to boil. Serve hot, swirled with a little extra cream.

Chilli Prawns

*This delightful, spicy combination
makes a tempting light main course
for a casual supper. Serve with rice,
noodles or freshly cooked pasta and
a leafy salad.*

INGREDIENTS

Serves 3–4

45ml/3 tbsp olive oil

2 shallots, chopped

2 garlic cloves, chopped

1 fresh red chilli, chopped

450g/1lb ripe tomatoes, peeled, seeded
   and chopped

15ml/1 tbsp tomato purée

1 bay leaf

1 thyme sprig

90ml/6 tbsp dry white wine

450g/1lb peeled cooked large prawns

salt and ground black pepper

roughly torn basil leaves, to garnish

1 Place the oil, shallots, garlic
and chilli in a microwaveproof
bowl and microwave on HIGH for
2 minutes, stirring once.

2 Add the tomatoes, tomato
purée, bay leaf, thyme,
wine and seasoning. Cover and
microwave on HIGH for 6–7
minutes, stirring twice. Discard
the herbs.

3 Stir the prawns into the sauce
and microwave on HIGH
for 2–3 minutes, stirring once.
Taste and adjust the seasoning.
Garnish with torn basil leaves and
serve at once.

COOK'S TIP

For a milder flavour, scrape and
then rinse out all the seeds from
the chilli before chopping it.

Scallops with Ginger

*Scallops cook very well in the
microwave. Rich and creamy, this
dish is very simple to make and
quite delicious.*

INGREDIENTS

Serves 4

40g/1½oz/3 tbsp butter

8–12 scallops, shelled

2.5cm/1in piece fresh root ginger,
   finely chopped

1 bunch spring onions, diagonally sliced

30ml/2 tbsp white vermouth

250ml/8fl oz/1 cup crème fraîche

salt and ground black pepper

chopped fresh parsley, to garnish

1 Place the butter in a shallow
microwaveproof dish.
Microwave on HIGH for
30 seconds to melt.

2 Remove the tough muscle
opposite the red coral on each
scallop. Separate the coral and cut
the white part of the scallop in
half horizontally. Add the scallops,
including the corals, to the dish,
cover and microwave on HIGH for
4–6 minutes, rearranging once.

3 Lift out the scallops with a
slotted spoon and transfer
them to a warmed serving dish.
Keep warm.

4 Add the ginger and spring
onions to the juices in the
bowl and microwave on HIGH for
1 minute. Pour in the vermouth
and microwave on HIGH for
30 seconds. Stir in the crème
fraîche and microwave on HIGH
for 1–1½ minutes, stirring twice.
Taste and adjust the seasoning.

5 Pour the sauce over the
scallops, sprinkle with fresh
parsley and serve.

Chicken Liver Pâté with Marsala

This pâté is really quick and simple to make, yet it has a delicious – and quite sophisticated – flavour. It contains Marsala, a soft and pungent fortified wine from Sicily. Brandy or a medium-dry sherry may be used instead.

INGREDIENTS

Serves 4

350g/12oz chicken livers, defrosted
   if frozen
225g/8oz/1 cup butter, softened
2 garlic cloves, crushed
15ml/1 tbsp Marsala
5ml/1 tsp chopped fresh sage
salt and ground black pepper
8 sage leaves, to garnish
Melba toast, to serve

1 Trim any membranes and sinew from the livers, then rinse and dry with kitchen paper. Place 25g/1oz/2 tbsp of the butter in a microwaveproof bowl with the chicken livers and the garlic. Cover loosely and microwave on HIGH for about 4 minutes, or until the livers are firm but pink in the middle, stirring twice.

2 Use a slotted spoon to transfer the livers to a blender or food processor. Add the Marsala and chopped sage.

3 Place 150g/5oz/10 tbsp of the remaining butter in a microwaveproof bowl and microwave on HIGH for 1½ minutes to melt, then pour it into the blender or processor and blend until smooth. Season well.

4 Spoon the pâté into four individual pots and smooth the surface. Place the remaining butter in a microwaveproof bowl and microwave on HIGH for 1 minute to melt and pour it over the pâtés. Garnish with sage leaves and chill until set. Serve with triangles of Melba toast.

COOK'S TIP
To make Melba toast, toast medium-thick bread. Cut off the crusts and slice the toast in half horizontally. Lightly brown the untoasted sides. Cool on a wire rack.

Mushroom Pâté

This is a vegetarian alternative to liver-based pâtés. Cooking the onion in butter gives a rich flavour, but you can use oil instead, if preferred.

INGREDIENTS

Serves 4

30ml/2 tbsp olive oil or butter

2 onions, chopped

350g/12oz/4½ cups mushrooms, chopped
   or roughly sliced

225g/8oz/1 cup ground almonds

a handful of parsley, stalks removed

salt and ground black pepper

flat leaf parsley, to garnish

thin slices of toast, cucumber, chicory and
   celery sticks, to serve

1 Place the olive oil or butter in a microwaveproof bowl with the onions. Microwave on HIGH for 5–7 minutes, stirring twice.

2 Add the mushrooms and microwave on HIGH for 3–3½ minutes, stirring halfway through cooking. Season well.

3 Transfer the cooked onion and mushrooms to a blender or food processor with their juices. Add the ground almonds and parsley, and process briefly. The pâté can either be smooth or you can leave it slightly chunky. Taste again for seasoning.

4 Spoon the pâté into individual pots. Garnish with flat leaf parsley and serve with thin slices of toast and sticks of cucumber, chicory and celery.

Eggs en Cocotte

A classic starter, these baked eggs are cooked on a flavoursome base of ratatouille, making them ideal for microwave cooking. They are also excellent for lunch or supper, with plenty of warm crusty bread.

INGREDIENTS

Serves 4

4 eggs

20ml/4 tsp freshly grated Parmesan cheese

chopped fresh parsley, to garnish

For the ratatouille

1 small red pepper

15ml/1 tbsp olive oil

1 onion, finely chopped

1 garlic clove, crushed

2 courgettes, diced

400g/14oz can chopped tomatoes
    with basil

salt and ground black pepper

1 First prepare the vegetables: cut the red pepper in half on a board and remove the seeds. Then dice the pepper flesh.

2 Place the oil in a microwave-proof bowl. Add the onion, garlic, courgettes and pepper, and microwave on HIGH for 3–4 minutes, stirring once, until softened. Stir in the tomatoes, with salt and pepper to taste, and microwave on HIGH for 3–4 minutes, stirring once.

3 Divide the ratatouille between four individual microwave-proof dishes or large ramekins, each with a capacity of about 300ml/½ pint/1¼ cups.

4 Make a small hollow in the centre of each portion of ratatouille and break in an egg.

5 Grind some black pepper over the top of each cocotte and sprinkle with the cheese. Gently prick each yolk with a needle or wooden cocktail stick. Microwave on HIGH for 4–6 minutes or until the eggs are just set. Sprinkle with the fresh parsley and serve at once.

Leeks with Mustard Dressing

Pencil-slim baby leeks are increasingly available, and are beautifully tender. Use three or four of these smaller leeks per serving.

INGREDIENTS

Serves 4

8 slim leeks, each about 13cm/5in long
45ml/3 tbsp water
5–10ml/1–2 tsp Dijon mustard
10ml/2 tsp white wine vinegar
1 hard-boiled egg, halved lengthways
75ml/5 tbsp light olive oil
10ml/2 tsp chopped fresh parsley
salt and ground black pepper

1 Place the leeks in a microwaveproof dish with the water. Cover and microwave on HIGH for 3–5 minutes, rearranging twice. Leave to stand for 2 minutes, then drain thoroughly.

2 Meanwhile, stir the mustard and vinegar together in a bowl. Scoop the egg yolk into the bowl and mash it thoroughly into the vinegar mixture using a fork.

3 Gradually work in the oil to make a smooth sauce, then season to taste.

4 Place the leeks on several layers of kitchen paper, then pat them dry with several more layers of kitchen paper.

5 Transfer the leeks to a serving dish. While they are still warm, spoon the dressing over them and leave to cool. Finely chop the egg white, then mix it with the chopped fresh parsley and scatter this over the leeks. Chill until ready to serve.

COOK'S TIP

Although this dish is served cold, make sure that the leeks are still warm when you pour over the dressing so that they will absorb the mustard flavours.

Leek Terrine with Deli Meats

This attractive starter is very simple to make yet looks spectacular. You can make the terrine a day ahead and keep it covered in the fridge. If your guests are vegetarian offer chunks of feta cheese with the terrine instead of the cooked meats.

Serves 6

20–24 small young leeks
45ml/3 tbsp water
60ml/4 tbsp walnut oil
60ml/4 tbsp olive oil
30ml/2 tbsp white wine vinegar
5ml/1 tsp wholegrain mustard
salt and ground black pepper
about 225g/8oz mixed sliced meats, such
   as Parma ham, coppa or pancetta
50g/2oz/²⁄₃ cup walnuts, toasted and
   chopped

1 Cut off the roots and most of the green parts from the leeks. Wash them thoroughly under cold running water to remove any grit or mud.

2 Place the leeks in a roasting bag with the water. Secure loosely with string or an elastic band and microwave on HIGH for 6–8 minutes, turning over and shaking to rearrange halfway through cooking. Leave to stand for 3–5 minutes, then drain well.

3 Fill a 450g/1lb loaf tin with the leeks, placing them alternately tops to root ends, sprinkling each layer with salt and pepper.

4 Put another loaf tin inside the first and gently press down on the leeks. Carefully invert both tins and drain out any water.

COOK'S TIP

It is important to use tender young leeks for this terrine. It is mainly the white part that is used in this recipe, but the green tops can be reserved for making soup. The terrine must be pressed for at least 4 hours – this makes it easier to carve into slices. You can vary the sliced meats as you like; try, for example, bresaola, salami, smoked venison or roast ham.

5 Place one or two weights on the top tin and chill the terrine for at least 4 hours, or overnight.

6 Meanwhile, make the dressing. Whisk together the walnut and olive oils, vinegar and whole-grain mustard in a small bowl. Add seasoning to taste.

7 Carefully turn out the terrine on to a board and cut it into slices using a large sharp knife. Lay the slices of leek terrine on serving plates and arrange the sliced meats alongside.

8 Spoon the dressing over the terrine and scatter over the chopped walnuts. Serve at once.

VARIATION

If you are short of time, serve the cooked leeks simply marinated in the walnut and mustard dressing.

Stuffed Vine Leaves

Based on the Greek dolmas (or dolmades) but with a wholegrain vegetarian stuffing, this makes an excellent low-fat, high-fibre starter, snack or buffet dish. This is a quick version of the traditional speciality – the leaves and filling are cooked separately, rather than by long, slow cooking together for the authentic dish.

INGREDIENTS

Makes about 40

15ml/1 tbsp sunflower oil
5ml/1 tsp sesame oil
1 onion, finely chopped
225g/8oz/1⅓ cups brown rice
600ml/1 pint/2½ cups hot vegetable stock
1 small yellow pepper, seeded and finely chopped
115g/4oz/⅔ cup ready-to-eat dried apricots, finely chopped
2 lemons
50g/2oz/½ cup pine nuts
45ml/3 tbsp chopped fresh parsley
30ml/2 tbsp chopped fresh mint
2.5ml/½ tsp mixed spice
225g/8oz packet vine leaves preserved in brine, drained
150ml/¼ pint/⅔ cup water
30ml/2 tbsp olive oil
ground black pepper
lemon wedges, to garnish

To serve
300ml/½ pint/1¼ cups low-fat natural yogurt
30ml/2 tbsp chopped fresh mixed herbs
cayenne pepper

1 Place the sunflower and sesame oils together in a large microwaveproof bowl. Microwave on HIGH for 30 seconds. Add the onion and microwave on HIGH for 2 minutes, stirring once.

2 Add the rice and stir to coat the grains in oil. Pour in the stock, cover loosely and microwave on HIGH for 3 minutes. Reduce the power setting to MEDIUM and microwave for a further 25 minutes, stirring two or three times.

3 Stir in the chopped pepper and apricots. Replace the cover and leave to stand for 5 minutes.

4 Grate the rind off 1 lemon, then squeeze both lemons. Drain off any stock that has not been absorbed by the rice. Stir in the pine nuts, herbs, mixed spice, lemon rind and half the juice. Season with pepper and set aside.

5 Place the vine leaves in a bowl with the water, cover and microwave on HIGH for 4 minutes. Drain the leaves well, then lay them shiny side down on a board. Cut out any coarse stalks.

6 Place a heap of the rice mixture in the centre of a vine leaf. Fold over first the stem end, then the sides and finally the pointed end to make a neat parcel. Repeat with the remaining leaves.

7 Pack the parcels closely together in a shallow serving dish. Mix the remaining lemon juice with the olive oil and pour over the vine leaves. Cover and chill before serving.

8 Serve the vine leaves, garnished with lemon wedges. Spoon the yogurt into a bowl, stir in the chopped herbs and sprinkle with a little cayenne. Offer this light sauce with the chilled stuffed vine leaves.

COOK'S TIP

If vine leaves are not available, the leaves of Swiss chard, young spinach or cabbage can be used instead.

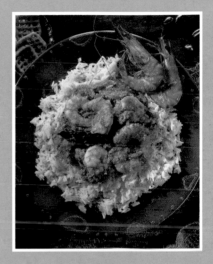

FISH AND
SHELLFISH

~

Fisherman's Casserole

A perfect dish for microwaving as it's cooked in one dish.

INGREDIENTS

Serves 4–6

450g/1lb mixed firm fish fillets, such as
   cod, haddock and monkfish
50g/2oz/4 tbsp butter
1 onion, sliced
1 celery stick, sliced
350g/12oz potatoes, cut into chunks
750ml/1¼ pints/3 cups hot fish stock
bouquet garni
150g/5oz frozen broad beans
300ml/½ pint/1¼ cups milk
115g/4oz peeled cooked prawns
8 mussels, shelled
salt and ground black pepper
chopped parsley, to garnish

1 Skin the fish and cut the flesh into bite-sized chunks using a large sharp knife. Place the butter in a microwaveproof dish and microwave on HIGH for 1 minute, until melted. Add the onion, celery and potatoes, cover and microwave on HIGH for 4 minutes, stirring once during cooking.

2 Stir in the stock, bouquet garni and beans. Cover and microwave on HIGH for 10 minutes, stirring twice.

3 Add the fish and milk, re-cover and microwave on HIGH for 5–7 minutes until the fish flakes. Stir in the prawns, mussels and seasoning and microwave on HIGH for 1–2 minutes to warm through. Sprinkle with parsley and serve.

Potato-topped Fish Pie

Cheese-topped potatoes enclose a creamy mixture of fish, prawns and hard-boiled eggs.

INGREDIENTS

Serves 4

400ml/14fl oz/1⅔ cups hot milk
1 bay leaf
¼ onion, sliced
450g/1lb haddock or cod fillet
225g/8oz smoked haddock fillet
3 hard-boiled eggs, chopped
65g/2½oz/5 tbsp butter
25g/1oz/2 tbsp plain flour
115g/4oz/1 cup frozen peas
75g/3oz peeled cooked prawns
30ml/2 tbsp chopped fresh parsley
lemon juice, to taste
500g/1¼lb cooked potatoes, mashed
60ml/4 tbsp grated Cheddar cheese
salt and ground black pepper

1 Place 120ml/4fl oz/½ cup of the milk, the bay leaf and onion in a microwaveproof dish, then add the white and smoked fish. Cover and microwave on HIGH for 7–8 minutes, rearranging once. Strain and reserve the milk. Flake the fish into a microwaveproof pie dish, discarding the skin and any bones. Add the eggs.

2 Place 25g/1oz/2 tbsp of the butter, the flour and remaining milk in a microwaveproof jug. Whisk in the reserved cooking liquid from the fish. Microwave on HIGH for 5–7 minutes, stirring every 1 minute, until the mixture is smooth, boiling and thickened. Stir in the peas and cooked prawns.

3 Add the parsley, lemon juice and seasoning to taste. Pour the sauce over the fish and eggs and carefully mix the ingredients.

4 Spoon the mashed potato evenly over the fish and fork up the surface. Dot with the remaining butter.

5 Sprinkle the cheese over the pie, then microwave on HIGH for 5–6 minutes. Brown under a preheated hot grill, if liked. Serve piping hot.

COMBINATION MICROWAVE

This recipe is suitable for cooking in a combination microwave. Follow your oven manufacturer's timing guide for good results.

Cod Creole

The lime or lemon juice and cayenne add piquancy to this dish.

INGREDIENTS

Serves 4

450g/1lb cod fillet, skinned
15ml/1 tbsp lime or lemon juice
10ml/2 tsp olive oil
1 onion, finely chopped
1 green pepper, seeded and sliced
2.5ml/½ tsp cayenne pepper
2.5ml/½ tsp garlic salt
400g/14oz can chopped tomatoes

1 Cut the cod fillet into bite-sized chunks and sprinkle with the lime or lemon juice.

2 Place the olive oil, onion and pepper in a large microwave-proof bowl. Cover and microwave on HIGH for 3 minutes, stirring once. Add the cayenne pepper and garlic salt.

3 Stir in the cod with the chopped tomatoes and cover. Microwave on HIGH for 8–10 minutes, stirring twice, until the fish is cooked and flakes easily. Serve with boiled rice or potatoes.

> ### COOK'S TIP
>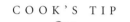
> Be careful not to overcook the fish – or to let it bubble too vigorously in the sauce – as the chunks will break up.

Five-spice Fish

Chinese mixtures of spicy, sweet and sour flavours are particularly successful with fish – and dinner is ready in minutes!

INGREDIENTS

Serves 4

5ml/1 tsp Chinese five-spice powder
20ml/4 tsp cornflour
4 portions white fish fillet, such as cod, haddock or hoki, about 175g/6oz each
15ml/1 tbsp sesame or sunflower oil
3 spring onions, shredded
5ml/1 tsp finely chopped fresh root ginger
150g/5oz button mushrooms, sliced
115g/4oz baby corn, sliced
30ml/2 tbsp soy sauce
45ml/3 tbsp dry sherry or apple juice
5ml/1 tsp sugar
salt and ground black pepper

1 Mix the five-spice powder and cornflour and use to coat the portions of fish.

2 Place the oil in a shallow microwaveproof dish with the spring onions, ginger, mushrooms and corn. Cover and microwave on HIGH for 2 minutes, stirring once. Add the fish and toss well to mix. Cover and microwave on HIGH for 4–6 minutes, stirring once.

3 Mix together the soy sauce, sherry or apple juice and sugar, then pour this mixture over the fish. Cover and microwave on HIGH for 2–3 minutes, stirring once. Adjust the seasoning, then serve with noodles and stir-fried vegetables.

Monkfish with Mexican Salsa

INGREDIENTS

Serves 4

675g/1½lb monkfish tail
45ml/3 tbsp olive oil
30ml/2 tbsp lime juice
1 garlic clove, crushed
15ml/1 tbsp chopped fresh coriander
salt and ground black pepper
coriander sprigs and lime slices, to garnish

For the salsa

4 tomatoes, peeled, seeded and diced
1 avocado, peeled, stoned and diced
½ red onion, chopped
1 green chilli, seeded and chopped
30ml/2 tbsp chopped fresh coriander
30ml/2 tbsp olive oil
15ml/1 tbsp lime juice

1 Prepare the monkfish. Using a sharp knife, remove the pinkish-grey membrane. Cut one fillet from either side of the backbone, then cut both fillets in half to make four steaks.

2 Mix together the oil, lime juice, garlic, coriander and seasoning in a shallow non-metallic dish. Add the monkfish steaks and turn them several times to coat with the marinade. Cover the dish and leave the fish to marinate at cool room temperature, or in the fridge, for several hours.

3 About 30 minutes before cooking the fish, mix all the salsa ingredients and leave to marinate at room temperature.

4 Remove the monkfish from the marinade and place in a shallow microwaveproof dish. Cover and microwave on HIGH for 4–6 minutes, turning once and brushing twice with the marinade, until cooked through.

5 Serve the monkfish garnished with coriander sprigs and lime slices and accompanied by the salsa.

COOK'S TIP

It is important to remove the tough, pinkish-grey membrane covering the monkfish tail before cooking, otherwise it will shrink and toughen the monkfish.

Spaghetti with Seafood Sauce

For speed, the sauce for this recipe is cooked in the microwave while the spaghetti is cooked on the hob.

INGREDIENTS

Serves 4

45ml/3 tbsp olive oil

1 onion, chopped

1 garlic clove, finely chopped

225g/8oz spaghetti

600ml/1 pint/2½ cups passata

15ml/1 tbsp tomato purée

5ml/1 tsp dried oregano

1 bay leaf

5ml/1 tsp sugar

115g/4oz/1 cup peeled cooked shrimps, drained and well rinsed if canned

115g/4oz/1 cup peeled cooked prawns

175g/6oz/1½ cups shelled cooked clams or cockles, drained and well rinsed if canned or bottled

15ml/1 tbsp lemon juice

45ml/3 tbsp chopped fresh parsley

25g/1oz/2 tbsp butter

salt and ground black pepper

4 whole cooked prawns, to garnish (optional)

1 Place the oil in a microwave-proof bowl and add the onion and garlic. Microwave on HIGH for 3 minutes, stirring halfway through cooking.

2 Meanwhile, cook the spaghetti in a large saucepan of boiling salted water for 10–12 minutes until *al dente*.

3 Stir the passata, tomato purée, oregano, bay leaf and sugar into the onions and season well. Cover and microwave on HIGH for 4 minutes, stirring twice during cooking.

4 Add the shrimps, prawns, clams or cockles, lemon juice and 30ml/2 tbsp of the parsley. Stir well, then cover and microwave on HIGH for 3–4 minutes, stirring once, until the shellfish are heated through.

5 Meanwhile, drain the cooked spaghetti and add the butter to the pan. Return the drained spaghetti to the pan and toss it in the butter. Season well with ground black pepper.

6 Divide the spaghetti between four warmed plates and top with the seafood sauce. Sprinkle with the remaining parsley, garnish with whole prawns and serve immediately.

Stuffed Plaice Rolls

Plaice fillets are a good choice because they are delicate in flavour, easy to cook, and free of bones.

INGREDIENTS

Serves 4

2 carrots, grated

1 courgette, grated

60ml/4 tbsp fresh wholemeal
   breadcrumbs

15ml/1 tbsp lime or lemon juice

4 plaice fillets

salt and ground black pepper

1 Mix together the grated carrots and courgette. Stir in the breadcrumbs, lime or lemon juice and seasoning.

2 Lay the fish fillets skin side up and divide the stuffing between them, spreading it evenly.

COOK'S TIP

The plaice rolls create their own delicious juices, but for additional sauce, stir chopped fresh parsley into a little low-fat fromage frais and serve this with the fish.

3 Roll up the fillets to enclose the stuffing and place in a microwaveproof dish. Cover and microwave on HIGH for 4–6 minutes, rearranging once. Leave to stand, covered, for 3 minutes before serving. Serve hot with new potatoes.

VARIATIONS

Lemon sole can be used instead of plaice. Alternatively, buy thick pieces of cod or salmon fillet and simply top them with the carrot and courgette mixture. The microwave cooking times will be a little longer if cod steaks are used.

Mediterranean Plaice

Sun-dried tomatoes, toasted pine nuts and anchovies make a flavoursome combination for the stuffing mixture.

INGREDIENTS

Serves 4

4 plaice fillets, about 225g/8oz each,
    skinned
75g/3oz/6 tbsp butter
1 small onion, chopped
1 celery stick, finely chopped
115g/4oz/2 cups fresh white breadcrumbs
45ml/3 tbsp chopped fresh parsley
30ml/2 tbsp pine nuts, toasted
3–4 pieces sun-dried tomatoes in oil,
    drained and chopped
50g/2oz can anchovy fillets, drained
    and chopped
75ml/5 tbsp fish stock
ground black pepper

1 Using a sharp knife, cut the plaice fillets in half lengthways to make eight smaller fillets.

2 Place the butter in a microwaveproof bowl and add the onion and celery. Cover and microwave on HIGH for 2 minutes, stirring halfway through cooking.

3 Mix together the breadcrumbs, parsley, pine nuts, sun-dried tomatoes and anchovies. Stir in the softened vegetables with their buttery juices and season with pepper.

4 Divide the stuffing into eight portions. Taking one portion at a time, form the stuffing into balls, then roll up each one inside a plaice fillet. Secure the rolls with wooden cocktail stick.

5 Place the rolled fillets in a buttered microwaveproof dish. Pour in the stock and cover the dish. Microwave on HIGH for 6–8 minutes, or until the fish flakes easily. Remove the cocktail sticks, then serve with a little of the cooking juices drizzled over.

Halibut with Fennel and Orange

The fennel for this recipe can be cooked in a roasting bag, but remember to replace the metal tie with an elastic band or a piece of string.

INGREDIENTS

Serves 4

1 fennel bulb, thinly sliced

30ml/2 tbsp water

grated rind and juice of 1 orange

150ml/¼ pint/⅔ cup dry white wine

4 halibut steaks, about 200g/7oz each

50g/2oz/4 tbsp butter

salt and ground black pepper

fennel fronds, to garnish

1 Place the fennel in a microwaveproof bowl with the water. Cover and microwave on HIGH for 4–5 minutes, until just tender.

2 Place the orange rind, juice and wine in a microwaveproof jug and microwave on HIGH for 2–3 minutes, until reduced by about half.

3 Drain the fennel well. Butter a shallow microwaveproof dish. Spread out the fennel in the dish and season it to taste. Arrange the halibut on the fennel, season the fish, dot it with butter, then pour over the reduced orange and wine.

4 Cover and microwave on HIGH for 7–8 minutes, rotating the dish twice, until the halibut flesh flakes. Serve garnished with fennel fronds.

Salmon with Cucumber Sauce

Cucumber and dill are classic accompaniments for delicate salmon; here they are used in a creamy sauce.

INGREDIENTS

Serves 6–8

1.8kg/4lb salmon, gutted and scaled

melted butter, for brushing

3 parsley or thyme sprigs

½ lemon, halved

1 large cucumber, peeled

25g/1oz/2 tbsp butter

50ml/2fl oz/¼ cup dry white wine

45ml/3 tbsp finely chopped fresh dill

60ml/4 tbsp soured cream

salt and ground black pepper

1 Season the salmon and brush it inside and out with melted butter. Place the parsley or thyme and lemon in the body cavity.

2 Prick the salmon skin in several places to prevent bursting and place the fish in a shallow microwaveproof dish. Shield the head and tail with small pieces of smooth foil to prevent them from overcooking. Cover and microwave on HIGH for 20–22 minutes, rotating the dish three times during cooking. Leave the salmon to stand for 1 hour, then remove the skin.

3 Meanwhile, halve the cucumber lengthways, scoop out the seeds and dice the flesh.

4 Place the cucumber in a colander, sprinkle it with salt and toss lightly. Leave for about 30 minutes to drain, then rinse well and pat dry.

5 Place the butter in a small microwaveproof bowl, add the cucumber and microwave on HIGH for 1 minute, until translucent but not soft. Add the wine and microwave on HIGH for a further 1–2 minutes.

6 Stir the chopped dill and soured cream into the cooked cucumber. Season the cucumber sauce to taste and serve immediately with the salmon.

Herby Fish Cakes with Lemon-Chive Sauce

The wonderful flavour of fresh herbs makes these fish cakes the catch of the day.

INGREDIENTS

Serves 4

350g/12oz potatoes, peeled
60ml/4 tbsp water
75ml/5 tbsp skimmed milk
350g/12oz haddock or hoki fillets, skinned
15ml/1 tbsp lemon juice
15ml/1 tbsp creamed horseradish sauce
30ml/2 tbsp chopped fresh parsley
flour, for dusting
115g/4oz/2 cups fresh wholemeal bread-
    crumbs
salt and ground black pepper
sprig of flat leaf parsley, to garnish
mangetouts and a sliced tomato and
    onion salad, to serve

For the lemon-chive sauce
thinly pared rind and juice of ½ small
    lemon
120ml/4fl oz/½ cup dry white wine
2 thin slices fresh root ginger
10ml/2 tsp cornflour
30ml/2 tbsp chopped fresh chives

1 Cut the potatoes into small cubes and place in a microwaveproof bowl with 45ml/3 tbsp of the water. Cover and microwave on HIGH for 6–8 minutes until tender, stirring halfway through cooking. Drain and mash with the milk and season to taste.

2 Purée the fish with the lemon juice and horseradish sauce in a blender or food processor, then mix the purée with the potatoes and parsley.

3 With floured hands, shape the mixture into eight cakes and coat them with the breadcrumbs. Chill the fish cakes for 30 minutes.

4 To make the sauce, cut the lemon rind into julienne strips and place it in a large microwave-proof bowl. Add the lemon juice, wine, ginger and seasoning to taste. Microwave on HIGH for 3–4 minutes, stirring twice.

5 Blend the cornflour with the remaining 15ml/1 tbsp cold water. Add to the sauce and stir until clear. If necessary, microwave on HIGH for 1 minute, stirring once, until clear and thickened.

6 To cook the fish cakes, place them in a shallow microwave-proof dish. Cover and microwave on HIGH for 7–8 minutes, turning the cakes over halfway through cooking. Brown lightly under a preheated hot grill, if liked.

7 Stir the chives into the hot sauce and serve immediately with the fish cakes, garnished with sprigs of flat leaf parsley. Mangetouts and a sliced tomato and onion salad are suitable accompaniments.

Mackerel Kebabs with Parsley Dressing

Fish kebabs cook quickly and evenly in the microwave.

Serves 1

450g/1lb mackerel fillets
finely grated rind and juice of 1 lemon
45ml/3 tbsp chopped fresh parsley
12 cherry tomatoes
8 black olives, stoned
salt and ground black pepper

1 Cut the fish into 4cm/1½in chunks and place in a bowl with half the lemon rind and juice, half the parsley and seasoning. Cover and leave to marinate for 30 minutes.

2 Thread the fish on to eight long wooden skewers, alternating the chunks with tomatoes and olives. Place the kebabs on a microwave-proof roasting rack or rest them across a shallow microwaveproof dish. Cover with greaseproof paper and microwave on HIGH for 4–6 minutes. Rearrange halfway through cooking, until the fish is cooked.

3 Mix the remaining lemon rind and juice with the remaining parsley in a small bowl, adding seasoning to taste. Spoon the dressing over the kebabs and serve hot, with plain boiled rice or noodles and a leafy green salad.

COOK'S TIP

When using wooden or bamboo kebab skewers, soak them first in a bowl of cold water for a few minutes to help prevent them from drying out and cracking.

VARIATIONS

Other firm-fleshed fish may be used in place of the mackerel – for a special occasion you could opt for monkfish tail or salmon fillet; or try a mixture of the two, threading the fish chunks alternately on to the skewers with the tomatoes and olives.

Tuna and Mixed Vegetable Pasta

Cook this simple and very speedy sauce in the microwave while the pasta cooks conventionally.

INGREDIENTS

Serves 4

30ml/2 tbsp olive oil

175g/6oz/1½ cups button mushrooms, sliced

1 garlic clove, crushed

½ red pepper, seeded and chopped

15ml/1 tbsp tomato purée

300ml/½ pint/1¼ cups tomato juice

115g/4oz frozen peas

15–30ml/1–2 tbsp drained pickled green peppercorns, crushed

275g/10oz/2½ cups wholewheat pasta shapes

200g/7oz can tuna chunks in brine, drained

6 spring onions, diagonally sliced

1 Place the oil in a microwave-proof bowl with the mushrooms, garlic and pepper. Cover and microwave on HIGH for 4 minutes, stirring halfway through cooking. Stir in the tomato purée, then add the tomato juice, peas and some or all of the crushed peppercorns, depending on how spicy you like the sauce.

2 Cover the bowl and microwave on HIGH for a further 4 minutes, stirring halfway through cooking.

3 Bring a large saucepan of lightly salted water to the boil on the hob and cook the pasta for about 12 minutes, or according to the packet instructions, until just tender. When the pasta is almost ready, add the tuna to the sauce and microwave on HIGH for 1 minute to heat though. Stir in the spring onions. Drain the pasta and tip it into a warmed bowl. Pour the sauce over the pasta and toss to mix. Serve at once.

Sweet and Sour Fish

Serve this tasty, nutritious dish with brown rice and stir-fried cabbage or spinach for a delicious, light lunch-time meal.

INGREDIENTS

Serves 4

60ml/4 tbsp cider vinegar

45ml/3 tbsp light soy sauce

50g/2oz/¼ cup granulated sugar

15ml/1 tbsp tomato purée

25ml/1½ tbsp cornflour

250ml/8fl oz/1 cup water

1 green pepper, seeded and sliced

225g/8oz can pineapple pieces in fruit juice

225g/8oz tomatoes, peeled and chopped

225g/8oz/2 cups button mushrooms, sliced

675g/1½lb chunky haddock fillets, skinned

salt and ground black pepper

1 Mix the vinegar, soy sauce, sugar and tomato purée in a microwaveproof bowl. Gradually blend the cornflour to a smooth paste with the water, then add to the bowl, stirring well. Microwave on HIGH for 2–2½ minutes, stirring three times during cooking, until smooth, boiling and thickened.

2 Add the green pepper, canned pineapple pieces (with juice), tomatoes and mushrooms to the sauce and microwave on HIGH for 2 minutes, stirring halfway through cooking. Season to taste with salt and pepper.

3 Place the fish in a single layer in a shallow microwaveproof dish and pour over the sauce. Cover and microwave on HIGH for 8–10 minutes, rotating the dish twice during cooking. Leave to stand for 5 minutes before serving.

Spiced Fish with Okra

INGREDIENTS

Serves 4

450g/1lb monkfish
5ml/1 tsp ground turmeric
2.5ml/½ tsp chilli powder
2.5ml/½ tsp salt
5ml/1 tsp cumin seeds
2.5ml/½ tsp fennel seeds
2 dried red chillies
45ml/3 tbsp oil
1 onion, finely chopped
2 garlic cloves, crushed
4 tomatoes, skinned and finely chopped
150ml/¼ pint/⅔ cup water
225g/8oz okra, trimmed and cut into
    2.5cm/1in lengths
5ml/1 tsp garam masala
tomato rice, to serve

1 Remove the membrane and bones from the monkfish. Cut the fillet into 2.5cm/1in cubes and place them in a dish. Mix the turmeric, chilli powder and 1.5ml/¼ tsp of the salt, then rub this mixture all over the fish. Marinate the fish for 15 minutes.

2 Mix the cumin seeds, fennel seeds and chillies in a large microwaveproof bowl, cover and microwave on HIGH for 1–2 minutes. Transfer the spices to a blender or mortar and process or grind them to a coarse powder.

3 Place 30ml/2 tbsp of the oil in a large microwaveproof bowl and microwave on HIGH for 30 seconds, until hot. Add the fish, turning the pieces in the oil. Cover and microwave on HIGH for 4–5 minutes, stirring halfway through cooking. Use a slotted spoon to remove the fish from the bowl.

4 Add the remaining oil to the bowl with the onion, garlic, ground spices and the remaining salt. Cover and microwave on HIGH for 2 minutes, stirring once. Stir in the tomatoes and water, cover and microwave on HIGH for 2–3 minutes, stirring once.

5 Add the okra, cover and microwave on HIGH for 4–6 minutes, stirring halfway through cooking.

6 Replace the fish. Add the garam masala and lightly mix both with the sauce. Cover and microwave on HIGH for 2–3 minutes, until the fish is hot and the okra is tender. Serve with rice flavoured with a little tomato purée during cooking.

COOK'S TIP
~

Yellow (flavoured with turmeric or saffron) and plain rice also go well with this spiced dish, and the two colours make an attractive presentation.

Coconut Salmon

This is an ideal dish to serve at dinner parties

INGREDIENTS

Serves 4

10ml/2 tsp ground cumin
10ml/2 tsp chilli powder
2.5ml/½ tsp ground turmeric
30ml/2 tbsp white wine vinegar
1.5ml/¼ tsp salt
4 salmon steaks, about 175g/6oz each
45ml/3 tbsp oil
1 onion, chopped
2 green chillies, seeded and chopped
2 garlic cloves, crushed
2.5cm/1in piece fresh root ginger, grated
5ml/1 tsp ground coriander
175ml/6fl oz/¾ cup coconut milk
fresh coriander sprigs, to garnish
spring onion rice, to serve

1 Mix 5ml/1 tsp of the ground cumin with the chilli powder, turmeric, vinegar and salt. Rub this spice paste over the salmon steaks and leave to marinate for about 15 minutes.

2 Place the oil in a large, deep microwaveproof dish. Add the onion, chillies, garlic and ginger. Cover and microwave on HIGH for 3 minutes, stirring halfway though cooking. Process this cooked mixture to a paste in a food processor or blender.

3 Return the paste to the dish. Stir in the remaining cumin, the ground coriander and coconut milk. Microwave on HIGH for 2–2½ minutes, stirring twice during cooking.

4 Add the salmon steaks, cover and microwave on MEDIUM for 9–10 minutes, rearranging halfway through cooking, until the fish is cooked. Leave to stand for 5 minutes before serving, garnished with coriander. Serve rice flavoured with spring onions with the salmon.

COOK'S TIP

To make coconut milk, dissolve grated creamed coconut in boiling water and strain it into a jug, if necessary.

Green Fish Curry

Serves 4

1.5ml/¼ tsp ground turmeric
30ml/2 tbsp lime juice
pinch of salt
4 portions cod fillets, skinned and cut into
    5cm/2in chunks
1 onion, chopped
1 green chilli, roughly chopped
1 garlic clove, crushed
25g/1oz/¼ cup cashew nuts
2.5ml/½ tsp fennel seeds
30ml/2 tbsp desiccated coconut
30ml/2 tbsp oil
1.5ml/¼ tsp cumin seeds
1.5ml/¼ tsp ground coriander
1.5ml/¼ tsp ground cumin
1.5ml/¼ tsp salt
150ml/¼ pint/⅔ cup water
175ml/6fl oz/¾ cup single cream
45ml/3 tbsp finely chopped fresh
    coriander
fresh coriander sprig, to garnish
rice with vegetables, to serve

1 Mix the turmeric, lime juice and pinch of salt, then rub the mixture over the fish. Cover and leave to marinate for 15 minutes.

2 Meanwhile, process the onion, chilli, garlic, cashew nuts, fennel seeds and coconut to a paste in a blender or food processor. Spoon the paste into a bowl and set it aside.

3 Place the oil in a large microwaveproof bowl. Add the cumin seeds and microwave on HIGH for 1–1½ minutes or until the seeds begin to splutter. Add the paste, ground coriander, cumin, salt and water and mix well. Cover and microwave on HIGH for 3–5 minutes, stirring twice during cooking.

4 Stir in the cream and fresh coriander. Microwave on HIGH for a further 2–3 minutes, stirring halfway through cooking.

5 Gently mix in the fish. Cover and microwave on HIGH for 7–10 minutes, stirring twice, until cooked. Serve, garnished with coriander, with rice and vegetables or pilau.

COOK'S TIP

Whole and ground spices, lime, garlic, chilli and coconut make a superb sauce. Fresh coriander and single cream balance and enliven the flavours.

Prawn Curry

This rich prawn curry is flavoured with coconut and a delicious blend of aromatic spices.

INGREDIENTS

Serves 4

675g/1½lb uncooked tiger prawns
4 dried red chillies
50g/2oz/1 cup desiccated coconut
5ml/1 tsp black mustard seeds
1 large onion, chopped
45ml/3 tbsp oil
4 bay leaves
2.5cm/1in piece fresh root ginger, finely
    chopped
2 garlic cloves, crushed
15ml/1 tbsp ground coriander
5ml/1 tsp chilli powder
5ml/1 tsp salt
4 tomatoes, finely chopped
175ml/6fl oz/¾ cup water
plain rice, to serve

1 Peel the prawns. Run a sharp knife along the back of each prawn to make a shallow cut and carefully remove the thin black intestinal vein.

2 Put the dried red chillies, coconut, mustard seeds and onion in a large microwaveproof bowl. Microwave on HIGH for 8 minutes, stirring twice. Process the mixture to a coarse paste in a blender or food processor.

3 Place the oil in a microwave-proof bowl with the bay leaves. Add the ginger and garlic, cover and microwave on HIGH for 2 minutes, stirring twice during cooking.

4 Stir in the coriander, chilli powder, salt and the paste. Cover and microwave on HIGH for 2–3 minutes, stirring halfway through cooking.

5 Stir in the tomatoes and water, cover and microwave on HIGH for 4–6 minutes, stirring halfway through cooking, until thickened slightly.

6 Mix in the prawns, cover and microwave on HIGH for 4 minutes or until they turn pink and their edges curl slightly. Serve with plain boiled rice.

Seafood Pilaff

This all-in-one main course makes a satisfying meal for any day of the week. For a special meal, substitute dry white wine for the orange juice.

INGREDIENTS

Serves 4

10ml/2 tsp olive oil

250g/9oz/1¼ cups long grain rice

5ml/1 tsp ground turmeric

1 red pepper, seeded and diced

1 small onion, finely chopped

2 courgettes, sliced

150g/5oz/2 cups button mushrooms, halved

350ml/12fl oz/1½ cups fish or chicken stock

150ml/¼ pint/⅔ cup orange juice

350g/12oz white fish fillets, skinned

12 cooked mussels, shelled

salt and ground black pepper

grated rind of 1 orange, to garnish

1 Mix the oil with the rice and turmeric in a large microwaveproof bowl. Microwave on HIGH for 1 minute.

2 Add the pepper, onion, courgettes and mushrooms. Stir in the stock and orange juice. Cover and microwave on HIGH for 13 minutes, stirring halfway through cooking. Leave to stand, covered.

3 Place the fish on a microwaveproof plate. Cover and microwave on HIGH for 4–5 minutes, until cooked. Flake the fish and stir it into the rice mixture. Stir in the mussels and microwave on HIGH for a further 1 minute. Adjust the seasoning, sprinkle with orange rind and serve hot.

Salmon Pasta with Parsley Sauce

INGREDIENTS

Serves 4

450g/1lb salmon fillet, skinned

225g/8oz/3 cups pasta shapes, such as penne or twists

175g/6oz cherry tomatoes, halved

150ml/¼ pint/⅔ cup low-fat crème fraîche

45ml/3 tbsp chopped fresh parsley

finely grated rind of ½ orange

salt and ground black pepper

COOK'S TIP

∾

If low-fat crème fraîche is not available, use ordinary crème fraîche or double cream instead.

1 Cut the salmon into bite-sized pieces, arrange them on a microwaveproof plate and cover with greaseproof paper. Microwave on HIGH for 2–2½ minutes, rearranging halfway through cooking. Leave to stand for 5 minutes.

2 Cook the pasta in a saucepan of boiling water on the hob, following the packet instructions.

3 Alternatively, cook the pasta in 1.2 litres/2 pints boiling water with 5ml/1 tsp oil in a large microwaveproof bowl. Microwave on HIGH for 10–12 minutes.

4 Drain the pasta and toss it with the tomatoes and salmon. Mix the crème fraîche, parsley, orange rind and pepper to taste, then toss this sauce into the salmon and pasta and serve hot.

Ginger and Lime Prawns

INGREDIENTS

Serves 4

225g/8oz raw tiger prawns, peeled

⅓ cucumber

15ml/1 tbsp sunflower oil

15ml/1 tbsp sesame seed oil

175g/6oz mangetouts, trimmed

4 spring onions, diagonally sliced

30ml/2 tbsp chopped fresh coriander, to
    garnish

For the marinade

15ml/1 tbsp clear honey

15ml/1 tbsp light soy sauce

15ml/1 tbsp dry sherry

2 garlic cloves, crushed

small piece of fresh root ginger, peeled
    and finely chopped

juice of 1 lime

1 Mix the marinade ingredients,
stir in the prawns and leave to
marinate for 1–2 hours.

2 Prepare the cucumber: slice
it in half lengthways, scoop
out the seeds, then slice each half
neatly into crescents. Set aside.

3 Place both types of oil in
a large microwaveproof
bowl. Microwave on HIGH for
30 seconds. Drain the prawns
(reserving the marinade) and
add them to the oils in the bowl.
Cover and microwave on HIGH
for 1½–2½ minutes, stirring
halfway through cooking, until
they begin to turn pink.

4 Add the mangetouts and
the cucumber, cover and
microwave on HIGH for a further
1–2 minutes, stirring once.

5 Stir in the reserved marinade
and microwave on HIGH for
a further 30 seconds. Stir in the
spring onions and serve, sprinkled
with fresh coriander.

Mediterranean Fish Cutlets

INGREDIENTS

Serves 4

4 white fish cutlets, about 150g/5oz each

45ml/3 tbsp fish stock

45ml/3 tbsp dry white wine

1 bay leaf, a few black peppercorns
    and a strip of pared lemon rind,
    for flavouring

chopped fresh parsley, to garnish

For the tomato sauce

400g/14oz can chopped tomatoes

1 garlic clove, crushed

15ml/1 tbsp sun-dried tomato paste

15ml/1 tbsp pastis or other aniseed-
    flavoured liqueur

15ml/1 tbsp drained capers

12–16 black olives, stoned

salt and ground black pepper

1 To make the tomato sauce,
place the tomatoes, garlic,
tomato paste, pastis or liqueur,
capers, olives and salt and pepper
in a microwaveproof bowl. Cover
and microwave on HIGH for 4–6
minutes, stirring twice.

2 Place the fish cutlets in a
microwaveproof dish, pour
over the stock and wine and
add the flavourings. Cover
and microwave on HIGH for
5 minutes, rotating the dish twice.
Leave to stand for 2 minutes.

3 Using a slotted spoon, transfer
the fish to a heated dish. Strain
the stock into the tomato sauce
and mix thoroughly. Season the
sauce, pour it over the fish and
serve immediately, garnished with
chopped parsley.

Whole Cooked Salmon

Farmed salmon has made this fish more affordable and less of a treat, but a whole salmon still features as a centrepiece at parties. As with all fish, the taste depends first on freshness and second on not overcooking it. Although you need to start early, the cooking time is short. Cooked salmon is, of course, also delicious served hot with a buttery hollandaise sauce. New potatoes and fine green beans are perfect accompaniments.

INGREDIENTS

Serves 6–8 as part of a buffet

1.8kg/4lb whole salmon
1 lemon, sliced
salt and ground black pepper
lemon wedges, cucumber ribbons and
    fresh dill sprigs, to garnish

1 Wash the salmon and dry it well, inside and out. Prick the skin in several places to prevent bursting and place the salmon in a shallow microwaveproof dish.

2 Put a few slices of lemon inside the salmon and arrange some more on the top. Season well and sprinkle a little boiling water over to moisten the fish.

3 Cover with greaseproof paper or vented clear film and microwave on HIGH for 20–22 minutes, rotating the dish three times during cooking. Leave to stand, covered, for 5 minutes, before serving hot. If serving cold, leave to cool completely before uncovering.

4 To serve hot with hollandaise sauce, peel away the skin and transfer the salmon to a heated serving dish. Keep warm while preparing the sauce.

5 To serve cold and on the same day, remove the skin from the cooked fish and arrange it on a large platter. Garnish with lemon wedges, cucumber cut into thin ribbons and sprigs of dill. If you intend serving the salmon the following day, leave the skin on and chill the fish overnight before adding the garnish.

HOLLANDAISE SAUCE

Place 115g/4oz/8 tbsp butter in a large microwaveproof jug and microwave on HIGH for 1½ minutes. Whisk in 45ml/3 tbsp lemon juice, 2 egg yolks, a pinch of mustard powder and salt and pepper to taste. Microwave on MEDIUM for 1 minute, then whisk and serve.

COOK'S TIP

To prevent the head and tail ends of fish from overcooking in the microwave, they can be shielded with small pieces of smooth foil. This may be done at the beginning of the cooking time or after a few minutes if cooking progress is being carefully watched.

MEAT AND
POULTRY

~

Stilton Burgers

Slightly more up-market than the traditional burger, this tasty recipe contains a delicious surprise. The lightly melted Stilton cheese encased in a burger is absolutely delicious.

INGREDIENTS

Serves 4

450g/1lb/4 cups minced beef
1 onion, finely chopped
1 celery stick, chopped
5ml/1 tsp dried mixed herbs
5ml/1 tsp prepared mustard
50g/2oz/½ cup Stilton cheese, crumbled
4 burger buns
salt and ground black pepper

1 Place the minced beef in a bowl together with the onion and celery. Season well.

2 Stir in the herbs and mustard, bringing all the ingredients together to form a firm mixture.

3 Divide the mixture into eight equal portions. Place four on a chopping board and flatten each one slightly.

4 Share the crumbled cheese between the burgers, placing a little in the centre of each.

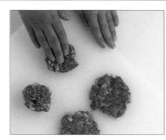

5 Flatten the remaining mixture and place on top. Mould the mixture carefully to encase the crumbled cheese and shape into four burgers.

6 To cook, place the burgers on a microwaveproof roasting rack and microwave, uncovered, for 6–7 minutes, turning over once. Leave to stand for 2–3 minutes. Alternatively, for a browner and crisper result, preheat a microwave browning dish or special microwave burger cooker according to the manufacturer's instructions. Add the burgers, pressing them down well on to the base, and microwave on HIGH for 5–5½ minutes, turning over once. If using a microwave burger cooker to cook the burgers individually, read and follow the manufacturer's instructions, particularly for timing. Leave to stand for 2–3 minutes.
  Serve in burger buns or pitta bread with salad leaves and a relish of your choice.

COMBINATION MICROWAVE

This recipe is suitable for cooking in a combination microwave. Follow the oven manufacturer's timing guide for good results.

Beef and Mushroom Burgers

It's worth making your own burgers to cut down on fat – in these, the meat is extended with mushrooms for extra fibre.

INGREDIENTS

Serves 4

1 small onion, chopped

150g/5oz/2 cups small cup mushrooms

450g/1lb lean minced beef

50g/2oz/1 cup fresh wholemeal
  breadcrumbs

5ml/1 tsp dried mixed herbs

15ml/1 tbsp tomato purée

plain flour, for shaping

salt and ground black pepper

relish, lettuce, burger buns or pitta bread,
  to serve

1 Place the onion and mushrooms in a food processor and process until finely chopped. Add the beef, breadcrumbs, herbs, tomato purée and seasoning. Process for a few seconds, until the mixture binds together but still has some texture.

2 Divide the mixture into four, then press into burger shapes using lightly floured hands.

3 To cook, place the burgers on a microwaveproof roasting rack and microwave, uncovered, for 6–7 minutes, turning over once. Leave to stand for 2–3 minutes.

4 Alternatively, for a browner and crisper result, preheat a microwave browning dish according to the manufacturer's instructions. Add the burgers, pressing down well on to the base and microwave on HIGH for 5–5½ minutes, turning over once. Leave to stand for 2–3 minutes. Serve with relish and lettuce, in burger buns or pitta bread.

VARIATION

To make Lamb and Mushroom Burgers, substitute lean minced lamb for the minced beef.

COMBINATION MICROWAVE

This recipe is suitable for cooking in a combination microwave. Follow the oven manufacturer's timing guide for good results.

Stuffed Tomatoes

*Ever popular, this simple recipe
demonstrates the versatility of
mince as a stuffing.*

INGREDIENTS

Serves 4

4 beef tomatoes
7.5ml/1½ tsp oil
75g/3oz/¾ cup minced beef
1 small red onion, thinly sliced
25g/1oz/¼ cup bulgur wheat
30ml/2 tbsp freshly grated
    Parmesan cheese
15g/½oz/1 tbsp cashew nuts, chopped
1 small celery stick, chopped
salt and ground black pepper
crisp green salad, to serve

1 Trim the tops from the
tomatoes, scoop out the flesh
with a teaspoon and reserve.

2 Place the oil in a large
microwaveproof bowl, add
the minced beef and onion, cover
and microwave on HIGH for
5–6 minutes or until the beef is
cooked, stirring twice to break up
the meat. Stir in the tomato flesh.

3 Place the bulgur wheat in a
bowl, cover with boiling water
and leave to soak for 10 minutes.
Drain if necessary.

4 Mix the mince and bulgur,
Parmesan cheese, nuts and
celery. Season well.

5 Spoon the filling into the
tomatoes and place in a
shallow microwaveproof dish.
Microwave on HIGH for
3–5 minutes or until the tomatoes
and their filling are tender. Serve
with a crisp green salad.

Beef Casserole and Dumplings

This delicious casserole is topped with light herby dumplings for a filling and nutritious meal. Accompany with broccoli florets.

Serves 4

15ml/1 tbsp oil

16 button onions

2 carrots, sliced

2 celery sticks, sliced

25g/1oz/2 tbsp flour

450g/1lb/4 cups minced beef

600ml/1 pint/2½ cups hot beef stock

salt and ground black pepper

For the dumplings

115g/4oz/1 cup plain flour

7.5ml/1½ tsp baking powder

2.5ml/½ tsp salt

50g/2oz soft margarine

15ml/1 tbsp chopped fresh parsley

60–75ml/4–5 tbsp water

1 Place the oil, onions, carrots and celery in a large microwaveproof casserole. Cover and microwave on HIGH for 6–8 minutes, stirring twice, until softened.

2 Stir in the flour, mixing well. Microwave for 1 minute, stirring halfway through cooking.

3 Stir in the minced beef, stock and salt and pepper to taste.

4 Three-quarters cover with clear film or the casserole lid. Microwave on HIGH for 20–25 minutes, stirring three times. Leave to stand while cooking the dumplings.

5 To make the dumplings, mix the flour, baking powder and salt. Rub in the margarine, then stir in the parsley and water to form a smooth dough.

6 Roll into eight equal-sized balls and place in a shallow microwaveproof dish in a ring pattern. Pour in 600ml/1 pint/ 2½ cups boiling water. Microwave on HIGH for 2 minutes. Rearrange and cover, then microwave on HIGH for a further 2 minutes. Remove the dumplings with a slotted spoon and serve with the beef casserole.

Beef and Lentil Pie

In this variation of cottage pie, lentils are substituted for some of the meat to produce a dish that is lower in fat and higher in fibre.

INGREDIENTS

Serves 4

175g/6oz/1 cup green lentils

1 onion, chopped

2 celery sticks, chopped

1 large carrot, chopped

1 garlic clove, crushed

225g/8oz lean minced beef

425g/15oz can chopped tomatoes

10ml/2 tsp yeast extract

1 bay leaf

For the topping

450g/1lb potatoes, peeled and cut into
    large chunks

450g/1lb parsnips, peeled and cut into
    large chunks

60ml/4 tbsp low-fat natural yogurt

45ml/3 tbsp chopped chives

20ml/4 tsp freshly grated Parmesan cheese

2 tomatoes, sliced

25g/1oz/¼ cup pine nuts (optional)

1 Place the lentils in a microwave-proof bowl and pour in boiling water to cover. Cover and microwave on HIGH for 6 minutes.

2 Place onion, celery, carrot and garlic in a microwaveproof bowl. Cover, microwave on HIGH for 4 minutes and stir once. Add mince, stir and microwave on HIGH for 2 minutes. Mix in tomatoes.

3 Drain the lentils, reserving 250ml/8fl oz/1 cup of the cooking water in a measuring jug. Add the lentils to the meat mixture, then dissolve the yeast extract in the cooking water and stir it in with the bay leaf. Cover loosely, then microwave on HIGH for 12–15 minutes, stirring twice.

4 Make the topping: place the potatoes and parsnips in a microwaveproof bowl with 75ml/5 tbsp water. Cover and microwave on HIGH for 11–13 minutes, stirring once, until tender. Mash the potatoes and parsnips together and stir in the yogurt and chives.

5 Remove the bay leaf and divide the meat mixture among four small dishes or one large dish suitable for grilling. Spoon over the potato mixture. Sprinkle with Parmesan and garnish with tomato slices. Sprinkle pine nuts over the top, if using, and grill the pies for a few minutes until the topping is crisp and golden brown.

Spicy Bolognese

A spicy version of a popular dish. Worcestershire sauce and chorizo sausages add an extra element to this perfect family standby.

INGREDIENTS

Serves 4

15ml/1 tbsp oil
1 onion, chopped
225g/8oz/2 cups minced beef
5ml/1 tsp ground chilli powder
15ml/1 tbsp Worcestershire sauce
25g/1oz/2 tbsp plain flour
150ml/¼ pint/⅔ cup beef stock
4 chorizo sausages
200g/7oz can chopped tomatoes
50g/2oz baby sweetcorn
15ml/1 tbsp chopped fresh basil
salt and ground black pepper

1 Place the oil and onion in a large microwaveproof bowl. Microwave on HIGH for 2 minutes. Add the minced beef and chilli powder, mixing well. Microwave on HIGH for 4–5 minutes, breaking up the mince twice during cooking.

2 Stir in the Worcestershire sauce and flour. Microwave on HIGH for 30 seconds, stirring once, before pouring in the stock.

3 Slice the chorizo sausages and halve the corn lengthways.

4 Stir in the sausages, tomatoes, sweetcorn and chopped basil. Season well, cover loosely and microwave on HIGH for 15–20 minutes, stirring twice. Serve with spaghetti, garnished with fresh basil.

COOK'S TIP

If you like, cool the Bolognese sauce and freeze it in conveniently sized portions for up to 2 months.

Chilli Con Carne

An American recipe that has become a regular feature in many homes. Simple and economical, it is one of the most popular minced beef recipes developed. This recipe isn't highly spiced and so is suitable for young children too.

Serves 4

15ml/1 tbsp oil
225g/8oz/2 cups minced beef
1 onion, quartered
5ml/1 tsp chilli powder
15g/½oz/2 tbsp plain flour
30ml/2 tbsp tomato purée
150ml/¼ pint/⅔ cup beef stock
200g/7oz can chopped tomatoes
200g/7oz can kidney beans, drained
1 green pepper, seeded and chopped
15ml/1 tbsp Worcestershire sauce
75g/3oz/½ cup long grain rice
salt and ground black pepper
soured cream, to serve
chopped fresh parsley, to garnish

1 Place the oil, minced beef, onion and chilli powder in a microwaveproof bowl and microwave on HIGH for 6–8 minutes, stirring twice.

2 Add the flour and tomato purée and microwave on HIGH for 30 seconds, stirring once. Stir in the stock and tomatoes, cover and microwave on HIGH for 12–15 minutes, stirring once.

3 Mix in the kidney beans, chopped green pepper and Worcestershire sauce. Cover and microwave on HIGH for 5–7 minutes, stirring once.

4 Place the rice in a large microwaveproof bowl. Add 250ml/8fl oz/1 cup boiling water and a pinch of salt. Cover loosely and microwave on HIGH for 3 minutes. Stir, re-cover and microwave on MEDIUM for 12 minutes. Leave to stand, covered, for 5 minutes.

5 Fluff up the rice and spoon it on to serving plates. Serve the chilli con carne on the rice. To complete the dish, add a spoonful of soured cream and garnish with fresh parsley.

Butterflied Cumin and Garlic Lamb

Ground cumin and garlic give the lamb a wonderful Middle-Eastern flavour. Vary the recipe by making a simple oil, lemon and herb marinade instead.

INGREDIENTS

Serves 6

1.75kg/4lb leg of lamb
60ml/4 tbsp olive oil
30ml/2 tbsp ground cumin
4–6 garlic cloves, crushed
salt and ground black pepper
pilaff with raisins and toasted almonds,
    to serve
coriander sprigs and lemon wedges,
    to garnish

1 To butterfly the lamb, cut away the meat from the bone using a small sharp knife. Remove any excess fat and the thin, parchment-like membrane. Bat out the meat to an even thickness, then prick the fleshy side well with a knife tip.

2 In a bowl, mix together the oil, cumin and garlic, and season with pepper. Spoon the mixture all over the lamb, then rub it well into the crevices. Cover and leave to marinate overnight.

3 Spread the lamb, skin-side down, on a microwave roasting rack or upturned saucer in a microwaveproof shallow dish. Season with salt and microwave on HIGH for 5 minutes. Reduce the power setting to MEDIUM and microwave for a further 30–35 minutes, or until the meat is cooked but still pink inside, turning it over once.

4 Brown the lamb under a preheated hot grill to crisp the outside, if liked. Leave to stand, covered with foil, for 10–15 minutes before carving.

5 Cut the lamb into diagonal slices and serve it with a rice pilaff with toasted almonds and raisins. Garnish with coriander sprigs and lemon wedges.

COMBINATION MICROWAVE

This recipe is suitable for cooking in a combination microwave. Follow the oven manufacturer's timing guide for good results.

Rack of Lamb with Redcurrant Bunches

Bunches of redcurrants tied with chives provide a strong colour contrast to glazed rack of lamb.

INGREDIENTS

Serves 4–6

45ml/3 tbsp redcurrant jelly

5ml/1 tsp wholegrain mustard

2 best ends of lamb, each with 6 chops, trimmed of all fat

120ml/4fl oz/½ cup red wine

120ml/4fl oz/½ cup stock or water

salt and ground black pepper

For the garnish

4–6 chives, wilted

8–12 small bunches of redcurrants

1 Place the redcurrant jelly with the mustard in a small microwaveproof bowl and microwave on HIGH for 1–2 minutes, stirring once, until the jelly has melted. Brush the mixture over the lamb.

2 Place the racks of lamb on a microwave roasting rack or upturned saucer in a microwave-proof shallow dish. Microwave on HIGH for 18–22 minutes, or until cooked to your taste, rotating the dish and basting the lamb four times during cooking. Transfer the lamb to a warm platter, loosely cover it with foil and allow to rest for 10 minutes.

3 Drain the fat from the roasting dish, leaving the sediment behind. Stir in the red wine and microwave on HIGH for 2–3 minutes, until most of the liquid has evaporated.

4 Add the stock or water. Microwave on HIGH for 3–4 minutes until reduced and very slightly syrupy. Season, strain into a sauceboat and keep hot.

5 Wrap the chives around the redcurrant stems, tie them in a neat knot and then trim the ends. Make four bunches of redcurrants in this way. Carve the lamb into cutlets, arrange them on four or six dinner plates and spoon over a little of the sauce. To complete the dish, garnish with the redcurrant bunches.

COMBINATION MICROWAVE

This recipe is suitable for cooking in a combination microwave. Follow the oven manufacturer's timing guide for good results.

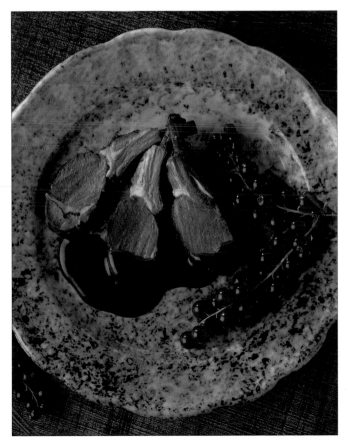

Turkish Lamb and Apricot Stew

Cooking this stew on medium power ensures that the lamb is deliciously moist and tender.

INGREDIENTS

Serves 4

1 large aubergine, cubed
30ml/2 tbsp sunflower oil
1 onion, chopped
1 garlic clove, crushed
5ml/1 tsp ground cinnamon
3 whole cloves
450g/1lb boned leg of lamb, cubed
400g/14oz can chopped tomatoes
300ml/½ pint/1¼ cups boiling water
115g/4oz/⅔ cup ready-to-eat dried
   apricots
115g/4oz canned chick-peas, drained
5ml/1 tsp clear honey
salt and ground black pepper
couscous, to serve
30ml/2 tbsp olive oil
30ml/2 tbsp chopped almonds, fried in a
   little oil
chopped fresh parsley

2 Stir in the ground cinnamon and cloves and microwave on HIGH for 30 seconds. Add the lamb and microwave on HIGH for 5 minutes, stirring once.

3 Rinse, drain and pat dry the aubergine, then add it to the casserole with the tomatoes, boiling water, apricots and seasoning. Cover and microwave on MEDIUM for 30 minutes, or until the meat is almost tender.

4 Stir in the chick-peas and honey. Cover and microwave on HIGH for 3–5 minutes, or until the lamb is tender. Serve the stew accompanied by couscous with the olive oil, fried almonds and chopped parsley stirred in.

1 Place the aubergine in a colander, sprinkle with salt and leave for 30 minutes. Place the oil in a microwaveproof casserole, add the onion and garlic, cover and microwave on HIGH for 2 minutes, until softened.

Lamb Pie with a Potato Crust

INGREDIENTS

Serves 4

675g/1½lb potatoes, diced

45ml/3 tbsp water

30ml/2 tbsp skimmed milk

15ml/1 tbsp wholegrain or
    French mustard

1 onion, chopped

2 celery sticks, sliced

2 carrots, diced

450g/1lb lean minced lamb

150ml/¼ pint/⅔ cup beef stock

60ml/4 tbsp rolled oats

15ml/1 tbsp Worcestershire sauce

30ml/2 tbsp chopped fresh rosemary

salt and ground black pepper

1 Place the potatoes in a microwaveproof bowl with the water. Cover and microwave on HIGH for 8–10 minutes, until tender, stirring once. Drain and mash until smooth, then stir in the milk and mustard.

2 Place the onion, celery and carrots in a large microwave-proof bowl. Cover and microwave on HIGH for 5 minutes, stirring once. Add the minced lamb, mixing well. Microwave on HIGH for 2 minutes, stirring once.

3 Stir in the stock, rolled oats, Worcestershire sauce and rosemary, and season to taste with salt and pepper. Cover loosely and microwave on HIGH for 20–25 minutes, until cooked, stirring twice.

4 Turn the meat mixture into a 1.75 litre/3 pint/7½ cup microwaveproof dish that is suitable for grilling. Swirl the potato evenly over the top. Microwave, uncovered, on HIGH for 4–5 minutes until hot. Brown under a grill, if liked. Serve with freshly cooked vegetables.

COMBINATION MICROWAVE

This recipe is suitable for cooking in a combination microwave. Follow the oven manufacturer's timing guide for good results.

Rogan Josh

For this popular Indian dish, the lamb is traditionally marinated in yogurt, then cooked with spices and tomatoes to give the dish its rich, red appearance.

INGREDIENTS

Serves 4

900g/2lb lamb fillet
45ml/3 tbsp lemon juice
250ml/8fl oz/1 cup natural yogurt
5ml/1 tsp salt
2 garlic cloves, crushed
2.5cm/1in piece fresh root ginger, grated
30ml/2 tbsp oil
2.5ml/½ tsp cumin seeds
2 bay leaves
4 green cardamom pods
1 onion, finely chopped
10ml/2 tsp ground coriander
10ml/2 tsp ground cumin
5ml/1 tsp chilli powder
400g/14oz can chopped tomatoes
30ml/2 tbsp tomato purée
150ml/¼ pint/⅔ cup water
toasted cumin seeds and bay leaves,
    to garnish
plain rice, to serve

1 Discard any excess fat from the meat and cut it into 2.5cm/1in cubes.

2 In a bowl, mix the lemon juice, yogurt, salt, 1 garlic clove and the ginger. Add the lamb and leave to marinate overnight.

3 Place the oil in a large microwaveproof bowl and microwave on HIGH for 1 minute. Add the cumin seeds, bay leaves and cardamom pods and microwave on HIGH for 2 minutes.

4 Add the onion and remaining garlic, cover and microwave on HIGH for 3 minutes, stirring once. Stir in the ground coriander, cumin and chilli powder, then microwave on HIGH for 1 minute, stirring once.

5 Stir in the marinated lamb, cover and microwave on HIGH for 10 minutes, stirring once.

6 Mix in the tomatoes, tomato purée and water. Cover and microwave on HIGH for 5–8 minutes until hot and bubbling. Reduce the power setting to MEDIUM and microwave for 30–40 minutes, until tender. Leave to stand, covered, for 10 minutes before serving, garnished with cumin seeds and bay leaves, with plain rice.

Spicy Lamb Curry

*One of the simplest Indian dishes
to make, this spicy mixture can be
used as a tasty filling for stuffing
vegetables, such as peppers and large
beefsteak tomatoes.*

INGREDIENTS

Serves 4

45ml/3 tbsp oil

1 onion, finely chopped

2 garlic cloves, crushed

2.5cm/1in piece fresh root ginger, grated

2 green chillies, finely chopped

675g/1½lb minced lamb

5ml/1 tsp ground cumin

5ml/1 tsp ground coriander

5ml/1 tsp chilli powder

5ml/1 tsp salt

250ml/8fl oz/1 cup water

175g/6oz frozen peas, thawed

30ml/2 tbsp lemon juice

naan bread and natural yogurt, to serve

1 Place the oil, onion, garlic,
ginger and chillies in a large
microwaveproof bowl. Cover
and microwave on HIGH for
5 minutes, stirring once.

2 Add the minced lamb and
stir well to break up the
meat. Microwave on HIGH for
5 minutes, stirring once.

3 Stir in the cumin, coriander,
chilli powder, salt and water.
Cover and microwave on HIGH
for 10 minutes, stirring once.

4 Finally, mix in the peas and
lemon juice. Microwave
on HIGH, uncovered, for 6−8
minutes, or until the meat is
tender. Serve with naan bread and
natural yogurt.

Curried Lamb and Lentils

This colourful curry is packed with protein and is low in fat too.

INGREDIENTS

Serves 4

8 lean, boneless lamb leg steaks, about
    500g/1¼lb total weight
1 onion, chopped
2 carrots, diced
1 celery stalk, chopped
15ml/1 tbsp hot curry paste
30ml/2 tbsp tomato purée
475ml/16fl oz/2 cups stock
175g/6oz/1 cup green lentils
salt and ground black pepper
fresh coriander leaves, to garnish
boiled rice, to serve

1 Preheat a large browning dish according to the manufacturer's instructions. Add the lamb steaks, pressing them down well on the dish and microwave on HIGH for 7–8 minutes, turning over halfway through cooking. Alternatively, cook the lamb steaks on a microwave-proof plate, but they will not brown in the same way.

2 Place the onion, carrots and celery in a microwaveproof casserole. Cover and microwave on HIGH for 4 minutes, stirring once. Stir in the curry paste, tomato purée, stock and lentils. Cover and microwave on HIGH for 10–15 minutes or until the lentils are almost cooked.

3 Add the lamb steaks, cover and microwave on HIGH for 5–10 minutes, until tender. Season the lamb to taste, sprinkle with coriander and serve with rice.

Golden Pork and Apricot Casserole

The rich golden colour and warm spicy flavour of this simple casserole make it ideal for chilly winter days.

INGREDIENTS

Serves 4

4 lean pork loin chops
1 onion, thinly sliced
2 yellow peppers, seeded and sliced
10ml/2 tsp medium-hot curry powder
15ml/1 tbsp plain flour
250ml/8fl oz/1 cup chicken stock
115g/4oz/²⁄₃ cup ready-to-eat
    dried apricots
30ml/2 tbsp wholegrain mustard
salt and ground black pepper
rice or new potatoes, to serve

1 Preheat a large browning dish according to the manufacturer's instructions.

2 Meanwhile, trim the rind and fat off the pork chops. Place them in the browning dish, pressing them down well, and microwave on HIGH for 5–6 minutes, turning halfway through cooking. Alternatively, cook the chops on a microwaveproof plate, but they will not brown in the same way.

3 Place the onion and peppers in a microwaveproof casserole. Cover and microwave on HIGH for 4 minutes, stirring once. Stir in the curry powder and flour.

4 Pour in the stock, stirring, then add the apricots, mustard and pork chops. Cover and microwave on HIGH for 8–10 minutes, stirring once. Leave to stand, covered, for 10 minutes. Adjust the seasoning and serve hot, with rice or new potatoes.

Hot and Sour Pork

Chinese five-spice powder, made from a mixture of ground star anise, Szechuan pepper, cassia, cloves and fennel seed, has a flavour similar to liquorice. If you can't find any, use mixed spice instead.

INGREDIENTS

Serves 4

350g/12oz pork fillet
5ml/1 tsp sunflower oil
2.5cm/1in piece fresh root ginger, grated
1 red chilli, seeded and finely chopped
5ml/1 tsp Chinese five-spice powder
15ml/1 tbsp sherry vinegar
15ml/1 tbsp soy sauce
225g/8oz can pineapple chunks in
     natural juice
175ml/6fl oz/³/₄ cup chicken stock
20ml/4 tsp cornflour
15ml/1 tbsp water
1 small green pepper, seeded and sliced
115g/4oz baby sweetcorn, halved
salt and ground black pepper
sprig of flat leaf parsley, to garnish
boiled rice, to serve

1 Trim away any visible fat from the pork and cut the meat into 1cm/¹/₂in thick slices.

2 Brush the sunflower oil over the base of a microwaveproof casserole. Microwave on HIGH for 3 minutes, stirring once.

3 Blend the ginger, chilli, five-spice powder, sherry vinegar and soy sauce. Drain the pineapple, reserving the juice. Make the stock up to 300ml/ ¹/₂ pint/1¹/₄ cups with the juice and mix it with the spices, then pour over the pork.

4 Blend the cornflour with the water and gradually stir it into the pork. Add the vegetables and season to taste.

5 Cover loosely and microwave on HIGH for 14–16 minutes, stirring twice, until the pork and vegetables are almost tender. Stir in the pineapple, cover and microwave on HIGH for 3 minutes, stirring once, until the pineapple is hot and the pork tender. Garnish with flat leaf parsley and serve with rice.

Chow Mein

*One of the best known and most
popular of Chinese dishes, this
recipe is easy to prepare and a
healthy choice for everyday meals.*

INGREDIENTS

Serves 4

225g/8oz dried egg noodles

30ml/2 tbsp oil

1 onion, chopped

1cm/½in piece fresh root ginger,
    chopped

2 garlic cloves, crushed

30ml/2 tbsp soy sauce

50ml/2fl oz/¼ cup dry white wine

10ml/2 tsp Chinese five-spice powder

450g/1lb/4 cups minced pork

4 spring onions, sliced

50g/2oz oyster mushrooms

75g/3oz canned bamboo shoots, sliced
    if necessary

15ml/1 tbsp sesame oil

prawn crackers, to serve

1 Place the noodles in a
microwaveproof bowl, cover
with boiling water, then microwave
on HIGH for 4 minutes, stirring
once. Drain thoroughly.

2 Place the oil in a large
microwaveproof bowl and add
the onion, ginger, garlic, soy sauce
and wine. Cover and microwave
on HIGH for 2–3 minutes, stirring
once. Stir in the Chinese five-spice
powder.

3 Add the minced pork, cover
and microwave on HIGH for
6 minutes, stirring three times
to break up the meat during
cooking. Mix in the spring onions,
mushrooms and bamboo shoots.
Cover and microwave on HIGH
for 3 minutes, stirring once.

4 Stir in the noodles and sesame
oil. Mix all the ingredients
together well and serve with prawn
crackers.

COOK'S TIP

Lean minced lamb also makes
delicious chow mein. Canned
bamboo shoots can be replaced
by canned water chestnuts for a
crunchy texture.

Pork Crumble

Minced pork combines well with the sweetness of apple and the texture of crunchy vegetables. Served with the satisfying oat topping, this is a meal to tempt all the family.

INGREDIENTS

Serves 4

15ml/1 tbsp oil
1 onion, sliced
450g/1lb/4 cups minced pork
25g/1oz/2 tbsp plain flour
150ml/¼ pint/⅔ cup hot milk
150ml/¼ pint/⅔ cup hot vegetable
   stock
50g/2oz broccoli florets
50g/2oz/½ cup canned sweetcorn,
   drained
1 green eating apple, cored
   and diced
salt and ground black pepper

For the topping
50g/2oz/½ cup instant oatmeal
50g/2oz/½ cup plain flour
15g/½oz/1 tbsp butter
25g/1oz/¼ cup Red Leicester
   cheese, grated

1 Place the oil in a large microwaveproof bowl with the onion. Cover and microwave on HIGH for 2 minutes. Stir in the pork, cover and microwave on HIGH for 4–6 minutes, stirring twice to break up the meat.

2 Stir in the flour, then stir in the milk and stock. Cover and microwave on HIGH for 3 minutes, stirring twice.

3 Mix the broccoli, sweetcorn and apple into the pork mixture and season.

4 Spoon the mixture into four individual microwaveproof dishes that are suitable for grilling.

5 To make the crumble topping, mix the oatmeal and flour, then rub in the butter.

6 Spoon the topping on to the pork mixture and press down with the back of a spoon. Sprinkle the cheese over the top and microwave on HIGH for 6–8 minutes, repositioning the dishes halfway through cooking. Brown under a preheated hot grill, if you like.

VARIATION

For a rich cheesy topping, mix together crushed potato crisps and grated cheese. Cook as before.

COOK'S TIP
~

Vary the choice of vegetables according to personal preference. For example, try finely shredded white cabbage instead of the broccoli and/or frozen peas instead of the sweetcorn.

Chicken Roll

The roll can be prepared and cooked the day before and it will also freeze well. Remove from the fridge about an hour before serving.

INGREDIENTS

Serves 8
1.75kg/4lb chicken

For the stuffing
1 onion, finely chopped
50g/2oz/4 tbsp melted butter
350g/12oz lean minced pork
115g/4oz streaky bacon, chopped
15ml/1 tbsp chopped fresh parsley
10ml/2 tsp chopped fresh thyme
115g/4oz/2 cups fresh white breadcrumbs
30ml/2 tbsp sherry
1 large egg, beaten
25g/1oz/¼ cup shelled pistachio nuts
25g/1oz/¼ cup black olives,
   about 12, stoned
salt and ground black pepper

1 To make the stuffing, place the onion and 25g/1oz/2 tbsp of the butter in a microwaveproof bowl. Cover and microwave on HIGH for 2 minutes, until softened.

2 Turn into a bowl and cool slightly before adding the remaining ingredients. Mix thoroughly and season with salt and ground black pepper.

3 To bone the chicken, use a small, sharp knife to remove the wing tips. Turn the chicken on to its breast and cut a line down the back bone.

4 Cut the flesh away from the carcass, scraping the bones clean. Carefully cut through the sinews around the leg and wing joints and scrape down the bones to free them. Remove the carcass, taking care not to cut through the skin along the breast bone.

5 To stuff the chicken, lay it flat, skin side down and smooth the flesh out as much as possible. Shape the stuffing down the centre of the chicken and fold the sides over the stuffing.

6 Sew the flesh neatly together, using a needle and dark thread. Tie with fine string into a roll. Weigh the stuffed chicken roll. Brush with the remaining butter.

7 Place the roll, with the join underneath, in a roasting bag. Secure with string or an elastic band, making sure there is room for steam to escape. Place in a shallow microwaveproof dish. Microwave0 on MEDIUM for 9 minutes per 450g/1lb, turning over twice during cooking.

8 Remove the chicken from the bag and brown it under a preheated hot grill, if liked. Leave to cool completely before removing the string and thread. Wrap in foil and chill until ready for serving or freezing.

COMBINATION MICROWAVE

This recipe is suitable for cooking in a combination microwave. Follow the oven manufacturer's timing guide for good results.

COOK'S TIP

Use dark thread for sewing, as it is much easier to see so that you can remove it once the roll is cooked.

Spiced Chicken with Spinach

A mildly spiced dish using a popular combination of spinach and chicken. This recipe is best made using fresh spinach, but if this is unavailable you can use frozen instead.

Serves 4

225g/8oz fresh spinach leaves, washed but
   not dried
2.5cm/1in piece fresh root ginger, grated
2 garlic cloves, crushed
1 green chilli, roughly chopped
200ml/7fl oz/scant 1 cup water
30ml/2 tbsp oil
2 bay leaves
1.5ml/¼ tsp black peppercorns
1 onion, finely chopped
4 tomatoes, skinned and finely chopped
10ml/2 tsp curry powder
5ml/1 tsp salt
5ml/1 tsp chilli powder
45ml/3 tbsp natural yogurt
8 chicken thighs, skinned
natural yogurt and chilli powder,
   to garnish
masala naan, to serve

1 Place the spinach, without water, in a microwaveproof bowl. Cover and microwave on HIGH for 4 minutes, stirring once. Purée the spinach, ginger, garlic and chilli with 50ml/2fl oz/¼ cup of the water in a food processor or blender.

2 Place the oil in a large microwaveproof dish. Add the bay leaves, black peppercorns and onion, cover and microwave on HIGH for 4 minutes, stirring once.

3 Stir in the tomatoes, curry powder, salt and chilli powder. Cover and microwave on HIGH for 3 minutes, stirring once.

4 Mix in the purée and remaining water. Cover and microwave on HIGH for 2 minutes.

5 Stir in half the yogurt and add the chicken, arranging the pieces in the sauce. Cover and microwave on HIGH for 10 minutes, stirring once.

6 Add the remaining yogurt. Cover and microwave on HIGH for a further 7–8 minutes, or until the chicken is tender. Serve on masala naan, drizzle over some natural yogurt and dust with chilli powder.

Hot Chilli Chicken

Not for the faint-hearted, this fiery, hot curry is made with a spicy chilli masala paste.

Serves 4

30ml/2 tbsp tomato purée
2 garlic cloves, roughly chopped
2 green chillies, roughly chopped
5 dried red chillies
2.5ml/¹/₂ tsp salt
1.5ml/¹/₄ tsp sugar
5ml/1 tsp chilli powder
2.5ml/¹/₂ tsp paprika
15ml/1 tbsp curry paste
30ml/2 tbsp oil
2.5ml/¹/₂ tsp cumin seeds
1 onion, finely chopped
2 bay leaves
5ml/1 tsp ground coriander
5ml/1 tsp ground cumin
1.5ml/¹/₄ tsp ground turmeric
400g/14oz can chopped tomatoes
150ml/¹/₄ pint/²/₃ cup water
8 chicken thighs, skinned
5ml/1 tsp garam masala
sliced green chillies, to garnish
chappatis and natural yogurt, to serve

1 Process the tomato purée, garlic, green and dried red chillies, salt, sugar, chilli powder, paprika and curry paste to a smooth paste in a food processor or blender.

2 Place the oil in a large microwaveproof bowl and add the cumin seeds. Microwave on HIGH for 1¹/₂ minutes. Add the onion and bay leaves, cover and microwave on HIGH for 3 minutes.

3 Stir in the chilli paste. Cover and microwave on HIGH for 1¹/₂ minutes, then mix in the remaining ground spices, chopped tomatoes and water. Cover and microwave on HIGH for 3 minutes.

4 Add the chicken and garam masala. Cover and microwave on HIGH for 18–22 minutes, stirring twice, until the chicken is tender. Garnish with sliced green chillies and serve with chappatis and natural yogurt.

Dijon Chicken Salad

An attractive and elegant dish to serve for lunch with herb and garlic bread.

INGREDIENTS

Serves 4

4 boned and skinned chicken breasts
mixed salad leaves, such as frisée and
    oakleaf lettuce or radicchio, to serve

For the marinade
30ml/2 tbsp Dijon mustard
3 garlic cloves, crushed
15ml/1 tbsp grated onion
60ml/4 tbsp white wine

For the mustard dressing
30ml/2 tbsp tarragon wine vinegar
5ml/1 tsp Dijon mustard
5ml/1 tsp clear honey
90ml/6 tbsp olive oil
salt and ground black pepper

1 Mix all the marinade ingredients together in a shallow glass or earthenware dish that is large enough to hold the chicken in a single layer.

2 Turn the chicken over in the marinade to coat it completely, cover with clear film and then chill overnight.

3 Transfer the chicken and the marinade to a microwave-proof dish. Cover and microwave on HIGH for 4–5 minutes, turning over and rearranging twice during cooking.

4 Put all the mustard dressing ingredients into a screw-topped jar and shake it vigorously to emulsify the mixture. Adjust the seasoning. This dressing can be stored in the fridge for several days.

5 Cut the cooked chicken breasts into thin, even slices.

6 Fan out the chicken slices and arrange them on a serving dish with the salad leaves. Spoon over some of the mustard dressing and serve.

COMBINATION MICROWAVE

This recipe is suitable for cooking in a combination microwave. Follow the oven manufacturer's timing guide for good results.

COOK'S TIP
〜

Dijon mustard is smooth and fairly mild. A hot variety is not suitable for this dish.

Chicken and Fruit Salad

*The chicken may be cooked a
day before serving and the salad
assembled at the last minute. Serve
with warm garlic bread.*

INGREDIENTS

Serves 8

4 tarragon or rosemary sprigs

2 x 1.5kg/3–3½lb chickens

65g/2½oz/5 tbsp softened butter

150ml/¼ pint/⅔ cup chicken stock

150ml/¼ pint/⅔ cup white wine

1 small cantaloupe melon

115g/4oz/1 cup walnut pieces

lettuce leaves

450g/1lb seedless grapes or
    cherries, stoned

salt and ground black pepper

For the dressing

30ml/2 tbsp tarragon vinegar

120ml/8 tbsp light olive oil

30ml/2 tbsp chopped mixed fresh herbs,
    for example parsley, mint and tarragon

1 Put the sprigs of tarragon or
rosemary inside the chickens
and season with salt and pepper.
Tie the chickens in a neat shape
with string and spread with
50g/2oz/4 tbsp of the softened
butter. Place breast-side down in
a microwaveproof shallow dish
and pour round the stock. Cover
loosely and microwave on HIGH
for 30–35 minutes, turning breast-
side up halfway through cooking.
Cover with foil and leave to stand
for 10–15 minutes. Prick to release
excess juices and leave to cool.

2 Add the wine to the cooking
juices. Transfer to a microwaveproof jug or bowl and
microwave on HIGH for about
5 minutes or until syrupy. Strain
and leave the juices to cool. Scoop
the melon into balls or into cubes.
Joint the chickens.

3 Place the remaining butter in a
microwaveproof bowl with the
walnuts. Microwave on HIGH for
2–3 minutes to brown, stirring
once. Drain and cool.

4 To make the dressing, whisk
the vinegar and oil together
with some seasoning. Remove the
fat from the chicken juices and add
the juices to the dressing with the
herbs. Adjust the seasoning.

5 Arrange the chicken pieces
on a bed of lettuce, sprinkle
over the grapes or stoned cherries,
melon balls or cubes and coat with
the herb dressing. Sprinkle with
toasted walnuts and serve.

COMBINATION MICROWAVE

This recipe is suitable for cooking
in a combination microwave.
Follow the oven manufacturer's
timing guide for good results.

COOK'S TIP

The chickens can be cooked in
roasting bags, but do not use
metal ties for securing the bags;
replace with elastic bands
or string.

Chicken Liver Salad

This salad may be served as a first course on individual plates.

INGREDIENTS

Serves 4

mixed salad leaves, such as frisée and
    oakleaf lettuce or radicchio

1 avocado, diced

2 pink grapefruits, segmented

350g/12oz chicken livers

30ml/2 tbsp olive oil

1 garlic clove, crushed

salt and ground black pepper

crusty bread, to serve

For the dressing

30ml/2 tbsp lemon juice

60ml/4 tbsp olive oil

2.5ml/$\frac{1}{2}$ tsp wholegrain mustard

2.5ml/$\frac{1}{2}$ tsp clear honey

15ml/1 tbsp chopped fresh chives

1 First prepare the dressing: put all the ingredients into a screw-topped jar and shake vigorously to emulsify the mixture. Taste and adjust the seasoning.

2 Wash and dry the salad. Arrange attractively on a serving plate with the avocado and grapefruit.

3 Dry the chicken livers on paper towels and remove any sinew or membrane. Cut the larger livers in half and leave the smaller ones whole. Prick them thoroughly with a fork.

4 Place the oil in a large microwaveproof bowl. Add the livers and garlic, mixing well. Cover loosely and microwave on HIGH for 3–4 minutes, stirring twice, until cooked but still slightly pink inside.

5 Season with salt and ground black pepper and drain on paper towels.

6 Place the liver on the salad and spoon the dressing over the top. Serve immediately, with warm crusty bread.

PULSES, PASTA
AND GRAINS

~

Lemon and Ginger Spicy Beans

A quick meal, made with canned beans. You won't need extra salt as canned beans tend to be salted.

INGREDIENTS

Serves 4

5cm/2in piece fresh ginger root, peeled
and roughly chopped
3 garlic cloves, roughly chopped
250ml/8fl oz/1 cup cold water
15ml/1 tbsp sunflower oil
1 large onion, thinly sliced
1 fresh red chilli, seeded and
finely chopped
1.5ml/¼ tsp cayenne pepper
10ml/2 tsp ground cumin
5ml/1 tsp ground coriander
2.5ml/½ tsp ground turmeric
30ml/2 tbsp lemon juice
75g/3oz/⅓ cup chopped fresh
coriander leaves
400g/14oz can black-eyed beans, drained
and rinsed
400g/14oz can aduki beans, drained
and rinsed
400g/14oz can haricot beans, drained
and rinsed
ground black pepper

3 Add the cayenne pepper, cumin, ground coriander and turmeric, and microwave on HIGH for 1 minute.

4 Stir in the ginger and garlic paste and microwave on HIGH for 1 minute.

5 Stir in the remaining water, lemon juice and fresh coriander. Cover and microwave on HIGH for 4 minutes.

6 Add all the beans to the mixture in the bowl and stir well. Cover and microwave on HIGH for 4–6 minutes, stirring halfway through cooking. Season with pepper and serve.

1 Place the ginger, garlic and 60ml/4 tbsp of the cold water in a blender or food processor and process until smooth.

2 Place the oil in a large microwaveproof bowl with the onion and chilli. Microwave on HIGH for 3 minutes, stirring halfway through cooking.

Borlotti Beans with Mushrooms

A mixture of wild and cultivated mushrooms helps to give this dish a rich and nutty flavour.

INGREDIENTS

Serves 4

30ml/2 tbsp olive oil

50g/2oz/4 tbsp butter

2 shallots, chopped

2-3 garlic cloves, crushed

675g/1½lb mixed mushrooms, thickly sliced

4 sun-dried tomatoes in oil, drained and chopped

45ml/3 tbsp dry white wine

400g/14oz can borlotti beans

45ml/3 tbsp grated Parmesan cheese

30ml/2 tbsp chopped fresh parsley

salt and ground black pepper

freshly cooked pappardelle pasta, to serve

1 Place the oil and butter in a microwaveproof bowl with the shallots. Microwave on HIGH for 1 minute.

2 Add the garlic and mushrooms and microwave on HIGH for 3–4 minutes, stirring halfway through cooking. Stir in the sun-dried tomatoes, wine and seasoning to taste.

3 Stir in the borlotti beans and microwave on HIGH for 2–3 minutes or until the beans are heated through.

4 Stir in the grated Parmesan and sprinkle with parsley. Serve immediately with hot pappardelle pasta.

COOK'S TIP

When buying wild mushrooms, examine packs carefully and reject any mushrooms that have tiny holes or show signs of being eaten as they may contain tiny maggots.

Mung Beans with Potatoes

Mung beans are one of the quicker-cooking pulses that do not require soaking and are therefore very easy to use. In this recipe, they are cooked with potatoes and traditional Indian spices to give a tasty, nutritious dish.

INGREDIENTS

Serves 4

175g/6oz/1 cup mung beans
750ml/1¼ pints/3 cups boiling water
225g/8oz potatoes, cut into
   2cm/¾in chunks
30ml/2 tbsp oil
2.5ml/½ tsp cumin seeds
1 green chilli, seeded and finely chopped
1 garlic clove, crushed
2.5cm/1in piece fresh root ginger,
   finely chopped
1.5ml/¼ tsp ground turmeric
2.5ml/½ tsp chilli powder
5ml/1 tsp salt
5ml/1 tsp sugar
4 curry leaves
5 tomatoes, peeled and finely chopped
15ml/1 tbsp tomato purée
plain rice, to serve
curry leaves, to garnish

1 Wash the beans and place them in a large microwave-proof bowl with the boiling water and potatoes. Cover and microwave on HIGH for 4 minutes, stirring once. Reduce the power setting to MEDIUM and microwave for a further 12–15 minutes or until the beans are almost tender. Set aside to stand, covered, for 10 minutes.

2 Meanwhile, place the oil and cumin seeds in another large microwaveproof bowl and microwave on HIGH for 1½ minutes. Add the chilli, garlic and ginger, and microwave on HIGH for 2 minutes, stirring once.

3 Add the turmeric, chilli powder, salt and sugar, then microwave on HIGH for 1 minute, stirring once.

4 Stir in the curry leaves, tomatoes and tomato purée. Cover and microwave on HIGH for 3–4 minutes, stirring once, until the sauce thickens slightly. Drain the beans and potatoes, then mix them into the tomato sauce. Serve with plain boiled rice and garnish with curry leaves.

Chick-pea Curry

Chick-peas are used and cooked in a variety of ways all over India.

INGREDIENTS

Serves 4

225g/8oz/1¼ cups dried chick-peas
50g/2oz tamarind pulp
120ml/4fl oz/½ cup boiling water, plus
    extra for cooking chick-peas
45ml/3 tbsp oil
2.5ml/½ tsp cumin seeds
1 onion, finely chopped
2 garlic cloves, crushed
2.5cm/1in piece fresh root ginger, grated
1 green chilli, seeded and finely chopped
5ml/1 tsp ground cumin
5ml/1 tsp ground coriander
1.5ml/¼ tsp ground turmeric
2.5ml/½ tsp salt
225g/8oz tomatoes, peeled and
    finely chopped
2.5ml/½ tsp garam masala
chopped chillies and onion, to garnish

1 Put the chick-peas in a large bowl and cover with plenty of cold water. Leave to soak overnight.

2 Drain the chick-peas, place in a large microwaveproof bowl and pour in boiling water to cover them. Cover and microwave on HIGH for 10 minutes. Reduce the power setting to MEDIUM and microwave for a further 20–25 minutes, stirring twice and adding extra boiling water to cover the chick-peas, if necessary. Drain thoroughly.

3 Meanwhile, break up the tamarind and soak it in the measured boiling water for about 15 minutes. Rub the resulting tamarind pulp through a sieve into a bowl, discarding any stones and fibre. The tamarind gives the dish a delicious, sharp flavour.

4 Place the oil in a large microwaveproof bowl with the cumin seeds and microwave on HIGH for 1½ minutes. Add the onion, garlic, ginger and chilli, cover and microwave on HIGH for 3 minutes, stirring once.

5 Add the cumin, coriander, turmeric and salt and microwave on HIGH for 1 minute. Stir in the tomatoes and tamarind pulp. Cover and microwave on HIGH for 3 minutes, stirring once.

6 Mix in chick-peas and garam masala. Cover, microwave on HIGH for 6–8 minutes, stir once. Garnish with chillies and onion.

Cannelloni al Forno

Filled with chicken, this is a lighter alternative to the usual beef-filled, béchamel-coated version. For a vegetarian recipe, fill with ricotta cheese, onion and mushroom, then top with tomato sauce.

INGREDIENTS

Serves 4–6

450g/1lb/4 cups skinned and boned
   chicken breast, cooked
225g/8oz mushrooms
2 garlic cloves, crushed
30ml/2 tbsp chopped fresh parsley
15ml/1 tbsp chopped fresh tarragon
1 egg, beaten
fresh lemon juice
12–18 cannelloni tubes
300ml/½ pint/1¼ cups tomato sauce
50g/2oz/½ cup freshly grated
   Parmesan cheese
salt and ground black pepper
fresh parsley sprig, to garnish

1 Process the chicken in a blender or food processor until finely minced. Transfer to a bowl.

2 Process the mushrooms, garlic, parsley and tarragon until finely minced.

3 Beat the mushroom mixture into the chicken with the egg, salt and pepper, adding lemon juice to taste.

4 Place the cannelloni in a microwaveproof dish and cover with boiling water. Cover and microwave on HIGH for 1 minute. Drain well and dry on a clean tea towel.

5 Place the filling in a piping bag fitted with a large plain nozzle. Use this to fill each of the tubes of cannelloni.

6 Lay the filled cannelloni tightly together in a single layer in a buttered shallow microwaveproof dish that is suitable for grilling. Spoon over the tomato sauce and sprinkle with Parmesan cheese. Microwave on HIGH for 5–8 minutes. Reduce the power setting to MEDIUM and microwave for a further 5 minutes. Brown under a preheated hot grill, if you like. Garnish with a sprig of fresh parsley.

COMBINATION MICROWAVE

This recipe is suitable for cooking in a combination microwave. Follow the oven manufacturer's timing guide for good results.

Ravioli with Four Cheese Sauce

This is a smooth cheese sauce that coats the pasta very evenly.

INGREDIENTS

Serves 4

350g/12oz ravioli

1.75 litres/3 pints/7½ cups boiling water

50g/2oz/¼ cup butter

50g/2oz/¼ cup plain flour

475ml/16fl oz/2 cups milk

50g/2oz Parmesan cheese

50g/2oz Edam cheese

50g/2oz Gruyère cheese

50g/2oz fontina cheese

salt and ground black pepper

chopped fresh parsley, to garnish

1 Place the ravioli in a large microwaveproof bowl and pour in the boiling water. Microwave on HIGH for 10 minutes, stirring halfway through cooking. Leave to stand for 3 minutes.

2 Whisk the butter, flour and milk together in a microwave-proof jug. Microwave on HIGH for 5–7 minutes, whisking every minute, until smooth, boiling and thickened.

3 Grate the cheeses and stir them into the sauce until they are just beginning to melt. Add seasoning to taste.

4 Drain the pasta thoroughly and turn it into a large serving bowl. Pour over the sauce and toss to coat. Serve immediately, garnished with chopped parsley.

COOK'S TIP

If you cannot find all of the recommended cheeses, simply substitute your favourite types. Strong-flavoured hard cheeses are best for this type of sauce.

Turkey Lasagne

This delicious low-fat version of a classic lasagne is very easy to cook in the microwave.

INGREDIENTS

Serves 6–8

1 large onion, chopped
2 garlic cloves, crushed
500g/1¼lb minced turkey meat
450g/1lb carton passata (smooth, thick, sieved tomatoes)
5ml/1 tsp dried mixed herbs
200g/7oz lasagne verdi
900ml/1½ pints/3¾ cups boiling water
225g/8oz frozen leaf spinach, thawed
200g/7oz low-fat cottage cheese

For the sauce

25g/1oz low-fat margarine
25g/1oz plain flour
300ml/½ pint/1¼ cups skimmed milk
1.5ml/¼ tsp ground nutmeg
25g/1oz grated Parmesan cheese
salt and ground black pepper
mixed salad, to serve

1 Mix the onion, garlic and minced turkey in a microwaveproof bowl. Cover and microwave on HIGH for 4 minutes, stirring twice to separate the pieces.

2 Add the passata, herbs and seasoning. Cover and microwave on HIGH for 8 minutes, stirring once.

3 Whisk all the sauce ingredients, except the Parmesan cheese, together in a microwaveproof jug. Microwave on HIGH for 4–6 minutes, whisking every minute, until smooth, boiling and thickened. Adjust the seasoning and stir in the cheese.

4 Place the lasagne in a deep, rectangular microwaveproof dish. Add the boiling water. Cover and microwave on HIGH for 9 minutes. Leave to stand for 15 minutes, then drain well and rinse under cold water. Lay the spinach leaves out on kitchen paper and pat dry.

5 Layer the turkey mixture, prepared lasagne, cottage cheese and spinach in a 2-litre/3½-pint/8-cup microwaveproof dish suitable for grilling, starting and ending with a layer of turkey.

6 Spoon the sauce over the top to coat the turkey and microwave on HIGH for 2–3 minutes or until heated through. Brown under a preheated hot grill if you like. Serve with a mixed salad.

COMBINATION MICROWAVE

This recipe is suitable for cooking in a combination microwave. Follow the oven manufacturer's timing guide for good results.

Pasta Shells with Smoked Haddock

INGREDIENTS

Serves 4

450g/1lb smoked haddock fillet

1 small leek or onion, thickly sliced

300ml/½ pint/1¼ cups hot skimmed milk

1 bouquet garni (bay leaf, thyme and
parsley stalks)

25g/1oz low-fat margarine

25g/1oz plain flour

30ml/2 tbsp chopped fresh parsley

225g/8oz pasta shells

salt and ground black pepper

15g/½oz flaked almonds, toasted, to serve

1 While preparing the sauce in the microwave, cook the pasta conventionally in a large saucepan of boiling salted water on the hob according to the packet instructions.

2 Remove all the skin and any bones from the haddock. Arrange the fish fillets in a large microwaveproof dish with the thicker portions to the outside of the dish. Sprinkle with the leek or onion. Add half the milk and the bouquet garni. Cover and microwave on HIGH for 5–6 minutes, rearranging once. Leave to stand for 3 minutes.

3 Strain, reserving the milk for making the sauce, and discard the bouquet garni.

4 Whisk the margarine, flour and remaining milk together in a microwave jug. Microwave on HIGH for 4–6 minutes, whisking every minute, until smooth, boiling and thickened. Season and add the fish and leek or onion.

5 Drain the pasta thoroughly and stir it into the sauce with the chopped parsley. Serve immediately, sprinkled with toasted flaked almonds.

Pasta Bows with Smoked Salmon and Dill

In Italy, pasta cooked with smoked salmon has become very fashionable. This is a quick and quite luxurious sauce.

INGREDIENTS

Serves 4

50g/2oz/4 tbsp butter
6 spring onions, sliced
90ml/6 tbsp dry white wine or vermouth
475ml/16fl oz/2 cups double cream
freshly grated nutmeg
225g/8oz smoked salmon
30ml/2 tbsp chopped fresh dill or 15ml/
    1 tbsp dried dill
freshly squeezed lemon juice
450g/1lb/4 cups pasta bows (farfalle)
salt and ground black pepper

1 While preparing the sauce in the microwave, cook the pasta conventionally in a large saucepan of boiling salted water on the hob according to the packet instructions.

2 Place the butter and spring onions in a microwaveproof bowl. Cover and microwave on HIGH for 1 minute.

3 Add the wine and microwave on HIGH for 2–3 minutes to reduce the liquid to about 30ml/2 tbsp. Stir in the cream and add salt, pepper and nutmeg to taste. Microwave on HIGH for 1–2 minutes, stirring twice, until slightly thickened.

4 Cut the smoked salmon into 2.5cm/1in squares and stir into the sauce with the dill. Taste and add a little lemon juice.

5 Drain the pasta well. Toss the pasta with the sauce and serve immediately.

Pasta with Tuna, Capers and Anchovies

This piquant sauce can be made without the tomatoes – just heat the oil, add the other ingredients and microwave on HIGH for 2–3 minutes, stirring once, before tossing with the pasta.

INGREDIENTS

Serves 4

400g/14oz can tuna fish in oil
30ml/2 tbsp olive oil
2 garlic cloves, crushed
800g/1¾lb can chopped tomatoes
6 canned anchovy fillets, drained
30ml/2 tbsp capers in vinegar, drained
30ml/2 tbsp chopped fresh basil
450g/1lb/4 cups rigatoni, penne or
    garganelle
salt and ground black pepper
fresh basil sprigs, to garnish

1 While preparing the sauce in the microwave, cook the pasta conventionally in a large saucepan of boiling salted water on the hob according to the packet instructions.

2 Drain the oil from the tuna into a microwaveproof bowl, add the olive oil and microwave on HIGH for 1 minute.

3 Add the garlic and microwave on HIGH for 30 seconds. Stir in the tomatoes, cover and microwave on HIGH for 4–6 minutes, stirring twice, until thickened.

4 Flake the tuna and cut the anchovies in half. Stir into the sauce with the capers and chopped basil. Season well.

5 Drain the pasta well and toss it with the sauce. Garnish with fresh basil sprigs and serve at once.

COOK'S TIP

For a slightly lighter version of this recipe, use tuna canned in brine and drain off the brine. Use 15ml/1 tbsp olive oil and heat it with the garlic for 30 seconds; continue as in the main recipe.

Spaghetti with Tomato and Clam Sauce

Small sweet clams make this a delicately succulent sauce. Cockles would make a good substitute, or even mussels. Don't be tempted to use seafood pickled in vinegar – the result will be inedible!

INGREDIENTS

Serves 4

900g/2lb small clams or 2 x 400g/14oz
    cans clams in brine, drained
90ml/6 tbsp olive oil
2 garlic cloves, crushed
600g/1lb 5oz can chopped tomatoes
45ml/3 tbsp chopped fresh parsley
450g/1lb spaghetti
salt and ground black pepper

1 While preparing the sauce in the microwave, cook the pasta conventionally in a large saucepan of boiling salted water on the hob according to the packet instructions.

2 If using fresh (live) clams, rinse them in several changes of cold water to remove any grit or sand. Drain.

3 Heat the oil in a large microwaveproof bowl and add the clams. Cover loosely and microwave on HIGH for 4–5 minutes, stirring once, until the clams open. Throw away any that do not open. Transfer the clams to a bowl with a perforated spoon.

4 Microwave the clam juice on HIGH for 2–3 minutes to reduce it to about 15ml/1 tbsp. Add the garlic and microwave on HIGH for 30 seconds. Stir in the tomatoes and microwave on HIGH for 3–4 minutes.

5 Stir in the cooked or canned clams with half the parsley and microwave on HIGH for 2 minutes, until hot. Season to taste with salt and pepper.

6 Drain the pasta well and turn it into a warm serving dish. Pour over the sauce and sprinkle with the remaining parsley.

Rigatoni with Spicy Sausage and Tomato

This is really a cheat's Bolognese sauce using the wonderful fresh spicy sausages sold in every Italian delicatessen.

INGREDIENTS

Serves 4

450g/1lb fresh spicy Italian sausage

30ml/2 tbsp olive oil

1 onion, chopped

475ml/16fl oz/2 cups passata (smooth, thick, sieved tomatoes)

150ml/¼ pint/⅔ cup dry red wine

6 sun-dried tomatoes in oil, drained

450g/1lb/4 cups rigatoni or similar pasta

salt and ground black pepper

freshly grated Parmesan cheese, to serve

1 Squeeze the sausagemeat out of the skins into a bowl and break it up.

2 While preparing the sauce, cook the pasta conventionally in a saucepan of boiling salted water on the hob according to the packet instructions.

3 Place the oil in a microwave-proof bowl and add the onion. Microwave on HIGH for 3 minutes. Stir in the sausagemeat and microwave on HIGH for 5 minutes, stirring every minute to break up the meat. Stir in the passata and wine. Cover and microwave on HIGH for 4 minutes, stirring once.

4 Slice the sun-dried tomatoes and add them to the sauce. Microwave, uncovered, for 2 minutes, stirring once, then season to taste.

5 Drain the pasta well and top with the sauce. Serve with grated Parmesan cheese.

COOK'S TIP

If you cannot find fresh Italian sausage, season pork sausage-meat with a crushed garlic clove, a little dried oregano, grated nutmeg and a pinch of paprika. Mix well.

Pasta with Tomato and Smoky Bacon Sauce

A wonderful sauce to prepare in mid-summer when the tomatoes are ripe and sweet.

INGREDIENTS

Serves 4

900g/2lb ripe tomatoes

450g/1lb/4 cups pasta, any variety

6 rashers smoked streaky bacon

50g/2oz/4 tbsp butter

1 onion, chopped

15ml/1 tbsp chopped fresh oregano or
    5ml/1 tsp dried oregano

salt and ground black pepper

freshly grated Parmesan cheese, to serve

1 Plunge the tomatoes into boiling water for 1 minute, then into cold water to stop them from becoming mushy. Slip off the skins. Halve the tomatoes, remove the seeds and cores and roughly chop the flesh.

2 Cook the pasta in a saucepan of boiling water according to the packet instructions. Remove and discard the rind from the bacon and chop the rashers.

3 Place the butter in a microwaveproof bowl and add the bacon. Microwave on HIGH for 5 minutes, stirring once, then add the onion.

4 Microwave on HIGH for a further 1½ minutes. Add the tomatoes, seasoning and oregano. Cover and microwave on HIGH for 5–6 minutes, stirring twice.

5 Drain the pasta well and toss it with the sauce. Serve with grated Parmesan cheese.

Pasta Carbonara

Cooking the pasta conventionally on the hob and the sauce in the microwave makes this a very speedy dish to prepare.

INGREDIENTS

Serves 4

350–450g/12oz–1lb fresh tagliatelle
15ml/1 tbsp olive oil
225g/8oz ham, bacon or pancetta, cut into
   2.5cm/1in sticks
115g/4oz button mushrooms
   (about 10), sliced
4 eggs, lightly beaten
75ml/5 tbsp single cream
30ml/2 tbsp finely grated
   Parmesan cheese
salt and ground black pepper
fresh basil sprigs, to garnish

1 While preparing the sauce in the microwave, cook the pasta conventionally in a large saucepan of boiling salted water on the hob according to the packet instructions.

2 Meanwhile, place the oil and ham in a microwaveproof bowl. Microwave on HIGH for 3 minutes, then add the mushrooms. Microwave on HIGH for a further 3 minutes, stirring once during cooking. Meanwhile, lightly beat the eggs and cream together and season well.

3 Drain the cooked pasta well and add to the ham and mushroom mixture, mixing well.

4 Pour in the eggs and cream and add half the Parmesan cheese. Stir well and, as you do this, the eggs will cook in the heat of the pasta. If you like your sauce slightly thicker, then microwave on HIGH for 30 seconds, stirring once during cooking. Pile on to warmed serving plates, sprinkle with the remaining Parmesan and garnish with basil.

Baked Macaroni Cheese

A delicious supper-time dish – replace the Cheddar with your family's favourite cheese.

INGREDIENTS

Serves 4

275g/10oz/2⅓ cups macaroni
1.2 litres/2 pints/5 cups boiling water
15ml/1 tbsp olive oil
2 leeks, chopped
50g/2oz/4 tbsp butter
50g/2oz/½ cup plain flour
900ml/1½ pints/3¾ cups milk
225g/8oz/2 cups mature Cheddar
   cheese, grated
30ml/2 tbsp fromage frais
5ml/1 tsp wholegrain mustard
50g/2oz/1 cup fresh white breadcrumbs
25g/1oz/½ cup Double Gloucester
   cheese, grated
salt and ground black pepper
15ml/1 tbsp chopped fresh parsley,
   to garnish

1 Place the macaroni in a large microwaveproof bowl with the boiling water and the olive oil. Add the leeks and microwave on HIGH for 10 minutes, stirring once. Leave to stand, covered, while cooking the sauce.

2 Stir the butter with the flour and milk in a large microwaveproof jug. Microwave on HIGH for 6–8 minutes, whisking every minute, until smooth, boiling and thickened.

3 Whisk in the Cheddar cheese, fromage frais and mustard, adding salt and pepper to taste.

4 Drain the macaroni and leeks and rinse under cold water. Stir the drained macaroni and leeks into the cheese sauce and turn into a dish that is suitable for grilling. Level the top with the back of a spoon and sprinkle over the breadcrumbs and Double Gloucester cheese.

5 Cook under a preheated hot grill until golden and bubbly. Serve hot, garnished with chopped fresh parsley.

Tagliatelle with Tomatoes and Courgettes

INGREDIENTS

Serves 3–4

5–6 ripe tomatoes

225g/8oz wholewheat tagliatelle

1.2 litres/2 pints/5 cups boiling water

30ml/2 tbsp olive oil

1 onion, chopped

2 celery sticks, chopped

1 garlic clove, crushed

2 courgettes, sliced

30ml/2 tbsp sun-dried tomato paste

50g/2oz/½ cup flaked almonds, toasted, to serve

salt and ground black pepper

1 Place the tomatoes in a bowl and pour in boiling water to cover, then leave to stand for 30 seconds to loosen their skins. Peel, then chop.

2 Place the tagliatelle in a large microwaveproof bowl with the boiling water. Microwave on HIGH for 6 minutes, stirring once. Leave to stand, covered, while cooking the sauce.

3 Place the oil, onion, celery, garlic and courgettes in another microwaveproof bowl. Cover and microwave on HIGH for 3–4 minutes, or until the onions are softened.

4 Stir in the tomatoes and sun-dried tomato paste. Microwave on HIGH for 3–4 minutes, then add salt and pepper.

5 Drain the pasta, return it to the bowl and add the sauce. Toss well. Transfer to a serving dish and scatter the toasted almonds over the top to serve.

COOK'S TIP

If using fresh pasta, you'll need double the quantity (450g/1lb) to satisfy 3–4 hearty appetites. Fresh tagliatelle usually only takes 2–3 minutes to cook and is ready when it's tender but still *al dente*, with a bit of bite.

Rocket, Mangetouts and Pine Nut Pasta

A light but filling pasta dish flavoured with the peppery taste of fresh rocket.

INGREDIENTS

Serves 4

250g/9oz capellini or angel-hair pasta

50g/2oz/¼ cup pine nuts

225g/8oz mangetouts

30ml/2 tbsp water

175g/6oz rocket

30ml/2 tbsp finely grated Parmesan cheese (optional)

30ml/2 tbsp olive oil (optional)

1 While preparing the sauce in the microwave, cook the pasta conventionally in a large saucepan of boiling salted water on the hob according to the packet instructions.

2 Place the pine nuts in a microwaveproof dish and microwave on HIGH for 3–5 minutes, stirring every minute, until golden.

3 Carefully top and tail the mangetouts. Place them in a large microwaveproof bowl and add the water. Cover and microwave on HIGH for 2 minutes. Add the rocket and mix lightly.

4 As soon as the pasta is cooked, drain it immediately and toss it with the mangetouts and rocket.

5 Toss the pine nuts into the pasta. Add the Parmesan and olive oil if using. Serve at once.

Thai Fragrant Rice

A lovely, soft, fluffy rice dish, perfumed with fresh lemon grass.

INGREDIENTS

Serves 4

1 piece lemon grass

2 limes

225g/8oz/1 cup brown basmati rice

15ml/1 tbsp olive oil

1 onion, chopped

2.5cm/1in piece fresh ginger root,
   finely chopped

7.5ml/1½ tsp coriander seeds

7.5ml/1½ tsp cumin seeds

550ml/18fl oz/2¼ cups boiling
   vegetable stock

60ml/4 tbsp chopped fresh
   coriander leaves

lime wedges, to serve

3 Rinse the rice in plenty of cold water until the water runs clear, then drain it in a sieve.

4 Place the oil in a large microwaveproof bowl. Add the onion and ginger.

5 Stir in the coriander and cumin seeds, lemon grass and lime rind and microwave on HIGH for 2 minutes.

6 Add the rice and the stock. Cover loosely with a lid or vented clear film and microwave on HIGH for 3 minutes. Reduce the power setting to MEDIUM and microwave for a further 25 minutes, stirring two or three times during cooking.

7 Stir in the fresh coriander, fluff up the grains of rice, then cover and leave to stand for 5 minutes before serving. Serve lime wedges with the rice.

1 Finely chop the lemon grass using a sharp knife.

2 Remove the rind from the limes using a zester or fine grater. Avoid the white pith which has a bitter taste.

COOK'S TIP
❧

Other varieties of rice, such as white basmati or long grain, can be used for this dish but you will need to adjust the cooking times according to type.

Golden Vegetable Paella

Serves 4

pinch of saffron strands or 5ml/1 tsp
   ground turmeric
750ml/1¼ pints/3 cups boiling vegetable
   or spicy stock
90ml/6 tbsp olive oil
2 large onions, sliced
3 garlic cloves, chopped
275g/10oz/1½ cups long grain rice
50g/2oz/⅓ cup wild rice
175g/6oz pumpkin or butternut
   squash, chopped
175g/6oz carrots, cut into
   matchstick strips
1 yellow pepper, seeded and sliced
4 tomatoes, peeled and chopped
115g/4oz oyster mushrooms, quartered
salt and ground black pepper
strips of red, yellow and green pepper,
   to garnish

1 If using saffron, place it in a small bowl with 45–60ml/ 3–4 tbsp of the stock. Leave to stand for 5 minutes. Meanwhile, place the oil in a large microwave-proof bowl with the onions and garlic, then microwave on HIGH for 4–4½ minutes, stirring once.

2 Stir both types of rice into the onion mixture and toss until coated in oil. Add the remaining stock, with the pumpkin or squash, and the saffron strands and liquid or turmeric.

3 Cover and microwave on HIGH for 3 minutes. Add the carrots, pepper, tomatoes, salt and black pepper. Cover again and microwave on HIGH for 2 minutes. Reduce the power setting to MEDIUM and microwave for a further 12 minutes, stirring twice, or until the rice is almost tender.

4 Finally, add the oyster mushrooms, check the seasoning, cover and microwave on HIGH for 1 minute. Leave to stand for 10 minutes, fluff up the rice with a fork, top with the peppers and serve.

Spiced Lentils and Rice

Lentils are cooked with whole and ground spices, onions, potatoes and rice to produce an authentic Indian-style risotto.

INGREDIENTS

Serves 4

150g/5oz/³/₄ cup toovar dhal or split red lentils

115g/4oz basmati rice

1 large potato

1 large onion

30ml/2 tbsp sunflower oil

4 whole cloves

1.5ml/¼ tsp cumin seeds

1.5ml/¼ tsp ground turmeric

10ml/2 tsp salt

300ml/½ pint/1¼ cups boiling water

1 Wash the toovar dhal or lentils and rice in several changes of cold water. Then leave to soak in plenty of cold water for 15 minutes. Drain well.

2 Peel the potato and cut it into 2.5cm/1in chunks.

3 Thinly slice the onion and set it aside until the whole spices are lightly cooked.

4 Place the sunflower oil in a large microwaveproof bowl with the cloves and cumin seeds. Microwave on HIGH for 2 minutes.

5 Add the onion and potatoes, cover and microwave on HIGH for 4 minutes, stirring once. Stir in the lentils and rice, turmeric, salt and water.

6 Cover and microwave on HIGH for 3 minutes. Reduce the power setting to MEDIUM and microwave for a further 12 minutes, stirring twice. Leave to stand, covered, for about 10 minutes before serving.

Mushroom, Leek and Cashew Nut Risotto

INGREDIENTS

Serves 4

225g/8oz/1⅓ cups brown rice

900ml/1½ pints/3 cups boiling vegetable
stock or a mixture of boiling stock and
dry white wine in the ratio 5:1

15ml/1 tbsp walnut or hazelnut oil

2 leeks, sliced

225g/8oz/2 cups mixed wild or cultivated
mushrooms, trimmed and sliced

50g/2oz/½ cup cashew nuts

grated rind of 1 lemon

30ml/2 tbsp chopped fresh thyme

25g/1oz/scant ¼ cup pumpkin seeds

salt and ground black pepper

fresh thyme sprigs and lemon wedges,
to garnish

1 Place the rice in a large
microwaveproof bowl with the
boiling stock (or stock and wine).
Cover loosely and microwave
on HIGH for 3 minutes. Reduce
the power setting to MEDIUM
and microwave for a further
25 minutes, stirring twice. Leave to
stand, covered, while cooking the
vegetable and nut mixture.

2 Place the oil in a large
microwaveproof bowl with the
leeks and mushrooms. Cover and
microwave on HIGH for 3–4
minutes, stirring once.

3 Add the cashew nuts, grated
lemon rind and chopped
fresh thyme to the leeks and
mushrooms and microwave on
HIGH for 1 minute. Season to
taste with salt and freshly ground
black pepper.

4 Drain off any excess stock
from the cooked rice and stir
in the vegetable mixture. Turn the
risotto into a serving dish. Sprinkle
the pumpkin seeds over the top
and garnish with the fresh thyme
sprigs and lemon wedges. Serve the
risotto at once.

Chicken and Vegetable Risotto

An Italian dish made with short grain arborio rice, which gives this easy one-pot recipe a creamy consistency.

INGREDIENTS

Serves 4

15ml/1 tbsp oil
1 onion, chopped
225g/8oz/2 cups minced chicken
175g/6oz/1½ cups arborio rice
600ml/1 pint/2½ cups boiling
   chicken stock
1 red pepper, seeded and chopped
1 yellow pepper, seeded and chopped
75g/3oz frozen green beans
115g/4oz chestnut mushrooms, sliced
15ml/1 tbsp chopped fresh parsley
salt and ground black pepper
fresh parsley sprigs, to garnish

1 Place the oil, onion and chicken in a large microwave-proof bowl. Cover the bowl and microwave on HIGH for 6–7 minutes, stirring twice.

2 Stir in the rice, stock, red and yellow peppers and green beans. Cover the bowl and microwave on HIGH for 13 minutes, stirring twice.

3 Add the mushrooms and microwave on HIGH for 1 minute. Leave to stand, covered, for 10 minutes.

4 Stir in the chopped parsley and season well to taste. Serve, garnished with parsley sprigs.

VARIATIONS

Make a country-style risotto by using thinly sliced garlic sausage or spicy sausage instead of the chicken and replacing the peppers with shelled broad beans. The green beans can also be replaced with sliced courgettes. To enrich a risotto, use a proportion of dry white wine instead of all chicken stock. For example, try using about a third white wine, making it up to the full quantity with boiling stock. Heat the mixture in the microwave before adding it to the risotto, otherwise the overall cooking time will be longer to allow for the cool liquid.

COOK'S TIP

A traditional risotto has a moist, creamy consistency. Risotto rice, of which the best is arborio, is short in length but it has the capacity for absorbing a large proportion of liquid during cooking while retaining its shape and some texture. The cooked rice is slightly sticky, so it acts as a type of thickening agent for the excess liquid. In fact, a risotto rice is halfway between familiar long grain rice and traditional pudding rice in terms of cooking quality.

Creamy Risotto with Asparagus

*Fine asparagus spears look great
gathered in a bundle and tied with a
spring onion stem.*

INGREDIENTS

Serves 4

30ml/2 tbsp olive oil

1 onion, finely chopped

2 garlic cloves, crushed

225g/8oz/1 generous cup arborio rice

1.5 litres/2½ pints/6¼ cups hot
    vegetable stock

150ml/¼ pint/⅔ cup dry white wine

225g/8oz asparagus spears, cut into
    2.5cm/1in pieces

50g/2oz/¼ cup butter

45ml/3 tbsp freshly grated
    Parmesan cheese

salt and ground black pepper

For the garnish

12 slender asparagus spears

75ml/5 tbsp water

4 long green spring onion stems, wilted

1 Place the oil, onion and garlic
in a large microwaveproof
bowl. Cover and microwave on
HIGH for 3 minutes, stirring
once. Add the rice, stock and wine.
Cover and microwave on HIGH
for 7 minutes, stirring once. Stir
in the cut-up asparagus, cover and
microwave on HIGH for a further
6 minutes, stirring once. Leave to
stand, covered, for 10 minutes.

2 Meanwhile, place the whole
asparagus in a microwave-
proof bowl with the water. Cover
and microwave on HIGH for 3–5
minutes, stirring once, until the
spears are just tender.

3 Place three asparagus spears
together, positioning them
2cm/¾in below one another. Tie
the spears together with a wilted
spring onion stem. Make three
more asparagus bundles.

4 Trim the base of each bundle
of spears across at an angle.
Trim the ends of the ties neatly.

5 Stir the butter and Parmesan
into the risotto and check
the seasoning. Serve at once,
garnishing each portion with an
asparagus bundle.

Sweet Vegetable Couscous

*A wonderful combination of sweet
vegetables and spices, this makes a
substantial winter dish.*

INGREDIENTS

Serves 4-6

1 generous pinch of saffron threads

45ml/3 tbsp boiling water

15ml/1 tbsp olive oil

1 red onion, sliced

2 garlic cloves, crushed

1-2 fresh red chillies, seeded and
    finely chopped

2.5ml/½ tsp ground ginger

2.5ml/½ tsp ground cinnamon

400g/14oz can chopped tomatoes

300ml/½ pint/1¼ cups hot vegetable stock
    or water

4 carrots, peeled and cut into
    5mm/¼in slices

2 turnips, peeled and cut into
    2cm/¾in cubes

450g/1lb sweet potatoes, peeled and cut
    into 2cm/¾in cubes

75g/3oz/⅓ cup raisins

2 courgettes, cut into 5mm/¼in slices

400g/14oz can chick-peas, drained
    and rinsed

45ml/3 tbsp chopped fresh parsley

45ml/3 tbsp chopped fresh
    coriander leaves

450g/1lb quick-cook couscous

1 Sprinkle the saffron into the boiling water and set this aside to infuse.

2 Place the oil in a large microwaveproof bowl. Add the onion, garlic and chillies. Microwave on HIGH for 2 minutes, stirring halfway through cooking.

3 Add the ground ginger and cinnamon and microwave on HIGH for 1 minute.

4 Stir in the tomatoes, stock or water, infused saffron and liquid, carrots, turnips, sweet potatoes and raisins. Cover and microwave on HIGH for 15 minutes, stirring twice during cooking.

5 Add the courgettes, chick-peas, parsley and coriander, cover and microwave on HIGH for 5–8 minutes, stirring once, until the vegetables are tender.

6 Meanwhile, prepare the couscous following the packet instructions and serve it with the vegetables.

VEGETABLES
AND SALADS
∼

Ratatouille

INGREDIENTS

Serves 4

2 large aubergines, roughly chopped

4 courgettes, roughly chopped

150ml/¼ pint/⅔ cup olive oil

2 onions, sliced

2 garlic cloves, chopped

1 large red pepper, seeded and
  roughly chopped

2 large yellow peppers, seeded and
  roughly chopped

fresh rosemary sprig

fresh thyme sprig

5ml/1 tsp coriander seeds, crushed

3 plum tomatoes, peeled, seeded
  and chopped

8 basil leaves, torn

salt and ground black pepper

fresh parsley or basil sprigs, to garnish

1 Sprinkle the aubergines and
  courgettes with salt, then put
them in a colander. Cover with a
plate and place a weight on top to
press out the bitter juices. Leave for
about 30 minutes.

2 Place the olive oil in a large
  microwaveproof bowl. Add
the onions, cover and microwave
on HIGH for 5 minutes, until just
softened, then add the garlic and
microwave on HIGH for a further
1 minute.

3 Rinse the aubergines and
  courgettes and pat dry with
kitchen paper or a dish towel. Stir
into the onions with the red and
yellow peppers, rosemary, thyme
and coriander seeds.

4 Add the tomatoes and season
  well. Cover and microwave on
HIGH for 15−20 minutes, stirring
twice during cooking, until the
vegetables are soft but not too
mushy. Remove the sprigs of
herbs. Stir in the torn basil leaves
and check the seasoning. Leave to
cool slightly and serve warm or
cold, garnished with sprigs of
parsley or basil.

Herby Baked Tomatoes

*Dress up sliced, sweet tomatoes with
fresh herbs and a crisp topping.*

INGREDIENTS

Serves 4-6

675g/1½lb large red and yellow tomatoes
   (about 8)
10ml/2 tsp red wine vinegar
2.5ml/½ tsp wholegrain mustard
1 garlic clove, crushed
10ml/2 tsp water
10ml/2 tsp chopped fresh parsley
10ml/2 tsp chopped fresh chives
25g/1oz/½ cup fine fresh white
   breadcrumbs
salt and ground black pepper
sprigs of flat leaf parsley, to garnish

1 Thickly slice the tomatoes
and arrange half of them
in a 900ml/1½ pint/3¾ cup
microwaveproof dish which is
suitable for grilling.

2 Mix the vinegar, mustard,
garlic, seasoning and water
together. Sprinkle the tomatoes
with half the parsley and chives,
then drizzle over half the dressing.

3 Lay the remaining tomato
slices on top, overlapping
them slightly. Drizzle with
the remaining dressing. Cover
and microwave on HIGH for
6 minutes, rotating the dish twice
during cooking.

4 Uncover and sprinkle over
the breadcrumbs. Cook under
a preheated hot grill until the
topping is crisp. Sprinkle with
the remaining parsley and chives.
Serve immediately, garnished with
sprigs of flat leaf parsley.

COMBINATION MICROWAVE

This recipe is suitable for cooking
in a combination microwave.
Follow the oven manufacturer's
timing guide for good results.

Courgettes in Citrus Sauce

If baby courgettes are unavailable, use larger ones, but cook them whole. Then halve them lengthways and cut into 10cm/4in lengths.

INGREDIENTS

Serves 4

350g/12oz baby courgettes
30ml/2 tbsp plus 10ml/2 tsp water
4 spring onions, finely sliced
2.5cm/1in piece fresh root ginger, grated
30ml/2 tbsp cider vinegar
15ml/1 tbsp light soy sauce
5ml/1 tsp soft light brown sugar
45ml/3 tbsp vegetable stock
finely grated rind and juice of ½ lemon
    and ½ orange
5ml/1 tsp cornflour

1 Place the courgettes in a microwaveproof bowl with the 30ml/2 tbsp water. Cover and microwave on HIGH for 5 minutes, stirring once or twice during cooking.

2 Meanwhile, put all the remaining ingredients, except the cornflour, into a small microwaveproof jug. Microwave on HIGH for 1½ minutes, stirring halfway through cooking.

3 Blend the cornflour with the 10ml/2 tsp cold water and add to the sauce. Microwave on HIGH for 1 minute, stirring twice, until the sauce has thickened.

4 Pour the sauce over the courgettes and mix gently to coat evenly. Transfer to a warmed serving dish and serve.

Red Cabbage in Port and Red Wine

A sweet and sour, spicy red cabbage dish, with the added crunch of pears and walnuts.

INGREDIENTS

Serves 6

15ml/1 tbsp walnut oil
1 onion, sliced
2 whole star anise
5ml/1 tsp ground cinnamon
pinch of ground cloves
450g/1lb red cabbage, finely shredded
25g/1oz/2 tbsp dark brown sugar
15ml/1 tbsp red wine vinegar
60ml/4 tbsp red wine
30ml/2 tbsp port
2 pears, cut into 1cm/½in cubes
50g/2oz/¼ cup raisins
salt and ground black pepper
50g/2oz/¼ cup walnut halves

1 Place the oil in a large microwaveproof bowl. Add the onion and microwave on HIGH for 3 minutes, stirring halfway through cooking.

2 Stir in the star anise, cinnamon, cloves and cabbage.

3 Stir in the sugar, vinegar, red wine and port. Cover and microwave on HIGH for 12 –15 minutes, stirring twice during cooking, until the cabbage is almost tender.

4 Stir in the pears and raisins. Cover and microwave on HIGH for 5 minutes or until the cabbage and pears are tender. Season to taste, mix in the walnut halves and serve.

Spring Vegetable Medley

*A colourful, dazzling medley of fresh
and sweet young vegetables.*

INGREDIENTS

Serves 4

15ml/1 tbsp peanut oil

1 garlic clove, sliced

2.5cm/1in piece fresh ginger root,
    finely chopped

115g/4oz baby carrots

115g/4oz patty pan squash

115g/4oz baby sweetcorn

115g/4oz French beans, topped and tailed

115g/4oz sugar snap peas, topped
    and tailed

115g/4oz young asparagus, cut into
    7.5cm/3in pieces

8 spring onions, trimmed and cut into
    5cm/2in pieces

115g/4oz cherry tomatoes

For the dressing

juice of 2 limes

15ml/1 tbsp runny honey

15ml/1 tbsp soy sauce

5ml/1 tsp sesame oil

1 Place the peanut oil in a large
microwaveproof bowl.

2 Add the garlic and ginger,
and microwave on HIGH for
30 seconds.

3 Stir in the carrots, patty pan
squash, sweetcorn and beans.
Cover and microwave on HIGH
for 5 minutes, stirring halfway
through cooking.

4 Add the sugar snap peas,
asparagus, spring onions
and cherry tomatoes. Cover and
microwave on HIGH for 3–4
minutes, stirring halfway through
the cooking time.

5 Mix the dressing ingredients
together and add to the bowl.

6 Stir well, then cover again and
microwave on HIGH for 1–2
minutes, or until the vegetables are
just tender but still crisp.

Mushroom and Fennel Hotpot

Dried shiitake mushrooms add a wonderfully rich flavour to this vegetarian hotpot.

INGREDIENTS

Serves 4

25g/1oz dried shiitake mushrooms

1 small head of fennel or 4 celery sticks

30ml/2 tbsp olive oil

12 shallots, peeled

225g/8oz/2 cups button mushrooms, trimmed and halved

150ml/¼ pint/⅔ cup dry cider

25g/1oz sun-dried tomatoes

30ml/2 tbsp sun-dried tomato paste

1 bay leaf

chopped fresh parsley, to garnish

1 Place the dried shiitake mushrooms in a bowl. Pour over boiling water to cover and set aside for 10 minutes.

2 Roughly chop the fennel or celery sticks. Place the oil in a microwaveproof bowl. Add the shallots and fennel or celery. Cover and microwave on HIGH for 5–6 minutes stirring halfway through cooking. Add the button mushrooms, cover and microwave on HIGH for 1½ minutes.

3 Drain the shiitake mushrooms and reserve the liquid. Cut up any large pieces and add to the fennel or celery.

4 Stir in the cider, sun-dried tomatoes and sun-dried tomato paste. Add the bay leaf. Cover and microwave on HIGH for 2 minutes. Reduce the power setting to MEDIUM and microwave for a further 5–7 minutes, stirring halfway through cooking.

5 Stir in the reserved liquid from the soaked mushrooms. Cover and microwave on MEDIUM for 5–8 minutes until the mixture is very tender. Remove the bay leaf and serve, sprinkled with parsley.

COOK'S TIP

This makes an unusual vegetarian main course or accompaniment. Mushrooms provide useful amounts of vitamins, minerals and fibre.

Potato, Leek and Tomato Bake

This simple dish is delicious for lunch or supper – a real winner with all the family. Select the best tomatoes you can for a good flavour; if this means using small fruit, then add one or two extra.

INGREDIENTS

Serves 4
675g/1½lb potatoes
2 leeks, trimmed and sliced
3 large tomatoes, sliced
a few fresh rosemary sprigs, crushed
1 garlic clove, crushed
300ml/½ pint/1¼ cups hot vegetable stock
15ml/1 tbsp olive oil
salt and ground black pepper

1 Scrub and thinly slice the potatoes. Then layer them with the leeks and tomatoes in a 1.2 litre/2 pint/5 cup microwave-proof dish that is suitable for grilling, scattering some rosemary between the layers and ending with a layer of potatoes.

2 Add the garlic to the stock, stir in salt and pepper to taste and pour over the vegetables. Brush the top layer of potatoes with the olive oil.

3 Cover and microwave on HIGH for 15–18 minutes or until the potatoes are tender. Leave to stand for 5 minutes, then remove the cover. Brown under a preheated hot grill, if you like, and serve hot.

COMBINATION MICROWAVE

This recipe is suitable for cooking in a combination microwave. Follow the oven manufacturer's timing guide for good results.

Summer Vegetable Braise

Tender, young vegetables are ideal for speedy cooking methods and the microwave ensures they stay tender-crisp.

INGREDIENTS

Serves 4

175g/6oz/2½ cups baby carrots

175g/6oz/2 cups sugar snap peas or
   mangetouts

115g/4oz/1¼ cups baby corn

90ml/6 tbsp vegetable stock

10ml/2 tsp lime juice

salt and black pepper

chopped fresh parsley and chopped fresh
   chives, to garnish

1 Place the carrots, peas and baby corn in a large microwaveproof bowl with the vegetable stock and lime juice.

2 Cover and microwave on HIGH for 7–9 minutes, stirring halfway through cooking, until the vegetables are just tender.

COOK'S TIP

You can make this dish in the winter too, but cut larger, tougher vegetables into chunks and cook them for slightly longer.

3 Season the vegetables to taste with salt and pepper, then stir in the chopped fresh parsley and snipped chives. Microwave on HIGH for 1 minute, until the vegetables are well flavoured with the herbs. Then serve at once.

VARIATION

To make a more substantial dish, tip the cooked vegetables into a gratin dish and top with a mixture of grated cheese and breadcrumbs, then grill until crisp, golden and bubbling.

Mixed Pepper Pipérade

Serves 4

30ml/2 tbsp olive oil

1 onion, chopped

1 red pepper

1 green pepper

4 tomatoes, peeled and chopped

1 garlic clove, crushed

4 size 2 eggs, beaten with
    15ml/1 tbsp water

ground black pepper

4 large, thick slices of wholemeal toast,
    to serve

1 Place the oil in a large microwaveproof bowl with the onion.

2 Remove the seeds from the red and green peppers and slice them thinly. Stir the pepper slices into the onion, cover and microwave on HIGH for 5–6 minutes, stirring halfway through the cooking time.

3 Add the tomatoes and garlic, season with black pepper, cover again and microwave on HIGH for a further 6 minutes, stirring halfway through cooking, until pulpy.

4 Pour the egg mixture over the vegetables, microwave on HIGH for 4–4½ minutes, stirring twice during cooking, until the pipérade has thickened to the consistency of lightly scrambled eggs. Serve immediately, with warm wholemeal toast.

COOK'S TIP

Choose eggs that have been date-stamped for freshness. To rediscover the rich flavour of eggs, look for free-range varieties from an organic farm. Even if you do not use them in all your cooking, they are worth it for flavour in dishes of this type. Do not stir the pipérade too much or the eggs may become rubbery.

Middle-Eastern Vegetable Stew

*A spiced dish of mixed vegetables
makes a delicious and filling
vegetarian main course. Children
may prefer less chilli.*

INGREDIENTS

Serves 4-6

45ml/3 tbsp vegetable stock
1 green pepper, seeded and sliced
2 courgettes, sliced
2 carrots, sliced
2 celery sticks, sliced
2 potatoes, diced
400g/14oz can chopped tomatoes
5ml/1 tsp chilli powder
30ml/2 tbsp chopped fresh mint
15ml/1 tbsp ground cumin
400g/14oz can chick-peas, drained
salt and ground black pepper
mint sprigs, to garnish

2 Add the potatoes, tomatoes,
chilli powder, fresh mint,
ground cumin and chick-peas to
the vegetable dish and stir well.
Cover the dish and microwave
on HIGH for 15–20 minutes,
remembering to stir twice during
the cooking time.

3 Leave to stand, covered,
for 5 minutes, until all the
vegetables are tender. Season to
taste with salt and pepper and serve
hot, garnished with mint leaves.

VARIATION

Other vegetables can be
substituted for those in the
recipe, just use whatever you have
to hand – try swede, sweet potato
or parsnips.

1 Place the vegetable stock
in a large microwaveproof
casserole with the sliced pepper,
courgettes, carrots and celery.
Cover and microwave on HIGH
for 2 minutes.

COOK'S TIP

Chick-peas are traditional in this
type of Middle-Eastern dish, but
if you prefer, red kidney or
haricot beans can be used
instead.

Courgette and Potato Tortilla

INGREDIENTS

Serves 4

30ml/2 tbsp chopped fresh tarragon

4 size 2 eggs, beaten

30ml/2 tbsp olive oil

1 onion, finely chopped

450g/1lb potatoes, diced

1 garlic clove, crushed

2 courgettes, thinly sliced

salt and ground black pepper

1 Stir the tarragon into the eggs and season with salt and pepper. Set aside.

2 Place the oil and onion in a large, shallow microwaveproof dish which is suitable for grilling. Cover and microwave on HIGH for 3 minutes. Add the diced potatoes, garlic and sliced courgettes, cover again and microwave on HIGH for 10 minutes, stirring twice during cooking.

3 Pour the eggs over the vegetables, cover and microwave on HIGH for about 3–5 minutes, rotating the dish twice, until the eggs are beginning to set slightly. Meanwhile, preheat the grill.

4 Place the tortilla under the grill and cook for a few minutes until the top has set and is tinged golden. Cut into wedges and serve from the dish.

COMBINATION MICROWAVE

This recipe is suitable for cooking in a combination microwave. Follow the oven manufacturer's timing guide for good results.

Chicken and Pesto Jackets

Although it is usually served with pasta, pesto also gives a wonderful lift to rice, bread and potato dishes – all good starchy carbohydrates. Here, it is combined with chicken and yogurt to make a low-fat topping for jacket potatoes.

INGREDIENTS

Serves 4

4 baking potatoes, 175g/6oz each, pricked

15ml/1 tbsp pesto

250ml/8fl oz/1 cup low-fat natural yogurt

2 chicken breasts, cooked

1 Arrange the potatoes in a ring pattern on double thick absorbent kitchen paper. Microwave on HIGH for 12–15 minutes, turning over once halfway during cooking. Leave to stand for 3–4 minutes.

2 Stir the pesto into the yogurt until well combined.

> ### COOK'S TIP
>
> The chicken breasts can be cooked in the microwave, if you like. Microwave on HIGH for 3–4 minutes, turning over halfway through cooking.

3 Skin and slice the chicken. Cut the potatoes open and fill with the chicken slices. Top with the pesto-flavoured yogurt and garnish with basil.

Cauliflower with Three Cheeses

Serves 4

4 baby cauliflowers
120ml/4fl oz/½ cup water
250ml/8fl oz/1 cup single cream
75g/3oz dolcelatte cheese, diced
75g/3oz mozzarella cheese, diced
45ml/3 tbsp freshly grated
    Parmesan cheese
freshly grated nutmeg
ground black pepper
toasted breadcrumbs, to garnish

1 Place the cauliflowers
floret-side down in a
microwaveproof dish. Add the
water, cover and microwave on
HIGH for 9–11 minutes, rearranging once. Leave to stand for
3 minutes.

2 Place the cream in a small
microwaveproof bowl with the
cheeses. Microwave on HIGH for
2–3 minutes, stirring three times,
until the cheeses have melted.
Season with nutmeg and freshly
ground pepper.

3 Drain the cauliflowers
thoroughly and place one on
each of four warmed plates.

4 Spoon a little of the cheese
sauce over each cauliflower
and sprinkle with toasted breadcrumbs. Serve at once.

Winter Vegetable Hot-pot

*Use whatever vegetables you have to
hand in this richly flavoured and
substantial one-pot meal.*

Serves 4

2 onions, sliced
4 carrots, sliced
1 small swede, sliced
2 parsnips, sliced
3 small turnips, sliced
½ celeriac, cut into matchstick strips
2 leeks, thinly sliced
1 garlic clove, chopped
1 bay leaf, crumbled
30ml/2 tbsp chopped fresh mixed herbs,
    such as parsley and thyme
300ml/½ pint/1¼ cups vegetable stock
15ml/1 tbsp plain flour
675g/1½lb red-skinned potatoes,
    scrubbed and thinly sliced
50g/2oz/4 tbsp butter
salt and ground black pepper

1 Arrange all the vegetables,
except the potatoes, in layers
in a large microwaveproof dish
with a tight-fitting lid.

2 Season the vegetable layers
lightly with salt and pepper,
and sprinkle them with chopped
garlic, crumbled bay leaf and
chopped herbs.

3 Blend the stock into the flour
and pour over the vegetables.
Arrange the potatoes in overlapping layers on top. Dot with butter
and cover tightly.

4 Microwave on HIGH for
10 minutes. Reduce the
power setting to MEDIUM and
microwave for a further 25–30
minutes or until the vegetables are
tender. Remove the lid and cook
under a preheated hot grill until
golden and crisp. Serve hot.

COMBINATION MICROWAVE

This recipe is suitable for cooking
in a combination microwave.
Follow the oven manufacturer's
timing guide for good results.

Broccoli and Chestnut Terrine

Served hot or cold, this versatile terrine is equally suitable for a dinner party as for a picnic.

INGREDIENTS

Serves 4–6

450g/1lb broccoli, cut into small florets
60ml/4 tbsp water
225g/8oz cooked chestnuts,
   roughly chopped
50g/2oz/1 cup fresh wholemeal
   breadcrumbs
60ml/4 tbsp low-fat natural yogurt
30ml/2 tbsp freshly grated
   Parmesan cheese
salt and ground black pepper
grated nutmeg
2 eggs, beaten

1 Line a 900g/2lb glass loaf dish with clear film.

2 Place the broccoli in a microwaveproof bowl with the water. Cover and microwave on HIGH for 6 minutes, stirring once. Drain well. Reserve a quarter of the smallest florets and chop the rest finely.

3 Mix together the chestnuts, breadcrumbs, yogurt and Parmesan, adding seasoning and grated nutmeg to taste.

4 Fold in the chopped broccoli, reserved small florets and the beaten eggs.

5 Spoon the broccoli mixture into the prepared dish. Cover and microwave on HIGH for 3 minutes. Reduce the power setting to MEDIUM and microwave for a further 5–8 minutes, or until just firm and set. Leave to stand for 5 minutes.

6 Turn out the terrine on to a flat plate or tray, and serve cut into thick slices. New potatoes and salad are suitable accompaniments.

Mixed Mushroom Ragout

*These mushrooms are delicious
served hot or cold and can be made
up to two days in advance.*

INGREDIENTS

Serves 4

1 small onion, finely chopped
1 garlic clove, crushed
5ml/1 tsp coriander seeds, crushed
30ml/2 tbsp red wine vinegar
15ml/1 tbsp soy sauce
15ml/1 tbsp dry sherry
10ml/2 tsp tomato purée
10ml/2 tsp soft light brown sugar
75ml/5 tbsp hot vegetable stock
115g/4oz baby button mushrooms
115g/4oz chestnut mushrooms, quartered
115g/4oz oyster mushrooms, sliced
salt and ground black pepper
sprig of fresh coriander, to garnish

1 Mix the onion, garlic, coriander seeds, red wine vinegar, soy sauce, sherry, tomato purée, sugar and stock in a large microwaveproof bowl. Cover and microwave on HIGH for 3 minutes, stirring once. Uncover and microwave on HIGH for a further 2–3 minutes, or until the liquid has reduced by half.

2 Add the mushrooms, mixing well. Cover and microwave on HIGH for 3–4 minutes, stirring once, until tender.

3 Remove the mushrooms with a slotted spoon and transfer them to a warmed serving dish.

4 Microwave the juices on HIGH for about 3–5 minutes, or until reduced to about 75ml/5 tbsp. Season to taste with salt and ground black pepper.

COOK'S TIP

If coriander is a favourite spice of yours, then it is worth buying a pepper mill and filling it with coriander seeds. This way, you can grind a little coriander into all sorts of savoury dishes to add a hint of exotic seasoning.

5 Allow the sauce to cool for 2–3 minutes, then pour over the mushrooms. Serve piping hot or well chilled, garnished with a sprig of fresh coriander.

Mushroom and Okra Curry

This simple but delicious curry, with its fresh gingery mango relish, is best served with plain basmati rice.

INGREDIENTS

Serves 4

4 garlic cloves, roughly chopped

2.5cm/1in piece fresh ginger root, roughly chopped

1–2 fresh red chillies, seeded and chopped

175ml/6fl oz/¾ cup water

15ml/1 tbsp sunflower oil

5ml/1 tsp coriander seeds

5ml/1 tsp cumin seeds

5ml/1 tsp ground cumin

2 green cardamom pods, seeds removed and ground

pinch of ground turmeric

400g/14oz can chopped tomatoes

450g/1lb mushrooms, quartered if large

225g/8oz okra, trimmed and cut into 1cm/½in slices

30ml/2 tbsp chopped fresh coriander

basmati rice, to serve

For the mango relish

1 large ripe mango, about 500g/1¼lb in weight

1 small garlic clove, crushed

1 onion, finely chopped

10ml/2 tsp grated fresh root ginger

1 fresh red chilli, seeded and finely chopped

pinch each of salt and sugar

1 For the mango relish, peel the mango and cut the flesh from the stone.

2 Mash the mango flesh with a fork or lightly process it in a blender or food processor, and mix in the rest of the relish ingredients. Set the relish aside.

3 Process the garlic, ginger, chillies and 45ml/3 tbsp of the water to a smooth paste in a blender or food processor.

4 Place the sunflower oil in a large microwaveproof bowl. Add the coriander and cumin seeds, and microwave on HIGH for 30 seconds. Add the ground cumin, ground cardamom and turmeric, then microwave on HIGH for a further 30 seconds.

5 Stir in the spice paste, tomatoes, remaining water, mushrooms and okra. Cover and microwave on HIGH for 10–12 minutes, stirring halfway through cooking.

6 Leave to stand, covered, for 5 minutes, until the okra is tender. Stir in the fresh coriander and serve with rice and the mango relish.

COOK'S TIP

When buying okra, look for firm, bright green vegetables that are unblemished. Small to medium okra are best; large pods can be quite tough and coarse, therefore not ideal for microwave cooking. Avoid any that look browned or bruised in places, especially around the stalk end. As with most pre-packed produce, reject sealed packets that look damp inside.

New Potato and Chive Salad

The secret of a good potato salad is to mix the potatoes with the dressing while they are still hot so that they absorb it.

INGREDIENTS

Serves 4-6

675g/1½lb new potatoes (unpeeled)

60ml/4 tbsp water

4 spring onions

45ml/3 tbsp olive oil

15ml/1 tbsp white wine vinegar

3.75ml/¾ tsp Dijon mustard

175ml/6fl oz/¾ cup mayonnaise

45ml/3 tbsp snipped fresh chives

salt and ground black pepper

1 Place the potatoes and water in a microwaveproof dish. Cover and microwave on HIGH for 9–12 minutes, stirring halfway through cooking. Leave to stand, covered, for 3 minutes. Meanwhile, finely chop the white parts of the spring onions along with a little of the green parts.

2 Whisk together the oil, vinegar and mustard. Drain the potatoes well, then immediately toss them lightly with the dressing, seasoning and spring onions and leave to cool.

3 Stir the mayonnaise and chives into the potatoes and chill well until ready to serve. Potato salad is delicious with cooked sausages, chicken wings or cold meats.

COOK'S TIP
~

Look out for the small, waxy potatoes, sold especially for salads and cold dishes – they are particularly good in this recipe.

Salade Niçoise

INGREDIENTS

Serves 4

90ml/6 tbsp olive oil

30ml/2 tbsp tarragon vinegar

5ml/1 tsp tarragon or Dijon mustard

1 small garlic clove, crushed

12 small new or salad potatoes

115g/4oz/1 cup French beans

3–4 Little Gem lettuces, roughly chopped

200g/7oz can tuna in oil, drained

6 anchovy fillets, halved lengthways

12 black olives, stoned

4 tomatoes, chopped

4 spring onions, finely chopped

10ml/2 tsp capers

30ml/2 tbsp pine nuts

2 hard-boiled eggs, chopped

salt and ground black pepper

1 Mix the oil, vinegar, mustard, garlic and seasoning in a large salad bowl.

2 Place the potatoes in a microwaveproof bowl with 30ml/2 tbsp water. Cover and microwave on HIGH for 6–8 minutes, stirring halfway through cooking. Leave to stand, covered, for 3 minutes, then drain thoroughly.

3 Place the beans in a microwaveproof bowl with 15ml/1 tbsp water. Cover and microwave on HIGH for 3 minutes, stirring once. Leave to stand, covered, for 2 minutes, then drain.

4 Mix the potatoes and beans with the lettuce, tuna, anchovies, olives, tomatoes, spring onions and capers.

5 Just before serving, place the pine nuts on a small microwaveproof plate and microwave on HIGH for 3–4 minutes, stirring once every minute, until brown.

6 Sprinkle the pine nuts over the salad while still hot, add the eggs and toss all the ingredients together well. Serve with chunks of hot crusty bread.

Watercress and Potato Salad

New potatoes are equally good hot or cold, and this colourful, nutritious salad is an ideal way of making the most of them.

INGREDIENTS

Serves 4

450g/1lb small new potatoes (unpeeled)

45ml/3 tbsp water

1 bunch watercress

200g/7oz/1½ cups cherry
   tomatoes, halved

30ml/2 tbsp pumpkin seeds

45ml/3 tbsp low-fat fromage frais

15ml/1 tbsp cider vinegar

5ml/1 tsp brown sugar

salt

paprika

3 Place the fromage frais, vinegar, sugar, salt and paprika to taste in a screw-top jar and shake well to mix. Pour over the salad just before serving.

VARIATION

To make Spinach and Potato Salad, substitute about 225g/8oz fresh baby spinach leaves for the watercress.

COOK'S TIP

If you are preparing this salad in advance, mix the dressing in the jar and set aside. Mix the dressing again and toss it into the salad just before serving.

---

1 Place the potatoes and water in a microwaveproof bowl. Cover and microwave on HIGH for 7–10 minutes, stirring halfway through cooking. Leave to stand, covered, for 3 minutes, then drain and leave to cool.

2 Toss the potatoes, watercress, tomatoes and pumpkin seeds together.

Fruity Brown Rice Salad

An Oriental-style dressing gives this colourful rice salad extra piquancy. Whole grains, like brown rice, are unrefined, so they retain their natural fibre, vitamins and minerals.

INGREDIENTS

Serves 4-6

4 spring onions
115g/4oz/²⁄₃ cup long grain brown rice
300ml/¹⁄₂ pint/1¹⁄₄ cups boiling water
1 small red pepper, seeded and diced
200g/7oz can sweetcorn, drained
45ml/3 tbsp sultanas
225g/8oz can pineapple pieces in
    fruit juice
15ml/1 tbsp light soy sauce
15ml/1 tbsp sunflower oil
15ml/1 tbsp hazelnut oil
1 garlic clove, crushed
5ml/1 tsp finely chopped fresh root ginger
salt and ground black pepper

1 Slice the spring onions at a slant and set them aside ready for garnishing the salad.

2 Place the rice in a large microwaveproof bowl with the boiling water and a little salt. Cover loosely and microwave on HIGH for 3 minutes. Reduce the power setting to MEDIUM and microwave for a further 25 minutes, stirring twice during cooking. Leave to stand, covered, for 5 minutes.

3 Tip the rice into a serving bowl and add the red pepper, sweetcorn and sultanas. Drain the canned pineapple pieces, reserving the juice, then toss them lightly into the rice mixture. Do not overmix or you will break the grains of rice.

4 Pour the reserved pineapple juice into a clean screw-top jar. Add the soy sauce, sunflower and hazelnut oils, garlic and ginger. Add salt and pepper to taste, then shake well to combine.

5 Pour the dressing over the salad and toss well. Scatter the spring onions over the top.

Mediterranean Salad with Basil

A type of Salade Niçoise with pasta, conjuring up all the sunny flavours of the Mediterranean.

INGREDIENTS

Serves 4

450g/1lb chunky fresh pasta shapes

a little oil

1.5 litres/2½ pints/6¼ cups plus 30ml/
2 tbsp boiling water

175g/6oz fine green beans

2 large ripe tomatoes

50g/2oz fresh basil leaves

200g/7oz can tuna fish in oil, drained and
roughly flaked

2 hard-boiled eggs, shelled and sliced or
quartered

50g/2oz can anchovy fillets, drained

15ml/1 tbsp capers

about 4 black olives

For the dressing

90ml/6 tbsp extra virgin olive oil

30ml/2 tbsp white wine vinegar or lemon
juice

2 garlic cloves, crushed

2.5ml/½ tsp Dijon mustard

30ml/2 tbsp chopped fresh basil

salt and ground black pepper

1 Whisk all the ingredients for the dressing together and leave to infuse while you make the salad.

2 Place the fresh pasta in a large microwaveproof bowl with a little oil and the main quantity of boiling water. Cover and microwave on HIGH for 2–3 minutes, stirring halfway through cooking. Drain well and cool.

3 Place the beans in a microwaveproof bowl with the 30ml/2 tbsp boiling water. Cover and microwave on HIGH for 3–4 minutes. Drain and refresh in cold water.

4 Slice or quarter the tomatoes and arrange on the bottom of a bowl. Moisten with a little dressing and cover with a quarter of the basil leaves. Then cover with the beans. Moisten with a little more dressing and cover with a third of the remaining basil.

5 Toss the pasta in a little more dressing and spoon it over the salad with half the remaining basil and the tuna.

6 Arrange the eggs on top, then, finally, scatter over the anchovy fillets, capers and black olives. Pour over the remaining dressing and garnish with the remaining basil. Serve immediately. Don't be tempted to chill this salad – all the flavours will be dulled.

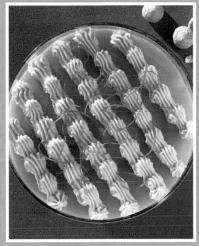

DESSERTS

~

Chocolate Amaretti Peaches

Quick and easy to prepare, this delicious dessert can also be made with fresh nectarines or apricots.

INGREDIENTS

Serves 4

115g/4oz amaretti biscuits, crushed
50g/2oz plain chocolate, chopped
grated rind of ½ orange
15ml/1 tbsp clear honey
1.5ml/¼ tsp ground cinnamon
1 egg white, lightly whisked
4 firm ripe peaches
75ml/5 tbsp white wine
15ml/1 tbsp caster sugar
whipped cream, to serve

1 Mix together the amaretti biscuits, chocolate, orange rind, honey and cinnamon in a bowl. Stir in the egg white to bind the mixture.

2 Halve and stone the peaches and fill the cavities with the chocolate mixture, mounding it up slightly.

3 Arrange the stuffed peaches in a lightly buttered, shallow microwaveproof dish which will just hold them. Pour the wine into a cup and stir in the sugar.

4 Pour the sweetened wine around the peaches. Cover loosely and microwave on HIGH for 2–3 minutes, until the peaches are tender. Serve at once with a little of the cooking juices spooned over and the whipped cream.

Plum and Walnut Crumble

Walnuts add a lovely crunch to the fruit layer in this crumble – almonds would be equally good.

Serves 4–6

1kg/2¼lb plums, halved and stoned
75g/3oz/¾ cup walnut pieces, toasted
175g/6oz/scant 1 cup demerara sugar
75g/3oz/6 tbsp butter or hard
   margarine, diced
175g/6oz/1½ cups plain flour

1 Butter a 1.2 litre/2 pint/5 cup microwaveproof dish that is suitable for grilling. Put the plums in the dish, then stir in the nuts and half the demerara sugar.

2 Rub the butter or margarine into the flour until the mixture resembles coarse crumbs. Stir in the remaining sugar and continue to rub in the fat until fine crumbs are formed.

3 Cover the fruit with the crumb mixture and press it down lightly. Microwave the crumble on HIGH for 14–16 minutes, rotating the dish three times during cooking. Brown the top under a preheated hot grill until golden and crisp, if liked, before serving.

VARIATION

To make Oat and Cinnamon Crumble, substitute rolled oats for half the flour in the crumble mixture and add 2.5–5ml/½–1 tsp ground cinnamon.

COMBINATION MICROWAVE

This recipe is suitable for cooking in a combination microwave. Follow your oven manufacturer's timing guide for good results.

Rhubarb and Strawberry Crisp

INGREDIENTS

Serves 4

225g/8oz strawberries, hulled and cut in
　half if large
450g/1lb rhubarb, cut into pieces
90g/3½oz/½ cup caster sugar
15ml/1 tbsp cornflour
85ml/3fl oz/⅓ cup fresh orange juice
115g/4oz/1 cup plain flour
75g/3oz/1 cup rolled oats
90g/3½oz/½ cup soft light brown sugar
2.5ml/½ tsp ground cinnamon
40g/1½oz/½ cup ground almonds
150g/5oz/10 tbsp butter, chilled
1 egg, lightly beaten

1 Mix the strawberries with
the rhubarb and sugar in a
1.75 litre/3 pint/7½ cup microwaveproof dish that is suitable
for grilling.

2 Blend the cornflour with the
orange juice in a small bowl,
then pour this mixture over the
fruit and stir gently to coat the
pieces.

3 Mix the flour, oats, brown
sugar, cinnamon and almonds
in a large bowl. Rub in the butter
using your fingertips until the
mixture resembles coarse breadcrumbs, then stir in the beaten egg.

4 Spoon the oat mixture evenly
over the fruit and press down
gently. Microwave on HIGH for
12–14 minutes, rotating the dish
twice during cooking. Brown
under a preheated hot grill until
golden and crisp, if liked.

COMBINATION MICROWAVE

This recipe is suitable for cooking
in a combination microwave.
Follow your oven manufacturer's
timing guide for good results.

Baked Apples with Apricots

INGREDIENTS

Serves 6

75g/3oz/¹/₂ cup ready-to-eat dried
   apricots, chopped
50g/2oz/¹/₂ cup walnuts, chopped
5ml/1 tsp grated lemon rind
2.5ml/¹/₂ tsp ground cinnamon
80g/3¹/₂oz/¹/₂ cup soft light brown sugar
15g/1oz/2 tbsp butter, at
   room temperature
6 large eating apples
15ml/1 tbsp melted butter
120ml/4fl oz/¹/₂ cup water or fruit juice

1 Place the apricots, walnuts, lemon rind and cinnamon in a bowl. Add the sugar and butter and stir until thoroughly mixed.

2 Core the apples, without cutting all the way through to the base. Peel the top of each apple and slightly widen the top of each opening to make plenty of room for the filling.

3 Spoon the filling into the apples, packing it down lightly into their middles.

4 Place the stuffed apples in a microwaveproof dish large enough to hold them neatly side by side.

5 Brush the apples with the melted butter and pour the water or fruit juice around them. Microwave on HIGH for 9–10 minutes, rearranging halfway through cooking, until the apples are tender. Serve hot.

Creole Bread and Butter Pudding

INGREDIENTS

Serves 4–6

4 ready-to-eat dried apricots, chopped
15ml/1 tbsp raisins
30ml/2 tbsp sultanas
15ml/1 tbsp chopped mixed peel
1 French loaf (about 200g/7oz),
    thinly sliced
50g/2oz/4 tbsp butter, melted
450ml/³⁄₄ pint/1⁷⁄₈ cups milk
150ml/¹⁄₄ pint/²⁄₃ cup double cream
115g/4oz/¹⁄₂ cup caster sugar
3 eggs
2.5ml/¹⁄₂ tsp vanilla essence
30ml/2 tbsp whisky

For the cream
150ml/¹⁄₄ pint/²⁄₃ cup double cream
30ml/2 tbsp Greek-style yogurt
15–30ml/1–2 tbsp whisky
15ml/1 tbsp caster sugar

1 Lightly butter a deep
1.5–1.75 litre/2¹⁄₂–3pint/
6¹⁄₂–7¹⁄₂ cup microwaveproof dish
that is suitable for grilling. Mix the
dried fruits and mixed peel, and
sprinkle a little over the base of the
dish. Brush both sides of the bread
slices with melted butter.

2 Fill the dish with alternate
layers of bread and dried fruit,
finishing with a layer of bread.

3 Pour the milk and cream into
a microwaveproof jug and
microwave on HIGH for 3–4
minutes, or until just boiling.
Meanwhile, whisk the sugar, eggs
and vanilla essence together.

4 Whisk the hot milk and cream
into the eggs and then strain
the mixture over the bread and
fruit. Sprinkle the whisky over the
top. Press the bread into the milk
and egg mixture, cover and leave to
stand for 20 minutes.

5 Microwave on MEDIUM
for 10–15 minutes, or until
the mixture is almost set in the
middle, rotating the dish four
times during cooking. Brown
under a preheated hot grill,
if liked.

6 Just before serving, mix the
cream, yogurt, whisky and
sugar into a small microwaveproof
bowl and microwave on HIGH for
1–2 minutes, stirring once. Serve
with the hot pudding.

Castle Puddings with Custard

INGREDIENTS

Serves 4–8

about 45ml/3 tbsp blackcurrant,
    strawberry or raspberry jam
115g/4oz/¹⁄₂ cup butter
115g/4oz/generous ¹⁄₂ cup caster sugar
2 eggs, beaten
few drops of vanilla essence
130g/3¹⁄₂oz/generous cup self-raising flour

For the custard
450ml/³⁄₄ pint/scant 2 cups milk
4 eggs
25–30ml/1¹⁄₂–2 tbsp sugar
few drops of vanilla essence

1 Butter eight microwaveproof individual pudding bowls or large teacups and put about 10ml/2 tsp of the jam in the base.

2 Cream the butter and sugar together in a bowl until light and fluffy, then gradually beat in the eggs, beating well after each addition and adding the vanilla essence towards the end. Fold in the flour, then divide the mixture between the bowls or cups.

3 Microwave on HIGH for 3–4 minutes, or until just set. Allow to stand for 3 minutes, then turn each out on to a warmed serving plate. Keep warm.

4 To make the custard, place the milk in a microwaveproof jug and microwave on HIGH for 4 minutes. Beat the eggs and sugar in a microwaveproof bowl, then gradually whisk in the hot milk.

5 Reduce the power setting to MEDIUM HIGH and microwave for 5–6 minutes, stirring every 1 minute until the custard is thick enough to coat the back of a spoon. Do not allow to boil. Stir in the vanilla essence. Serve with the warm puddings.

Gingerbread Upside-down Pudding

A proper pudding goes down well on a cold winter's day.

Serves 4–6

sunflower oil, for brushing

15ml/1 tbsp soft brown sugar

8 walnut halves

4 medium peaches, halved and stoned, or canned peach halves

For the base

130g/4½oz/½ cup wholemeal flour

2.5ml/½ tsp bicarbonate of soda

7.5ml/1½ tsp ground ginger

5ml/1 tsp ground cinnamon

115g/4oz/½ cup molasses sugar

1 egg

120ml/4fl oz/½ cup skimmed milk

50ml/2fl oz/¼ cup sunflower oil

1 For the topping, brush the base and sides of a 23cm/9in round deep microwaveproof dish with oil. Line the base with grease-proof paper, oil the paper then sprinkle the base with sugar.

2 Place a walnut half in each peach half, then arrange the peaches cut-side down in the dish.

3 For the base, sift together the flour, bicarbonate of soda, ginger and cinnamon, then stir in the sugar. Beat together the egg, milk and oil, then mix into the dry ingredients until smooth.

4 Pour the mixture evenly over the peaches and microwave on MEDIUM for 6–8 minutes, or until the mixture has shrunk away from the sides of the dish, but the surface still looks wet. Leave to stand for 5 minutes. Turn out into a serving plate. Serve hot with yogurt or custard.

Sticky Toffee Pudding

INGREDIENTS

Serves 6

115g/4oz/1 cup walnuts, toasted
  and chopped
175g/6oz/³⁄₄ cup butter
175g/6oz/scant 1 cup soft brown sugar
60ml/4 tbsp single cream
30ml/2 tbsp lemon juice
2 eggs, beaten
115g/4oz/1 cup self-raising flour

1 Grease a 900ml/1½ pint microwaveproof pudding basin and add half the walnuts.

2 Mix 50g/2oz/4 tbsp of the butter with 50g/2oz/4 tbsp of the sugar, the cream and 15ml/1 tbsp of the lemon juice in a small microwaveproof bowl. Microwave on HIGH for 1½–2 minutes, stirring once, until smooth. Pour half into the pudding basin, then swirl to coat it a little way up the sides.

3 Beat the remaining butter and sugar until light. Gradually beat in the eggs. Fold in the flour, remaining nuts and lemon juice; spoon into the bowl.

4 Three-quarters cover the basin with clear film and microwave on LOW for 7–10 minutes, until the mixture is well-risen and shrunk away from the sides of the bowl, but still wet on the surface. Leave to stand for 5 minutes.

5 Just before serving, microwave the remaining sauce on HIGH for 1–1½ minutes to reheat. Unmould the pudding on to a warm plate and pour over the warm sauce.

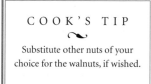

COOK'S TIP

Substitute other nuts of your choice for the walnuts, if wished.

Austrian Nut Pudding

This is a perfect pudding for the microwave.

INGREDIENTS

Serves 4

butter, for greasing

50g/2oz/4 tbsp caster sugar, plus a little
　　extra for sprinkling

115g/4oz/1 cup hazelnuts, chopped

50g/2oz/4 tbsp butter, softened

2 eggs, separated

25g/1oz/⅓ cup very fine fresh white
　　breadcrumbs

175g/6oz/1¼ cups fresh raspberries

icing sugar, to taste

cream, to serve

1 Lightly grease a 900ml/
1½ pint/3¾ cup microwave-
proof pudding basin and sprinkle
it evenly with a little caster sugar.

2 Spread the hazelnuts on a
microwaveproof plate and
microwave on HIGH for 5–6
minutes, until toasted and golden.
Leave to cool.

3 Meanwhile, place the butter
and sugar in a bowl and beat
until pale and creamy. Beat in the
egg yolks.

4 Place the cooled nuts in a food
processor and process until
finely ground.

5 Mix 15ml/1 tbsp water into
the breadcrumbs and beat
into the creamed mixture with the
hazelnuts.

6 Whisk the egg whites in a
clean bowl until stiff. Beat
about 30ml/2 tbsp into the
creamed mixture to loosen it
slightly, then carefully fold in
the remaining egg whites with a
metal spoon.

7 Spoon the mixture into
the prepared basin. Cover
and microwave on HIGH for
4–6 minutes.

8 Meanwhile, press the
raspberries through a sieve
into a bowl and add icing sugar to
sweeten the purée to taste. Turn
out the cooked pudding and serve
it hot, with the raspberry sauce
and cream.

Cinnamon and Coconut Rice

INGREDIENTS

Serves 4-6

40g/1½oz/¼ cup raisins
475ml/16fl oz/2 cups boiling water
225g/8oz/1 cup short grain rice
1 cinnamon stick
25g/1oz/2 tbsp caster sugar
475ml/16fl oz/2 cups milk
250ml/8fl oz/1 cup canned sweetened
    coconut milk
2.5ml/½ tsp vanilla essence
15ml/1 tbsp butter
25g/1oz/⅓ cup desiccated coconut
ground cinnamon, for sprinkling
single or double cream, to serve (optional)

3 Meanwhile, blend the milk, coconut milk and vanilla essence together in a bowl. Drain the raisins.

4 Remove the cinnamon stick from the rice. Stir in the raisins and the milk mixture. Cover and microwave on MEDIUM for a further 15–20 minutes, until the mixture is just thick. Do not overcook the rice.

5 Preheat the grill. Transfer the rice to a flameproof serving dish. Dot with the butter and sprinkle with coconut. Grill about 13cm/5in from the heat for about 3–5 minutes, until just browned. Sprinkle with cinnamon. Serve warm or cold, with cream if liked.

> ### COOK'S TIP
> ∼
> Select large plump raisins for
> this creamy dessert.

1 Soak the raisins in a small bowl in enough water to cover.

2 Place the boiling water in a microwaveproof bowl. Stir in the rice, cinnamon stick and sugar. Cover and microwave on HIGH for 3 minutes. Reduce the power setting to MEDIUM and microwave for a further 12 minutes, or until the liquid has been absorbed.

Hot Bananas with Rum and Raisins

Choose almost-ripe bananas with evenly coloured skins, either all yellow or just green at the tips. Black patches indicate that the fruit is over-ripe.

INGREDIENTS

Serves 4

40g/1½oz/¼ cup seedless raisins

75ml/5 tbsp dark rum

50g/2oz/4 tbsp unsalted butter

60ml/4 tbsp soft light brown sugar

4 ripe bananas, peeled and
    halved lengthways

1.5ml/¼ tsp grated nutmeg

1.5ml/¼ tsp ground cinnamon

30ml/2 tbsp slivered almonds, toasted

chilled cream or vanilla ice cream,
    to serve (optional)

1 Put the raisins in a bowl with the rum. Leave them to soak for about 30 minutes to plump up.

2 Place the butter in a shallow microwaveproof dish and microwave on HIGH for 1 minute or until the butter melts.

3 Stir in the sugar and microwave on HIGH for 1 minute. Add the bananas to the dish and coat them with the sugar mixture, then microwave on HIGH for 4 minutes, turning the fruit over once.

4 Sprinkle the spices over the bananas. Mix the rum and raisins in a small cup.

5 Microwave on HIGH for 30–45 seconds, and then pour them over the bananas. Carefully set alight using a long taper and stir gently to mix.

6 Scatter the slivered almonds over and serve immediately with chilled cream or vanilla ice cream, if you like.

Spiced Pears in Cider

INGREDIENTS

Serves 4

250ml/8fl oz/1 cup dry cider

thinly pared strip of lemon rind

1 cinnamon stick

30ml/2 tbsp soft brown sugar

4 firm pears

5ml/1 tsp arrowroot

15ml/1 tbsp water

ground cinnamon, to sprinkle

low-fat fromage frais, to serve

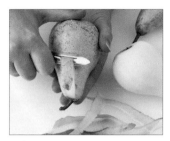

1 Place the cider, lemon rind, cinnamon stick and sugar in a microwaveproof bowl. Microwave on HIGH for 3–5 minutes until boiling, stirring frequently to dissolve the sugar. Meanwhile, peel the pears thinly, leaving them whole with the stems on.

2 Add the pears to the cider syrup. Spoon the syrup over the pears. Three-quarters cover the dish with clear film or with a lid. Microwave on HIGH for 5–6 minutes until the pears are just tender, turning and repositioning them in the bowl two or three times.

3 Carefully transfer the pears to another bowl using a slotted spoon. Microwave the cider syrup, uncovered, on HIGH for 15–17 minutes until it is reduced by half.

4 Mix the arrowroot with the water in a small bowl until smooth, then stir it into the syrup. Microwave on HIGH for 1 minute, stirring twice, until clear and thickened.

5 Pour the sauce over the pears and sprinkle with ground cinnamon. Leave to cool slightly, then serve warm with low-fat fromage frais.

VARIATIONS

Other fruits can be poached in this spicy liquid; try apples, peaches or nectarines. Cook the fruit whole or cut in half or quarters. The apples are best peeled before poaching, but you can cook the peaches and nectarines with their skins on.

COOK'S TIP

Any variety of pear can be used, but it is best to choose firm pears, or they will break up easily – Conference are a good choice.

Honey Fruit Yogurt Ice

INGREDIENTS

Serves 4–6

2 dessert apples, peeled, cored and finely
    chopped
4 ripe bananas, roughly chopped
15ml/1 tbsp lemon juice
30ml/2 tbsp clear honey
250g/9oz/1 cup Greek-style yogurt
2.5ml/½ tsp ground cinnamon
crisp biscuits, flaked hazelnuts and
    banana slices, to serve

1 Place the apples in a small
microwaveproof bowl,
cover and microwave on HIGH
for 2 minutes, stirring once.
Allow to cool.

2 Place the bananas in a food
processor or blender with the
lemon juice, honey, yogurt and
cinnamon. Process until smooth
and creamy. Add the cooked apples
and process briefly to mix.

3 Pour the mixture into a freezer
container and freeze until
almost solid. Spoon back into the
food processor and process again
until smooth.

4 Return to the freezer until
firm. Allow to soften at room
temperature for 15 minutes, then
serve in scoops, with crisp biscuits,
flaked hazelnuts and banana slices.

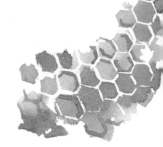

Autumn Pudding

INGREDIENTS

Serves 6

10 slices bread, at least one day old
1 Bramley cooking apple, peeled, cored
    and sliced
225g/8oz ripe red plums, halved
    and stoned
225g/8oz blackberries
60ml/4 tbsp water
75g/3oz/6 tbsp caster sugar

1 Remove the crusts from the
bread and stamp out a 7.5cm/
3in round from one slice. Cut the
remaining bread in half.

2 Place the bread round in the
base of a 1.2 litre/2 pint/5 cup
pudding basin, then overlap the
fingers around the sides, saving
some for the top.

3 Mix the apple, plums, blackberries, water and caster sugar
in a microwaveproof bowl. Cover
and microwave on HIGH for
7–8 minutes or until the sugar
dissolves, the juices begin to flow
and the fruit softens. Stir twice
during cooking.

4 Reserve the juice and spoon
the fruit into the bread-lined
basin. Top with the reserved bread,
then spoon over the reserved
fruit juices.

5 Cover the basin with a saucer
and place weights on top.
Chill the pudding overnight.
Turn out on to a serving plate
and serve with low-fat yogurt or
fromage frais.

Ruby Plum Mousse

INGREDIENTS

Serves 6

450g/1lb ripe red plums

45ml/3 tbsp granulated sugar

75ml/5 tbsp water

60ml/4 tbsp ruby port

15ml/1 tbsp/1 sachet powdered gelatine

3 eggs, separated

115g/4oz/½ cup caster sugar

150ml/¼ pint/⅔ cup double cream

skinned and chopped pistachio nuts, to
   decorate

crisp biscuits, to serve (optional)

1 Place the plums and granulated sugar in a microwaveproof bowl. Add 30ml/2 tbsp water. Cover and microwave on HIGH for 4–5 minutes, stirring once. Leave to stand for 3 minutes.

2 Press the fruit through a sieve to remove the stones and skins. Leave to cool, then stir in the port.

3 Pour the remaining 45ml/ 3 tbsp water into a small bowl, sprinkle over the gelatine and leave to soften. Microwave on HIGH for ½–¾ minute until clear and dissolved. Stir into the plum purée.

4 Whisk the egg yolks and caster sugar until thick and mousselike. Fold in the plum purée. Whip the cream until it stands in soft peaks and fold it in gently.

5 Whisk the egg whites until they hold stiff peaks, then carefully fold them in using a metal spoon. Divide among six glasses and chill until set.

6 Decorate the mousses with chopped pistachio nuts and serve with crisp biscuits, if liked.

Warm Autumn Compôte

*A simple yet quite sophisticated
dessert using autumnal fruits.*

INGREDIENTS

Serves 4

75g/3oz/6 tbsp caster sugar

1 bottle red wine

1 vanilla pod, split

thinly pared strip of lemon rind

4 pears

2 purple figs, quartered

225g/8oz raspberries

lemon juice, to taste

1 Put the sugar and wine in a large microwaveproof bowl. Stir in the vanilla pod and lemon rind. Microwave on HIGH for 4–6 minutes, stirring three times.

2 Peel and halve the pears, then scoop out the cores, using a melon baller. Add the pears to the syrup and mix well. Cover loosely and microwave on HIGH for 5–6 minutes, turning over two or three times during cooking so that they colour evenly.

3 Add the figs and microwave on HIGH for a further 2 minutes, until the fruits are tender.

4 Transfer the poached pears and figs to a serving bowl using a slotted spoon, then sprinkle over the raspberries.

5 Microwave the poaching liquid, uncovered, on HIGH for 5–7 minutes to reduce slightly and concentrate the flavour. Add a little lemon juice to taste. Strain the syrup over the fruits and serve warm.

Tangerine Trifle

*An unusual variation on a tradi-
tional trifle – of course, you can add
a little alcohol if you wish.*

INGREDIENTS

Serves 4

5 trifle sponges, halved lengthways

30ml/2 tbsp apricot conserve

15-20 ratafia biscuits

142g/4¾oz packet tangerine jelly

300g/11oz can mandarin oranges,
    drained, juice reserved

600ml/1 pint/2½ cups prepared custard

whipped cream and shreds of orange rind,
    to decorate

caster sugar, for sprinkling

1 Spread the halved sponge
cakes with apricot conserve
and arrange them in the base of
a deep serving bowl or glass dish.
Sprinkle over the ratafia biscuits.

2 Break up the jelly into a
microwaveproof jug, add the
juice from the canned mandarins
and microwave on HIGH for
2 minutes, then stir to dissolve
the jelly.

3 Make up the jelly to
600ml/1 pint/2½ cups with
ice-cold water, stir well and leave
to cool for up to 30 minutes.
Scatter the mandarin oranges over
the cakes and ratafias.

4 Pour the jelly over the
mandarin oranges, cake and
ratafias and chill for 1 hour, or
until the jelly has set.

5 Pour the custard over the trifle
and chill again. When ready
to serve, pipe the whipped cream
over the custard. Place the orange
rind shreds in a sieve and rinse
under cold water, then sprinkle
them with caster sugar and use to
decorate the trifle.

Chocolate Fudge Sundaes

What better way is there to give everyone a weekend treat than to make those fabulous sundaes for Sunday tea?

INGREDIENTS

Serves 4

4 scoops each vanilla and coffee ice cream
2 small ripe bananas, sliced
whipped cream
toasted flaked almonds

For the sauce

50g/2oz/¼ cup soft light brown sugar
120ml/4fl oz/½ cup golden syrup
45ml/3 tbsp strong black coffee
5ml/1 tsp ground cinnamon
150g/5oz plain chocolate, chopped
85ml/3fl oz/⅓ cup whipping cream
45ml/3 tbsp coffee liqueur (optional)

1 To make the sauce, place the sugar, syrup, coffee and cinnamon in a large microwave-proof jug. Microwave on HIGH for 3–4 minutes, stirring once, until boiling and slightly thickened.

2 Add the chocolate and stir until it has melted. When smooth, stir in the cream and liqueur, if using. Leave the sauce to cool slightly.

3 Fill four serving glasses with a scoop each of vanilla and coffee ice cream.

4 Scatter the sliced bananas over the ice cream. Pour the warm fudge sauce over the bananas, then top each sundae with a generous swirl of whipped cream. Sprinkle with toasted almonds and serve at once before the ice cream melts.

VARIATION

Ring the changes by choosing other flavours of ice cream such as strawberry, toffee or chocolate. In the summer, substitute raspberries or strawberries for the bananas, and sprinkle chopped roasted hazelnuts on top in place of the flaked almonds.

Apricots with Orange Cream

Mascarpone is a very rich cream cheese made from thick Lombardy cream. It is delicious flavoured with orange as a topping for these chilled, poached apricots.

Serves 4

450g/1lb/2½ cups ready-to-eat dried
   apricots
thinly pared strip of lemon peel
1 cinnamon stick
45ml/3 tbsp caster sugar
150ml/¼ pint/⅔ cup sweet dessert wine
   (such as Muscat de Beaumes de Venise)
115g/4oz/½ cup mascarpone cream cheese
45ml/3 tbsp orange juice
pinch of ground cinnamon and fresh mint
   sprig, to decorate

1 Place the apricots, lemon peel, cinnamon stick and 15ml/ 1 tbsp of the sugar in a pan and cover with 450ml/¾ pint/1⅞ cups cold water. Cover loosely and microwave on HIGH for 10 minutes. Leave to stand for about 5 minutes, then microwave on MEDIUM for 5–8 minutes until the fruit is tender.

2 Stir in the dessert wine. Leave until cold, then chill for 3–4 hours or overnight.

3 Mix together the mascarpone cheese, orange juice and remaining sugar in a bowl and beat well until smooth. Chill until required.

4 Just before serving, remove the cinnamon stick and lemon peel from the apricots. Serve with a spoonful of the chilled mascarpone orange cream, sprinkled with a little cinnamon and decorated with a sprig of fresh mint.

Rhubarb and Orange Fool

Perhaps this traditional English pudding got its name because it is so easy to make that even a 'fool' can attempt it.

Serves 4

30ml/2 tbsp orange juice
5ml/1 tsp finely shredded orange rind
1kg/2¼lb (about 10–12 stems) rhubarb,
   chopped
15ml/1 tbsp redcurrant jelly
45ml/3 tbsp caster sugar
150g/5oz prepared thick, creamy custard
150ml/¼ pint/⅔ cup double
   cream, whipped
sweet biscuits, to serve

1 Place the orange juice and rind, the rhubarb, redcurrant jelly and sugar in a microwave-proof bowl. Cover and microwave on HIGH for 8–10 minutes, stirring once, until the rhubarb is just tender but not mushy. Leave to cool completely.

2 Drain the cooled rhubarb to remove some of the liquid and reserve a few pieces with a little orange rind for decoration. Purée the remaining rhubarb in a food processor or blender, or press it through a sieve.

3 Stir the custard into the purée, then fold in the whipped cream. Spoon the fool into individual bowls, cover and chill. Just before serving, top with the reserved fruit and rind. Serve with crisp, sweet biscuits.

Fruit and Rice Ring

*This unusual rice pudding looks
beautiful turned out of a ring
mould, but if you prefer, stir the
fruit into the rice and serve it in
individual dishes.*

INGREDIENTS

Serves 4

65g/2½oz/5 tbsp short grain rice
900ml/1½ pints/3¾ cups semi-skimmed
  milk
1 cinnamon stick
45ml/3 tbsp sugar
finely grated rind of 1 small orange
175g/6oz/1½ cups mixed dried fruit
175ml/6fl oz/¾ cup orange juice

1 Place the rice, milk and
cinnamon stick in a large
microwaveproof bowl. Cover and
microwave on HIGH for 6–8
minutes until boiling, stirring two
or three times during this time.
Reduce the power setting to
MEDIUM and microwave for a
further 30 minutes, stirring twice,
until no liquid remains. Remove
the cinnamon stick and stir in the
sugar and orange rind.

2 Place the fruit and orange
juice in another microwaveproof bowl. Cover and microwave
on HIGH for 6 minutes, then
reduce the power setting to
MEDIUM and microwave for
10–15 minutes, until tender and
no liquid remains.

3 Tip the fruit into the base of a
lightly oiled 1.5 litre/2½ pint/
6¼ cup ring mould. Spoon the rice
over, smoothing it down firmly
and chill the pudding.

4 To serve the ring, run a knife
around the edge of the mould
and turn out the rice carefully on
to a serving plate.

Lemon Soufflé with Blackberries

The simple fresh taste of the cold lemon mousse combines well with the rich blackberry sauce, and the colour contrast looks wonderful, too. Blueberries or raspberries make equally delicious alternatives to blackberries.

Serves 6

grated rind of 1 lemon and juice
    of 2 lemons
15ml/1 tbsp/1 sachet powdered gelatine
5 x size 4 eggs, separated
150g/5oz/10 tbsp caster sugar
few drops vanilla essence
400ml/14fl oz/1²/₃ cups whipping cream
few fresh blackberries and blackberry
    leaves, to decorate

For the sauce

175g/6oz blackberries (fresh or frozen)
30–45ml/2–3 tbsp caster sugar

1 Place the lemon juice in a small microwaveproof bowl, sprinkle over the gelatine and leave to soften. Microwave on HIGH for 30–45 seconds until clear and dissolved. Allow to cool.

2 Put the lemon rind, egg yolks, sugar and vanilla into a large bowl and whisk until the mixture is very thick, pale and creamy.

3 Whisk the egg whites until stiff and almost peaky. Whip the cream until stiff and holding its shape.

4 Stir the gelatine mixture into the yolks, then fold in the cream and lastly the egg whites. When lightly, but thoroughly, blended turn into a 1.5 litre/2½ pint/6¼ cup soufflé dish and freeze for 2 hours.

5 To make the sauce, place the blackberries in a microwaveproof bowl with the sugar. Cover and microwave on HIGH for 2–3 minutes, stirring twice, until the juices begin to run and all the sugar has dissolved. Pass through a sieve to remove the seeds, then chill until ready to serve.

6 When the soufflé is almost frozen, but still spoonable, scoop or spoon it on to individual plates and decorate with blackberries and blackberry leaves. Serve with the blackberry sauce.

Summer Berry Medley

*Make the most of glorious seasonal
fruits in this refreshing dessert. The
sauce is also good swirled into plain
or strawberry-flavoured fromage
frais or yogurt.*

INGREDIENTS

Serves 4-6

175g/6oz redcurrants

175g/6oz raspberries

50g/2oz caster sugar

30–45ml/2–3 tbsp crème de framboise

450–675g/1–1½lb mixed soft summer
    fruits, such as strawberries, raspberries,
    blueberries, redcurrants and
    blackcurrants

vanilla ice cream, to serve

1 Strip the redcurrants from
their stalks using a fork
and place in a bowl with the
raspberries, sugar and crème de
framboise. Cover and leave to
macerate for 1–2 hours.

2 Put this fruit with its macerat-
ing juices in a microwaveproof
bowl. Cover and microwave on
HIGH for 3 minutes, stirring once,
until the fruit is just tender.

3 Pour the fruit into a blender
or food processor and blend
until smooth. Press through a
nylon sieve to remove any pips.
Leave to cool, then chill.

4 Divide the mixed soft fruit
between four glass serving
dishes and pour over the sauce.
Serve with scoops of good-quality
vanilla ice cream.

Poached Pears in Red Wine

Serves 4

300ml/½ pint /1¼ cups red wine

75g/3oz caster sugar

45ml/3 tbsp honey

juice of ½ lemon

1 cinnamon stick

1 vanilla pod, split open lengthways

5cm/2in thinly pared strip of orange rind

1 clove

1 black peppercorn

4 firm, ripe pears

whipped cream or soured cream, to serve

1 Place the wine, sugar, honey, lemon juice, cinnamon stick, vanilla pod, orange rind, clove and peppercorn in a microwaveproof bowl just large enough to hold the pears standing upright. Microwave on HIGH for 3–5 minutes, until boiling, stirring frequently to dissolve the sugar.

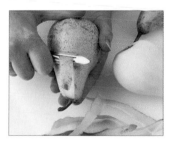

2 Meanwhile, peel the pears, leaving their stems intact. Take a thin slice off the base of each pear so that it will stand neatly square and upright.

COOK'S TIP

Remember that vanilla pods can be used more than once. Drain and dry a pod thoroughly then store for future use.

3 Place the pears in the wine mixture, spooning it over them. Three-quarters cover the dish with clear film or a lid. Microwave on HIGH for 5–6 minutes until the pears are just tender when pierced with the tip of a knife. Turn and reposition the pears in the bowl two or three times during cooking.

4 Carefully transfer the pears to another bowl using a slotted spoon. Microwave the poaching liquid, uncovered, on HIGH for 15–17 minutes, until the syrup is reduced by half. Leave to cool. Strain the cooled liquid over the pears and chill them for at least 3 hours.

5 Place the pears in individual serving dishes and spoon over a little of the red wine syrup. Serve with whipped or soured cream.

BAKING

~

Brown Soda Bread

INGREDIENTS

Makes two 450g/1lb loaves

450g/1lb/4 cups plain flour

450g/1lb/4 cups wholemeal flour

10ml/2 tsp salt

15ml/1 tbsp bicarbonate of soda

20ml/4 tsp cream of tartar

10ml/2 tsp caster sugar

50g/2oz/4 tbsp butter

900ml/1½ pints/3¾ cups buttermilk or
    skimmed milk

extra wholemeal flour, to sprinkle

1 Sift all the dry ingredients into a large bowl, tipping any bran from the flour back into the bowl.

2 Rub the butter into the flour mixture, then add enough buttermilk or milk to make a soft dough. You may not need all of it, so add it cautiously.

3 Knead the dough lightly until smooth, then divide and shape it into two large rounds and place on lightly oiled plates. Make a deep cross in the top of each loaf.

4 Sprinkle over a little extra wholemeal flour. Cook each loaf separately.

5 Microwave on MEDIUM for 5 minutes, give the plate a half turn and microwave on HIGH for a further 3 minutes. Brown the top under a preheated grill if you like. Allow to stand for 10 minutes, then transfer to a wire rack to cool. Repeat with the second loaf. This bread is best eaten on the day of making.

COMBINATION MICROWAVE

This recipe is suitable for cooking in a combination microwave. Follow the oven manufacturer's timing guide for good results.

Sage Soda Bread

This wonderful loaf, quite unlike bread made with yeast, has a velvety texture and a powerful sage aroma.

INGREDIENTS

Makes 1 loaf

350g/12oz/3 cups wholemeal flour
115g/4oz/1 cup strong white flour
5ml/1 tsp salt
10ml/2 tsp bicarbonate of soda
30ml/2 tbsp shredded fresh sage
300–450ml/½–¾ pint/1¼–1¾ cups
   buttermilk

1 Sift the dry ingredients into a large mixing bowl.

2 Stir in the sage and add enough buttermilk to make a soft dough.

3 Shape the dough into a round loaf and place on a lightly oiled plate and cut a deep cross in the top.

4 Microwave on MEDIUM for 5 minutes, give the plate a half turn and microwave on HIGH for a further 3 minutes. Brown the top under a preheated hot grill, if you like. Allow to stand for 10 minutes, then transfer to a wire rack to cool. Best eaten on the day of making.

COMBINATION MICROWAVE

This recipe is suitable for cooking in a combination microwave. Follow the oven manufacturer's timing guide for good results.

COOK'S TIP

As an alternative to the sage, try using finely chopped rosemary.

Cheese and Marjoram Scones

INGREDIENTS

Makes 18

115g/4oz/1 cup wholemeal flour
115g/4oz/1 cup self-raising flour
pinch of salt
40g/1½oz/3 tbsp butter
1.5ml/¼ tsp dry mustard
10ml/2 tsp dried marjoram
50–75g/2–3oz/½–⅔ cup Cheddar cheese,
    finely grated
about 125ml/4fl oz/½ cup milk
50g/2oz/⅓ cup pecans or walnuts,
    chopped

1 Sift the two types of flour into a bowl and add the salt. Cut the butter into small pieces, and rub it into the flour until the mixture resembles fine bread-crumbs.

2 Add the mustard, marjoram and grated cheese, then mix in sufficient milk to make a soft dough. Knead the dough lightly.

3 Roll out the dough on a floured surface to about a 2cm/¾in thickness and cut out about 18 scones using a 5cm/2in square cutter.

4 Brush the scones with a little milk and sprinkle the chopped pecans or walnuts over the top. Place the scones on a piece of non-stick parchment in the microwave, spacing them well apart. Microwave on HIGH for 3–3½ minutes, repositioning the scones twice during cooking.

5 Insert a skewer into the centre of each scone: if it comes out clean, the scone is cooked. Return any uncooked scones to the microwave and microwave on HIGH for a further 30 seconds. Brown under a preheated hot grill until golden, if liked. Serve warm, split and buttered.

VARIATION

For Herb and Mustard Scones, use 30ml/2 tbsp chopped fresh parsley or chives instead of the dried marjoram and 5ml/1 tsp Dijon mustard instead of the dry mustard. Substitute 50g/2oz chopped pistachio nuts for the pecans or walnuts.

Feta Cheese and Chive Scones

INGREDIENTS

Makes 9

115g/4oz/1 cup self-raising flour

150g/5oz/1¼ cups self-raising wholemeal
flour

2.5ml/½ tsp salt

75g/3oz feta cheese

15ml/1 tbsp snipped fresh chives

150ml/¼ pint/⅔ cup skimmed milk, plus
extra for glazing

1.5ml/¼ tsp cayenne pepper

3 Turn out the dough on to a floured surface and lightly knead until smooth. Roll out to 2cm/¾in thick and stamp out nine scones with a 6cm/2½in biscuit cutter. Brush with skimmed milk, then sprinkle over the cayenne pepper. Place the scones on a piece of non-stick parchment in the microwave, spacing them well apart.

4 Microwave on HIGH for 3–3½ minutes, repositioning the scones twice during cooking. Insert a skewer into the centre of each scone; if it comes out clean, the scone is cooked. Return any uncooked scones to the microwave and microwave for a further 30 seconds. Brown under a preheated hot grill until golden, if liked.

1 Sift the flours and salt into a mixing bowl, adding any bran left over from the flour in the sieve.

2 Crumble the feta cheese and rub into the dry ingredients. Stir in the chives, then add the milk and mix to a soft dough.

Oatmeal Tartlets with Minted Hummus

Serve these wholesome little tartlets with a crisp salad of cos lettuce.

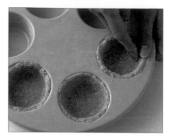

INGREDIENTS

Serves 6

225g/8oz/1½ cups medium oatmeal

2.5ml/½ tsp bicarbonate of soda

5ml/1 tsp salt

25g/1oz/2 tbsp butter

1 egg yolk

30ml/2 tbsp skimmed milk

400g/14oz can chick-peas, rinsed
   and drained

juice of 1–2 lemons

350g/12oz/1½ cups low-fat fromage blanc

60ml/4 tbsp tahini

45ml/3 tbsp chopped fresh mint

25g/1oz/2 tbsp pumpkin seeds

paprika, for dusting

ground black pepper

1 Mix together the oatmeal, bicarbonate of soda and salt in a large bowl. Rub in the butter until the mixture resembles fine breadcrumbs. Stir in the egg yolk and add the milk if the mixture seems too dry.

2 Press the mixture into six 9cm/3½in microwaveproof tartlet or mini flan dishes and prick the base and sides well with a fork. Microwave on HIGH for 4–6 minutes, repositioning twice during cooking, until cooked.

3 Purée the chick-peas, the juice of 1 lemon, fromage blanc and tahini in a blender or food processor until smooth. Spoon into a bowl and season with black pepper and more lemon juice to taste. Stir in the chopped mint. Divide among the tartlet moulds, sprinkle with pumpkin seeds and dust with paprika.

Courgette and Walnut Loaf

Cardamom seeds impart their distinctive aroma to this loaf. Serve spread with ricotta and honey for a delicious snack.

INGREDIENTS

Makes 1 loaf

3 eggs
75g/3oz/⅓ cup light muscovado sugar
120ml/4fl oz/½ cup sunflower oil
225g/8oz/2 cups wholemeal flour
5ml/1 tsp baking powder
5ml/1 tsp bicarbonate of soda
5ml/1 tsp ground cinnamon
3ml/¾ tsp ground allspice
7.5ml/1½ tsp green cardamoms, seeds
   removed and crushed
150g/5oz courgette, coarsely grated
115g/4oz/½ cup walnuts, chopped
50g/2oz/¼ cup sunflower seeds

1 Line the base and sides of a 900g/2lb loaf dish with non-stick baking paper.

2 Beat the eggs and sugar together in a large bowl and gradually add the oil.

3 Sift the flour into a separate bowl, adding the baking powder, bicarbonate of soda, cinnamon and allspice.

4 Mix the dry ingredients into the egg mixture, adding the cardamoms, courgette and walnuts. Reserve 15ml/1 tbsp of the sunflower seeds, then add the remainder to the mixture.

5 Spoon the mixture into the loaf dish, level the top and sprinkle with the reserved sunflower seeds.

6 Shield each end of the dish with a smooth piece of foil, shiny side in. Cover with clear film and microwave on HIGH for 8–9 minutes, giving the dish a quarter turn three or four times.

7 Remove the clear film and foil for the last 1½ minutes, until the loaf is cooked, when a skewer inserted in the centre comes out clean. Allow to cool for 5 minutes before turning out on to a rack to cool. Brown under a preheated hot grill before serving, if liked.

COMBINATION MICROWAVE

This recipe is suitable for cooking in a combination microwave. Follow the oven manufacturer's timing guide for good results.

Blueberry Crumble Tea Bread

INGREDIENTS

Makes 8 pieces

50g/2oz/4 tbsp butter or margarine, at
   room temperature
175g/6oz/²/₃ cup caster sugar
1 egg, at room temperature
120ml/4fl oz/¹/₂ cup milk
225g/8oz/2 cups plain flour
10ml/2 tsp baking powder
2.5ml/¹/₂ tsp salt
275g/10oz fresh blueberries or bilberries

For the topping

115g/4oz sugar
40g/1¹/₂oz/6 tbsp plain flour
2.5ml/¹/₂ tsp ground cinnamon
50g/2oz/4 tbsp butter, cut in pieces

1 Grease a 23 x 18cm/9 x 7in
microwaveproof dish.

2 Cream the butter or
margarine with the caster
sugar until light and fluffy. Beat in
the egg, then mix in the milk.

3 Sift over the flour, baking
powder and salt and stir just
enough to blend the ingredients.

4 Add the berries and stir them
in lightly. Spoon the mixture
into the prepared dish.

5 For the topping, place the
sugar, flour, ground cinnamon
and butter in a mixing bowl. Rub
in the butter until the mixture
resembles coarse breadcrumbs;
alternatively, cut in the butter with
a pastry blender.

6 Sprinkle the topping over the
mixture in the baking dish.
Microwave on MEDIUM for
12 minutes, rotating the dish twice
during cooking. Brown under a
preheated hot grill, if liked. Leave
to stand for 5 minutes. Serve warm
or cold.

Gingerbread

INGREDIENTS

Serves 8–10

15ml/1 tbsp vinegar
175ml/6fl oz/¾ cup milk
200g/7oz/1⅓ cups plain flour
10ml/2 tsp baking powder
1.5ml/¼ tsp bicarbonate of soda
2.5ml/½ tsp salt
10ml/2 tsp ground ginger
5ml/1 tsp ground cinnamon
1.25ml/¼ tsp ground cloves
115g/4oz butter/½ cup, at room
    temperature
90g/3½oz/½ cup caster sugar
1 egg, at room temperature
225g/8oz/¾ cup molasses
whipped cream, to serve
chopped stem ginger, to decorate

1 Line the base of a 20cm/8in square shallow microwave-proof dish with greaseproof paper and grease the paper and sides of the dish.

2 Add the vinegar to the milk and set aside. The vinegar will curdle the milk.

3 Sift all the dry ingredients together three times in a mixing bowl and set aside.

4 Cream the butter and sugar until light and fluffy. Beat in the egg until well combined. Then stir in the molasses.

5 Fold in the dry ingredients in four batches, alternately adding the curdled milk. Mix only enough to blend the ingredients.

6 Pour into the prepared dish and microwave on HIGH for 7–8 minutes, until the cake is cooked and a skewer inserted into the centre of the cake comes out clean. Leave to cool in the dish until warm.

7 Cut into squares and serve warm, with whipped cream. Decorate with the stem ginger.

COMBINATION MICROWAVE

This recipe is suitable for cooking in a combination microwave. Follow the oven manufacturer's timing guide for good results.

Spiced Banana Muffins

Wholemeal muffins, with banana for added fibre, make a delicious, healthy treat at any time of the day. If liked, slice off the tops and fill with a teaspoon of jam or marmalade.

INGREDIENTS

Makes 12

75g/3oz/³/₄ cup wholemeal flour
50g/2oz/¹/₂ cup plain flour
10ml/2 tsp baking powder
pinch of salt
5ml/1 tsp mixed spice
40g/1¹/₂oz/¹/₄ cup soft light brown sugar
50g/2oz/1/4 cup soft margarine
1 egg, beaten
150ml/¹/₄ pint/²/₃ cup semi-skimmed milk
grated rind of 1 orange
1 ripe banana
20g/³/₄oz/¹/₄ cup porridge oats
20g/³/₄oz/scant ¹/₄ cup chopped hazelnuts

1 Sift together both flours, the baking powder, salt and mixed spice into a bowl, then tip the bran remaining in the sieve into the bowl. Stir in the sugar.

2 Place the margarine in a microwaveproof bowl and microwave on HIGH for 1 minute, until melted. Cool the margarine slightly, then beat in the egg, milk and grated orange rind.

3 Gently fold in the dry ingredients. Mash the banana with a fork, then stir it gently into the mixture, being careful not to overmix.

4 Use the mixture to half-fill twelve double-thick bun cases. Cook six at a time, by placing them in a microwave muffin tray or in ramekin dishes. Combine the oats and hazelnuts and sprinkle a little of the mixture over each muffin.

5 Place in the microwave, arranging the dishes in a ring pattern. Microwave on HIGH for 2¹/₂–3 minutes, rearranging once during cooking. Repeat with the remaining six muffins. Transfer to a wire rack and remove from their paper cases when cool enough to handle. Serve warm or cold.

Chocolate and Orange Angel Cake

This light-as-air sponge with its fluffy icing is virtually fat-free, yet tastes heavenly. Make the icing conventionally on the hob for best results.

Serves 10

25g/1oz/¼ cup plain flour
15g/½oz/2 tbsp reduced-fat cocoa powder
15g/½oz/2 tbsp cornflour
pinch of salt
5 egg whites
2.5ml/½ tsp cream of tartar
115g/4oz/scant ½ cup caster sugar
blanched and shredded rind of 1 orange,
    to decorate

For the icing
200g/7oz/1 cup caster sugar
75ml/5 tbsp water
1 egg white

1 Sift the flour, cocoa powder, cornflour and salt together three times. Lightly whisk the egg whites in a large bowl until foamy. Add the cream of tartar, then whisk until soft peaks form.

2 Add the caster sugar to the egg whites a spoonful at a time, whisking after each addition. Sift a third of the flour and cocoa mixture over the meringue and gently fold in. Repeat, sifting and folding in the flour and cocoa mixture twice more.

3 Spoon the mixture into a microwaveproof 20cm/8in ring mould and level the top. Microwave on MEDIUM for 10–12 minutes, rotating the dish twice. Leave to stand for 5–10 minutes. Turn upside-down on a wire rack and leave to cool in the dish. Carefully ease out of the dish.

4 Make the icing conventionally: put the sugar in a saucepan with the water and stir over low heat until dissolved. Boil until the syrup reaches a temperature of 120°C/240°F on a sugar thermometer or when a drop of the syrup forms a soft ball when dropped into a cup of cold water. Remove from the heat.

5 Whisk the egg white until stiff. Add the syrup in a thin stream, whisking all the time. Continue to whisk until the mixture is very thick and fluffy.

6 Spread the icing over the top and sides of the cooled cake. Sprinkle the orange rind over the top of the cake and serve.

Hot Chocolate Cake

This is wonderfully wicked, either hot as a pudding, to serve with a white chocolate sauce, or cold as a cake. The basic cake freezes well – thaw, then warm it in the microwave before serving.

INGREDIENTS

Makes 10–12 slices

200g/7oz/1¾ cups self-raising
   wholemeal flour
25g/1oz/¼ cup cocoa powder
pinch of salt
175g/6oz/¾ cup soft margarine
175g/6oz/¾ cup soft light brown sugar
few drops vanilla essence
4 eggs
75g/3oz white chocolate, roughly chopped
chocolate leaves and curls, to decorate

For the white chocolate sauce
75g/3oz white chocolate
150ml/¼ pint/⅔ cup single cream
30–40ml/2–3 tbsp milk

1 Sift the flour, cocoa powder and salt into a bowl, adding the bran from the sieve.

2 Cream the margarine, sugar and vanilla essence together until light and fluffy, then gently beat in one egg.

3 Gradually stir in the remaining eggs, one at a time, alternately folding in some of the flour, until all the flour mixture is well blended in.

4 Stir in the white chocolate and spoon the mixture into a 675–900g/1½–2lb greased microwaveproof loaf dish. Shield each end of the dish with a small piece of smooth foil, shiny side in. Cover with clear film and microwave on HIGH for 8–9 minutes, giving the dish a quarter turn three or four times during cooking. Remove the clear film and foil for the last 1½ minutes of the cooking time. The cake is cooked when a skewer inserted in the centre comes out clean. Leave to stand while making the sauce.

5 Place the chocolate and cream for the sauce in a microwave-proof bowl and microwave on MEDIUM for 2–3 minutes, until the chocolate has melted. Add the milk and stir until cool.

6 Serve the cake sliced, in a pool of sauce, decorated with chocolate leaves and curls.

COMBINATION MICROWAVE

This recipe is suitable for cooking in a combination microwave. Follow your oven manufacturer's timing guide for good results.

Apple and Hazelnut Shortcake

INGREDIENTS

Serves 8–10

150g/5oz/1 cup wholemeal flour
50g/2oz/4 tbsp ground hazelnuts
50g/2oz/4 tbsp icing sugar, sifted
150g/5oz/10 tbsp unsalted butter or
    margarine
3 sharp eating apples
5ml/1 tsp lemon juice
15-30ml/1-2 tbsp caster sugar, or to taste
15ml/1 tbsp chopped fresh mint or 5ml/
    1 tsp dried mint
250ml/8fl oz/1 cup whipping cream or
    crème fraîche
few drops vanilla essence
few mint leaves and whole hazelnuts,
    to decorate

1 Process the flour, ground hazelnuts and icing sugar with the butter in a food processor in short bursts. Alternatively, rub the butter into the dry ingredients until they come together. Do not overwork the mixture. Bring the dough together, adding a very little iced water, if necessary. Knead briefly, wrap in greaseproof paper and chill for 30 minutes.

2 Line the base of a 23cm/9in round shallow microwave-proof dish with greaseproof paper. Roll out the shortcake mixture on a lightly floured surface to a round measuring about 23cm/9in in diameter.

3 Lift into the dish and press down well with the back of a spoon to level the surface and sides. Microwave on LOW for 8 minutes or until a skewer, inserted into the centre of the shortcake, comes out clean. Give the dish a quarter-turn every 2 minutes during cooking. Brown under a preheated hot grill until golden, if liked. Allow to cool.

4 Meanwhile, peel, core and chop the apples. Place in a microwaveproof bowl with the lemon juice. Add sugar to taste, cover and microwave on HIGH for 5–7 minutes, stirring once, until tender. Mash the apple gently with the chopped fresh mint and leave to cool.

5 Whip the cream with the vanilla essence. Place the shortcake on a serving plate and top with the cooked apple.

6 Top the shortcake with the cream, swirling it into a decorative pattern. Decorate with a few mint leaves and whole hazelnuts. Serve immediately.

COMBINATION MICROWAVE

This recipe is suitable for cooking in a combination microwave. Follow the oven manufacturer's timing guide for good results.

Strawberry and Hazelnut Roulade

INGREDIENTS

Serves 6–8

2 large eggs

50g/2oz/¼ cup caster sugar

50g/2oz/½ cup plain flour, sifted twice

40g/1½oz shelled hazelnuts, ground

120ml/4fl oz/½ cup double cream

1 egg white

175g/6oz/1½ cups strawberries, sliced

1 Line a 28 x 18cm/11 x 7in shallow rectangular microwaveproof dish with lightly oiled greaseproof paper, leaving about 5cm/2in of paper overlapping at the edges.

2 Whisk the eggs and caster sugar in a bowl until the mixture is very thick and has trebled in volume. Sift the flour over the egg mixture and fold it in with a metal spoon. Pour the mixture into the prepared dish, spreading it evenly.

3 Microwave on HIGH for 2½–3 minutes, until it is just firm in the centre, giving the dish a half turn once during the cooking time. Leave to stand for 3 minutes.

4 Sprinkle a sheet of greaseproof paper with the ground hazelnuts. Turn the sponge out on to the hazelnuts. Remove the lining paper. Hold another piece of greaseproof paper under a tap for a few seconds to dampen it; crumple it up, spread it out again and lay it on top of the cooked sponge. Roll the cake up from one of the shorter edges, enclosing the paper. Let the cake cool completely on a wire rack.

5 Meanwhile, whip the cream until it stands in soft peaks. In another bowl, beat the egg white until stiff and fold into the cream, mixing well.

6 Unroll the sponge, remove the paper, spread the cream over the surface and dot with the sliced strawberries. Roll up the cake again and place on a serving plate, seam side down. Chill the roulade for at least 1 hour, until it becomes firm enough to slice. Just before serving, trim the ends to neaten.

Fruit-topped Baked Cheesecake

Serves 6–8

50g/2oz/4 tbsp butter

115g/4oz/2 cups digestive biscuits,
    crushed

115g/4oz ricotta cheese

225g/8oz quark

2 eggs, separated

15ml/1 tbsp wholemeal flour

45ml/3 tbsp clear honey

10ml/2 tsp fresh orange juice

150ml/¼ pint/⅔ cup natural yogurt

50g/2oz/⅓ cup sultanas, chopped

about 225g/8oz mixed prepared fresh
    fruits, to decorate

1 Grease an 18cm/7in
microwaveproof flan dish.
Line the base with greaseproof
paper and grease the paper.

2 Place the butter in a
microwaveproof bowl and
microwave on HIGH for about
1 minute to melt. Add the digestive
biscuit crumbs and mix well. Use
to line the base of the flan dish,
pressing the mixture down flat
with the back of a spoon.

3 Place the ricotta in a bowl
with the quark, egg yolks,
flour, honey, orange juice and
yogurt. Beat until smooth.
Microwave the mixture on
MEDIUM for 7–8 minutes
until thickened, whisking every
2 minutes.

4 Stir in the sultanas. Whisk the
egg whites until they stand
in stiff peaks, and fold into the
cheesecake mixture. Spoon over
the prepared biscuit base.

5 Microwave on MEDIUM for
10–12 minutes, or until the
cheesecake is just set in the centre,
giving the dish a quarter turn
every 3 minutes. Leave to stand
until cool, then chill for 2 hours or
until firm enough to unmould, if
liked. Alternatively, serve straight
from the dish.

6 Top the cheesecake just before
serving with the prepared
fresh fruit or a favourite single fruit.

Carrot and Pecan Cake

Fructose is used as the sweetening agent in this recipe. It has one and a half times the sweetening power as the same weight of sugar, but only has the same number of calories.

Serves 6–8

175g/6oz/1¼ cups carrots, grated
90ml/3fl oz/⅓ cup sunflower oil
30ml/2 tbsp milk
2 eggs, beaten
75g/3oz/6 tbsp fructose
75g/3oz/⅔ cup plain flour
5ml/1 tsp baking powder
5ml/1 tsp bicarbonate of soda
10ml/2 tsp ground cinnamon
75g/3oz/½ cup raisins
25g/1oz/¼ cup shelled pecans, chopped
icing sugar, to dust

1 Grease an 18cm/7in microwaveproof round cake dish and line it with greaseproof paper.

2 In a large bowl, mix the carrots with the oil, milk, eggs and fructose, beating well.

3 Sift in the flour with the baking powder, bicarbonate of soda and cinnamon. Fold the dry mixture into the egg mixture, then stir in the raisins and pecans. Spoon into the prepared cake dish and level the surface.

4 Place the cake dish on an inverted saucer in the microwave. Microwave on MEDIUM for 9 minutes, giving the dish a quarter turn every 3 minutes. Increase the power setting to HIGH and microwave for a further 2–3 minutes, giving the dish a quarter turn after 1½ minutes.

5 The cake is cooked when it shrinks from the sides of the dish. Leave the cake to stand for 10 minutes before turning it out of the dish to cool on a wire rack.

6 Sprinkle with sifted icing sugar to serve.

Maple and Banana Teabread

INGREDIENTS

Serves 8–10

115g/4oz/1 cup wholemeal flour

5ml/1 tsp bicarbonate of soda

2 bananas, mashed

60ml/4 tbsp natural yogurt

50g/2oz/4 tbsp soft light brown sugar

65g/2½oz/5 tbsp unsalted butter

1 egg, beaten

30ml/2 tbsp maple syrup

75g/3oz/½ cup dried dates,
    coarsely chopped

icing sugar, to dust

1 Lightly grease a 23 x 13cm/
9 x 5in microwaveproof loaf
dish and line the base with greaseproof paper.

2 Sift the wholemeal flour
with the bicarbonate of soda,
adding the bran left in the sieve.

3 Mix the bananas with the
yogurt, brown sugar, butter,
egg and syrup, blending well. Add
the flour mixture and dates and
mix into a smooth batter. Spoon
the mixture evenly into the loaf
dish and spread it out slightly.

4 To prevent the ends of the
cake from over-cooking, wrap
a 5cm/2in wide strip of smooth
foil over each end of the dish. Place
the dish on an inverted plate in the
oven and microwave on MEDIUM
for 10 minutes, giving the dish a
quarter turn every 2½ minutes.

5 Increase the power setting to
HIGH and microwave for a
further 2 minutes. Remove the foil,
give the dish a quarter turn and
microwave for a further 1–3
minutes, until the teabread shrinks
from the sides of the dish. Leave
to stand for 10 minutes before
turning out to cool on a wire rack.

6 Sift a light coating of icing
sugar over the top of the cake
before serving. Serve warm or cold.

Kugelhopf

Serves 10–12

50g/2oz/1 cup digestive biscuits, crushed
15 blanched almonds
300ml/½ pint/1¼ cups milk
25g/1oz fresh yeast or 15g/½oz dried yeast
25g/1oz/2 tbsp caster sugar
450g/1lb/4 cups plain flour
175g/6oz/10 tbsp butter or margarine
3 large eggs, beaten
2.5ml/½ tsp salt
75g/3oz/½ cup sultanas
50g/2oz/⅓ cup raisins
25g/1oz/2 tbsp currants
grated rind of 1 lemon
icing sugar, to dust
strawberries, to serve

1 Grease a 23cm/9in diameter microwaveproof ring mould and sprinkle the mould with the digestive biscuit crumbs. Arrange the almonds on the base.

2 Pour the milk into a jug and microwave on HIGH for 1 minute or until tepid. Stir in the fresh yeast; or reconstitute the dried yeast with the milk according to the packet instructions, adding 5ml/1 tsp of the caster sugar.

3 Place 175g/6oz/1½ cups of the flour in a microwaveproof bowl and gradually beat in the yeast mixture.

4 Cover loosely with clear film and microwave on DEFROST for 1½–2 minutes. Leave to stand until well risen and frothy, about 10–15 minutes.

5 Place the butter or margarine in a microwaveproof bowl and microwave on HIGH for 1–1½ minutes to melt. Add to the risen batter, together with the remaining sugar and flour, the eggs and salt. Beat the mixture well with a wooden spoon. Stir in the sultanas, raisins, currants and lemon rind, mixing well. Spoon into the prepared mould and smooth the surface with a knife.

6 Cover the batter loosely with clear film and microwave on DEFROST for 8–9 minutes, or until the batter has risen to the top of the mould. Leave to stand for 10 minutes, then microwave, uncovered, on HIGH for 6 minutes, giving the dish a quarter turn three times during cooking. Leave to stand for 5 minutes before turning out on to a wire rack.

7 When cool, dust the top with icing sugar and fill the centre with strawberries before serving.

Oat Florentines

These irresistible "bakes" make the best of familiar flapjacks and old-fashioned, chocolate-coated florentine biscuits.

INGREDIENTS

Makes 16

75g/3oz/6 tbsp butter

45ml/3 tbsp/¼ cup golden syrup

115g/4oz/1¼ cups rolled oats

25g/1oz/2 tbsp soft brown sugar

25g/1oz/2 tbsp chopped mixed
   candied peel

25g/1oz/2 tbsp glacé cherries,
   coarsely chopped

25g/1oz/¼ cup hazelnuts,
   coarsely chopped

115g/4oz/⅔ cup plain chocolate

1 Lightly grease a 20cm/8in square microwaveproof shallow dish and line the base with a sheet of rice paper.

2 Place the butter and golden syrup in a microwaveproof bowl and microwave on HIGH for 1½ minutes to melt. Stir well.

3 Add the oats, sugar, peel, cherries and hazelnuts, mixing well to blend.

COOK'S TIP
Rice paper is used for cooking in traditional recipes as well as in microwave methods. It prevents mixtures, such as this sweet oat base, from sticking by cooking on to them. When cooked, the rice paper can be eaten with the biscuits or other items.

4 Spoon the mixture into the dish and level the surface with the back of a spoon. Microwave on MEDIUM HIGH for 6 minutes, giving the dish a half turn every 2 minutes. Allow to cool slightly then cut into 16 fingers and place on a wire rack to cool.

5 Break the chocolate into pieces and place in a microwaveproof bowl. Microwave on HIGH for 2–3 minutes, stirring twice, until melted and smooth. Spread over the tops of the florentines and mark in a zig-zag pattern with the prongs of a fork. Leave to set.

Iced Cup Cakes

INGREDIENTS

Makes about 24

115g/4oz/1 cup self-raising flour
pinch of salt
50g/2oz/4 tbsp butter or margarine
50g/2oz/4 tbsp soft brown sugar
1 egg, beaten
milk, to mix
whipped cream or glacé icing, to top
glacé cherries, chocolate vermicelli, grated
  chocolate, angelica, candied orange
  slices or toasted coconut, to decorate

1 Sift the flour with the salt into a bowl, rub in the butter or margarine finely, then stir in the sugar.

2 Mix in the egg and enough milk to form a mixture with a soft dropping consistency.

3 Place six paper cases in a six-hole microwaveproof muffin pan and place spoonfuls of the prepared cake mixture into each, filling them each about two-thirds full.

4 Microwave on HIGH for 2 minutes, giving the dish a half-turn after 1 minute. Transfer to a cool rack. Repeat with the remaining mixture, cooking in batches of six. Allow to cool completely before decorating.

5 To finish, pipe the tops of the cakes with swirls of whipped cream or coat with soft glacé icing. Decorate the cakes with an assortment of toppings. Serve on the day of making.

COOK'S TIP

Make and eat microwave-cooked cup cakes on the same day. Alternatively, freeze them before adding any topping and decorations.

VARIATIONS

Chocolate Cup Cakes Prepare the mixture as above but add 15ml/ 1 tbsp sifted cocoa powder to the flour mixture.

Lemon Cup Cakes Prepare the mixture as above but add the grated rind of 1 lemon to the mixture after mixing. Top with lemon flavoured glacé icing if you like.

Coffee Cup Cakes Prepare the mixture as above but add 5ml/ 1 tsp coffee granules dissolved in a little boiling water to the mixture with the eggs and milk. Top with coffee flavoured glacé icing if you like.

Chocolate Chip Cakes Prepare the mixture as above but add 25g/1oz/1 tbsp plain chocolate chips to the mixture with the eggs and milk.

Fairy Currant Cakes Prepare the mixture as above but add 25g/1oz/2 tbsp currants to the mixture with the eggs and milk.

Date-filled Pastries

From Gibraltar to Baghdad, traditionally, Jewish women get together to make hundreds of these labour-intensive pastries. Making a small quantity in the microwave is not so lengthy.

INGREDIENTS

Makes about 25

75g/3oz/6 tbsp margarine or
    butter, softened
175g/6oz/1½ cups plain flour
5ml/1 tsp rose water
5ml/1 tsp orange flower water
45ml/3 tbsp water
20ml/4 tsp sifted icing sugar, for
    sprinkling

For the filling
115g/4oz/⅔ cup stoned dried dates
50ml/2fl oz/¼ cup boiling water
2.5ml/½ tsp orange flower water

1 To make the filling, chop the dates finely. Add the boiling water and orange flower water, then beat the mixture vigorously and leave to cool.

2 For the pastries, rub the margarine or butter into the flour. Mix in the rose and orange flower waters and the water to make a firm dough.

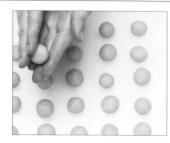

3 Shape the dough into about 25 small balls.

4 Press your finger into a ball of dough to make a small container, pressing the sides round and round to make the sides thinner. Put about 1.5ml/¼ tsp of the date mixture into the dough.

5 Seal by pressing the pastry together. Repeat with the remaining dough and filling.

6 Arrange the date pastries, seam side down, on lightly greased greaseproof paper and prick each one with a fork. Microwave on HIGH for 3–5 minutes, rearranging twice during cooking. Leave to stand for 5 minutes before transferring to a rack to cool.

7 Put the cooled pastries on a plate and sprinkle over the icing sugar. Shake lightly to make sure they are covered.

Coconut Pyramids

Without the danger of using a conventional cooker, making a batch of these all-time favourites is an ideal wet-afternoon occupation for young children.

INGREDIENTS

Makes about 15

225g/8oz/1 cup unsweetened
   desiccated coconut
115g/4oz/½ cup caster sugar
2 egg whites
oil, for greasing

1 Mix together the desiccated coconut and sugar. Lightly whisk the egg whites. Fold enough egg white into the coconut to make a fairly firm mixture. You may not need quite all the egg whites.

2 Form the mixture into pyramid shapes by taking a teaspoonful and rolling it first into a ball. Flatten the base and press the top into a point. Arrange the pyramids on greaseproof paper, leaving space between them.

3 Microwave on HIGH for 2–3 minutes or until the pyramids are just firm, but still soft inside. Transfer to a baking sheet and place under a preheated hot grill to tinge the tops golden, if liked.

4 Slide a palette knife under the pyramids to loosen them, and leave to cool before removing from the baking sheet.

COOK'S TIP

To freeze biscuits, arrange in a single layer on a tray. When hard, pack in bags or boxes. Thaw for 1 hour before use.

Cinnamon Balls

Ground almonds make these little cakes very moist. When cooked, they should be soft inside, with a very strong cinnamon flavour. They harden however with keeping, so it is a good idea to freeze some as they can be thawed very quickly when required.

INGREDIENTS

Makes about 15

175g/6oz/1½ cups ground almonds

75g/3oz/⅓ cup caster sugar

15ml/1 tbsp ground cinnamon

2 egg whites

oil, for greasing

icing sugar, for dredging

1 Mix together the ground almonds, sugar and cinnamon. Whisk the egg whites until they begin to stiffen, then fold enough into the almonds to make a fairly firm mixture.

2 Wet your hands with cold water and roll small spoonfuls of the mixture into smooth balls. Place these well apart on grease-proof paper.

3 Microwave on HIGH for 2½–3½ minutes, rearranging twice, until cooked but still slightly soft inside.

4 Slide a palette knife under the balls to release them from the paper and leave to cool. Sift a few tablespoons of icing sugar on to a plate and when the cinnamon balls are cold slide them on to the plate. Shake gently to completely cover the cinnamon balls in sugar.

COOK'S TIP

When completely cold, store the cinnamon balls in an airtight container. Alternatively, they keep well for up to about six months in the freezer.

Boston Banoffee Pie

INGREDIENTS

Makes a 20cm/8in pie

225g/8oz/1 cup butter
150g/5oz/1¼ cups plain flour
50g/2oz/4 tbsp caster sugar
200g/7oz can skimmed, sweetened
    condensed milk
115g/4oz/⅔ cup soft light brown sugar
30ml/2 tbsp golden syrup
2 small bananas, sliced
a little lemon juice
whipped cream, to decorate
5ml/1 tsp grated plain chocolate

1 Rub 115g/4oz/½ cup of the butter into the flour. Alternatively, process in a food processor until crumbled. Stir in the caster sugar.

2 Squeeze the mixture together with your hands until it forms a dough. Press into the base of a 20cm/8in microwaveproof flan dish. Cut the pastry away, leaving a 5mm/¼in overlap above the dish to allow for any shrinkage. Prick the base and sides well with a fork.

3 Place a double-thick layer of absorbent kitchen paper over the base, easing it into position around the edges. Microwave on HIGH for 3½ minutes, giving the dish a quarter turn every minute. Remove the paper and microwave on HIGH for a further 1½ minutes. Allow to cool.

4 Place the remaining 115g/4oz/½ cup butter in a large microwaveproof bowl or jug with the condensed milk, brown sugar and golden syrup. Microwave on HIGH for 3 minutes, mixing well twice during cooking.

5 Microwave on HIGH for a further 3–5 minutes, until the mixture thickens and turns a light caramel colour, stirring three times. Pour into the cooked pastry base and leave until cold.

6 Sprinkle the bananas with lemon juice and arrange on top of the caramel filling. Pipe a swirl of whipped cream in the centre and sprinkle with the grated chocolate.

COOKING AND
DEFROSTING
CHARTS

~

Cooking Fish and Shellfish

COD
steamed steaks and fillets

450g/1lb fillets
2 x 225g/8oz steaks
4 x 225g/8oz steaks

HIGH

Arrange fish fillets in a microwaveproof dish so that the thinner tail ends are to the centre. Fold in any flaps of skin on steaks and secure with wooden cocktail sticks. Dot with a little butter, sprinkle with seasoning and add a dash of lemon juice. Cover and microwave for 5–7 minutes for 450g/1lb fillets; 5 minutes for 2 x 225g/8oz steaks; and 8–9 minutes for 4 x 225g/8oz steaks, rearranging once halfway through cooking. Leave to stand, covered, for 3 minutes before serving.

FISH CAKES

4 x 75g/3oz

HIGH

Place in a shallow microwaveproof dish and brush with a little melted butter if liked. Microwave for 5 minutes, turning over once, halfway through cooking. Times refer to chilled or fresh fish cakes (thaw frozen fish cakes before cooking). Leave to stand for 2–3 minutes before serving. If liked, the fish cakes can be cooked in a preheated browning dish.

FISH FINGERS

2
4
6
8
12

HIGH

For best results cook in a preheated browning dish. Microwave for 1½ minutes for 2; 2 minutes for 4; 3 minutes for 6; 4 minutes for 8; and 5 minutes for 12 fish fingers, turning over once, halfway through cooking. Times refer to frozen fish fingers. Leave to stand for 1–2 minutes before serving.

FISH ROES

115g/4oz
225g/8oz

LOW

Rinse the fish roes and place in a microwaveproof dish with a large knob of butter and seasoning to taste. Cover and microwave for 4–4½ minutes for 115g/4oz; and 6–8 minutes for 225g/8oz fish roes, stirring once halfway through cooking. Leave to stand, covered, for 2 minutes before serving.

HADDOCK
steamed steaks and fillets

450g/1lb fillets
2 x 225g/8oz steaks
4 x 225g/8oz steaks

HIGH

Arrange the fish fillets in a microwaveproof dish so that the thinner tail ends are to the centre. Fold in any flaps of skin on steaks and secure with wooden cocktail sticks. Dot with a little butter, sprinkle with seasoning and add a dash of lemon juice. Cover and microwave for 5–7 minutes for 450g/1lb fillets; 5 minutes for 2 x 225g/8oz steaks; and 8–9 minutes for 4 x 225g/8oz steaks, rearranging once halfway through cooking. Leave to stand, covered, for 3 minutes before serving.

HALIBUT
steaks

2 x 225g/8oz steaks

HIGH

Fold in any flaps of skin and secure with wooden cocktail sticks. Place in a shallow microwaveproof dish and dot with a little butter. Season with salt, pepper and lemon juice. Cover and microwave for 4–5 minutes. Leave to stand, covered, for 2–3 minutes before serving.

HERRING
fresh whole

per 450g/1lb

HIGH

Remove heads and clean and gut before cooking. Slash the skin in several places to prevent bursting during cooking. Place in a shallow microwave-proof dish and season to taste. Shield the tail ends of the fish if liked. Cover with greaseproof paper and microwave for 3–4 minutes per 450g/1lb, turning over once halfway through cooking. Leave to stand, covered, for 2–3 minutes before serving.

KIPPERS
fillets

2
4
8

HIGH

If buying whole fish then remove heads and tails. Place skin-side down in a shallow microwaveproof cooking dish. Cover loosely and microwave for 1–2 minutes for 2 fillets; 3–4 minutes for 4 fillets; and 6–7 minutes for 8 fillets, rearranging once halfway through cooking. Leave to stand, covered, for 2–3 minutes before serving.

LOBSTER
to reheat cooked whole lobster and tails

450g/1lb whole
450g/1lb tails

HIGH

Place in a shallow microwaveproof dish and cover loosely. Microwave for 6–8 minutes for 450g/1lb whole; and 5–6 minutes for 450g/1lb tails, turning over once halfway through cooking. Leave to stand, covered, for 5 minutes before serving.

MACKEREL fresh whole	per 450g/1lb	HIGH		Remove heads and clean and gut before cooking. Slash the skin in several places to prevent bursting during cooking. Place in a shallow microwave-proof dish and season to taste. Shield the tail ends of the fish if liked. Cover with greaseproof paper and microwave for 3–4 minutes per 450g/1lb, turning over once halfway through cooking. Leave to stand, covered, for 2–3 minutes before serving.
MUSSELS fresh steamed	675g/1½lb	HIGH		Sort the mussels and scrub thoroughly with cold running water. Place in a microwaveproof dish with 75ml/5 tbsp water, fish stock or dry white wine. Cover loosely and microwave for 5 minutes, stirring once halfway through cooking. Remove with a slotted spoon, discarding any mussels that do not open. Thicken the cooking juices with a little beurre manié, (butter and flour paste), if liked, to serve with the mussels.
PLAICE steamed fillets	450g/1lb fillets	HIGH		Arrange fish fillets in a microwaveproof dish so that the thinner tail ends are to the centre of the dish. Dot with a little butter, sprinkle with seasoning and add a dash of lemon juice. Cover and microwave for 4–6 minutes, rearranging once halfway through cooking. Leave to stand, covered, for 3 minutes before serving.
RED OR GREY MULLET fresh whole	2 x 250g/9oz 4 x 250g/9oz	HIGH		Clean and gut before cooking. Place in a shallow microwaveproof dish and slash the skin in several places to prevent bursting during cooking. Cover and microwave for 4–5 minutes for 2 x 250g/9oz mullet; and 8–9 minutes for 4 x 250g/9oz mullet, turning over once halfway through cooking. Leave to stand, covered, for 5 minutes before serving.
SALMON steamed steaks	2 x 225g/8oz 4 x 225g/8oz	HIGH		Place in a shallow microwaveproof dish so that the narrow ends are to the centre of the dish. Dot with butter and sprinkle with lemon juice and salt and pepper. Cover with greaseproof paper and microwave for 2½–3 minutes for 2 x 225g/8oz steaks; and 4½–5¾ minutes for 4 x 225g/8oz steaks, turning over once halfway through cooking. Leave to stand, covered, for 5 minutes before serving.
	4 x 175g/6oz steaks	MEDIUM		Prepare and cook as above but use MEDIUM power and allow 10½–11½ minutes.
whole salmon and salmon trout	450g/1lb 900g/2lb 1.5kg/3–3½lb 1.75kg/4–4½lb	HIGH		Remove the head if liked. Slash or prick the skin in several places to prevent bursting during cooking. Place in a microwaveproof dish with 150ml/¼ pint/⅔ cup boiling water and a dash of lemon juice. Cover and microwave for 4½–5 minutes for a 450g/1lb fish, 8½–10½ minutes for a 900g/2lb fish; 11–14½ minutes for a 1.5kg/3–3½lb fish; and 14½–18½ minutes for a 1.75kg/4–4½lb fish, rotating 3 times during cooking. Leave to stand, covered, for 5 minutes before serving.
SCALLOPS steamed fresh	450g/1lb	MEDIUM		Remove from their shells. Place in a shallow microwaveproof dish and cover with absorbent kitchen paper. Microwave for 8–12 minutes, rearranging once, halfway through cooking. Leave to stand, covered, for 3 minutes before serving.
SHRIMPS AND PRAWNS to boil	450g/1lb 900g/2lb	HIGH		Rinse and place in a microwaveproof dish with 600ml/1 pint/2½ cups water, a dash of vinegar or lemon juice and a bay leaf if liked. Cover and microwave for 6–8 minutes for 450g/1lb; 8–10 minutes for 900g/2lb, stirring once halfway through cooking. Leave to stand, covered, for 3 minutes before draining and shelling.

SOLE
steamed fillets 450g/1lb HIGH Arrange fish fillets in a microwaveproof dish so that the thinner tail ends are to the centre of the dish. Dot with a little butter, season and add a dash of lemon juice. Cover and microwave for 4–6 minutes, rearranging once half-way through cooking. Leave to stand, covered, for 3 minutes before serving.

SMOKED HADDOCK
steamed fillets 450g/1lb HIGH Arrange fish fillets in a microwaveproof dish so that the thinner tail ends are to the centre of the dish. Dot with butter, sprinkle with seasoning and add a dash of lemon juice. Cover and microwave for 5–6 minutes, rearranging once halfway through cooking. Leave the fish to stand, covered, for 3 minutes before serving.

poached fillets 450g/1lb HIGH Place the fillets in a shallow microwaveproof dish with the thinner tail ends to the centre. Pour over 120ml/4fl oz/½ cup milk, dot with a little butter and season to taste. Cover and microwave for 5–6 minutes, rearranging once halfway through cooking. Leave to stand, covered, for 3 minutes before serving.

TROUT
whole 2 x 250g/9oz HIGH Clean and gut before cooking. Place in a shallow microwaveproof dish.
4 x 250g/9oz Slash the skin in several places to prevent bursting during cooking. Dot with butter if liked and season to taste. Cover and microwave for 4–5 minutes for 2 x 250g/9oz trout; and 8–9 minutes for 4 x 250g/9oz trout, turning over once halfway through cooking. Leave the fish to stand, covered, for 5 minutes before serving.

WHITING
steamed fillets 450g/1lb HIGH Arrange fish fillets in a microwaveproof dish so that the thinner tail ends are to the centre of the dish. Dot with a little butter, sprinkle with seasoning and add a dash or two of lemon juice. Cover and microwave for 4–6 minutes, rearranging once halfway through cooking. Leave to stand, covered, for 3 minutes before serving.

Monkfish with Mexican Salsa.

Cooking Poultry and Game

CHICKEN whole roast fresh chicken	1kg/2¼lb 1.5kg/3–3½lb 1.75kg/4–4½lb	HIGH	Rinse, dry and truss the chicken into a neat shape. Season and calculate the cooking time after weighing (and stuffing). Cook breast-side down for half of the cooking time and breast-side up for the remaining cooking time. Brush with a browning agent if liked and shield the wing tips with foil if necessary. Microwave for 12–16 minutes for a 1kg/2¼lb chicken; 18–24 minutes for a 1.5kg/3–3½lb chicken; 25–36 minutes for a 1.75kg/4–4½lb chicken. Cover with foil and leave to stand for 10–15 minutes before carving.
portions	1 x 225g/8oz portion 2 x 225g/8oz portions 4 x 225g/8oz portions	HIGH	Prick with a fork and brush with a browning agent if liked. Alternatively, crisp and brown under a preheated hot grill after cooking. Cover with buttered greaseproof paper to cook. Microwave for 5–7 minutes for 225g/8oz portion; 10–12 minutes for 2 x 225g/8oz portions; 18–24 minutes for 4 x 225g/8oz portions. Leave to stand, covered, for 5–10 minutes before serving.
drumsticks	2 4 8	HIGH	Prick with a fork and brush with a browning agent if liked. Alternatively, crisp and brown under a preheated hot grill after cooking. Cover with buttered greaseproof paper to cook. Microwave for 3–5 minutes for 2 drumsticks; 8–9 minutes for 4 drumsticks; 16–19 minutes for 8 drumsticks. Leave to stand, covered, for 5–10 minutes before serving.
thighs	8	HIGH	Prick with a fork and brush with a browning agent if liked. Alternatively, crisp and brown under a preheated hot grill after cooking. Cover with buttered greaseproof paper to cook. Microwave 8 thighs for 17–20 minutes. Leave to stand, covered, for 5–10 minutes before serving.
breasts	2 4	HIGH	Prick with a fork and brush with a browning agent if liked. Alternatively, crisp and brown under a preheated hot grill after cooking. Cover with buttered greaseproof paper to cook. Microwave for 2–3 minutes for 2 breasts; 3½–4 minutes for 4 breasts. Leave to stand, covered, for 5–10 minutes before serving.
livers, fresh or thawed frozen	225g/8oz 450g/1lb	HIGH	Rinse well and prick to prevent bursting during cooking. Place in a microwaveproof dish with a knob of butter. Cover loosely and microwave for 2–3 minutes for 225g/8oz; and 5–6 minutes for 450g/1lb, stirring twice during cooking. Leave to stand for 2 minutes before serving or using.
DUCK whole roast fresh duck	1.75kg/4–4½lb 2.25kg/5–5¼lb per 450g/1lb	HIGH	Rinse, dry and truss the duck into a neat shape, securing any tail-end flaps of skin to the main body. Prick thoroughly and place on a rack or upturned saucer in a microwaveproof dish for cooking. Cook breast-side down for half of the cooking time, and breast-side up for the remaining cooking time. Microwave for 28–32 minutes for a 1.75kg/4–4½lb duck; 35–40 minutes for a 2.25kg/5–5¼lb duck; or calculate times at 7–8 minutes per 450g/1lb. Drain away excess fat 3 times during cooking and shield tips, tail end and legs with foil if necessary. Cover with foil and leave to stand for 10–15 minutes before serving. Crisp the skin under a preheated hot grill if liked.
GAME BIRDS whole roast	1 x 450g/1lb 2 x 450g/1lb 1 x 900g/2lb 2 x 900g/2lb	HIGH	Rinse, dry and truss the birds into a neat shape. Brush with a browning agent if liked. Cover with greaseproof paper to cook. Microwave for 9–10 minutes for 450g/1lb bird; 18–22 minutes for 2 x 450g/1lb birds; 20–22 minutes for 900g/2lb bird; and 35–40 minutes for 2 x 900g/2lb birds, turning over twice during cooking. Leave to stand, covered, for 5 minutes before serving.

TURKEY			
whole roast fresh	2.75kg/6lb 4kg/9lb 5.5kg/12lb larger birds over 5.5kg/12lb *per* *450g/1lb*	HIGH	Rinse, dry and stuff the turkey if liked. Truss into a neat shape and weigh to calculate the cooking time. Brush with melted butter or browning agent if liked. Divide the cooking time into quarters and cook breast-side down for the first quarter, on one side for the second quarter, on the remaining side for the third quarter and breast-side up for the final quarter. Shield any parts that start to cook faster than others with small strips of foil. Microwave for 42 minutes for a 2.75kg/6lb bird; 63 minutes for a 4kg/9lb bird; 84 minutes for a 5.5kg/12lb bird; or allow 7 minutes per 450g/1lb for larger birds. When cooked, cover with foil and leave to stand for 10–25 minutes (depending upon size of bird) before carving.
drumsticks	2 x 350g/12oz	HIGH *then* MEDIUM	Place on a roasting rack, meaty sections downwards. Baste with a browning agent if liked. Cover and microwave on HIGH for 5 minutes, then on MEDIUM for 13–15 minutes, turning once. Leave to stand, covered, for 5 minutes before serving.
breasts	2 x 225g/8oz breasts 4 x 225g/8oz breasts	MEDIUM	Beat out flat if preferred and place in a shallow dish. Baste with browning agent if liked. Microwave for 8–10 minutes for 2 x 225g/8oz breasts; and 16–18 minutes for 4 x 225g/8oz breasts, turning over once. Leave to stand for 2–3 minutes before serving.

Dijon Chicken Salad.

Hot Chilli Chicken.

Cooking Meat

BACON

back and streaky rashers	4 rashers 450g/1lb	HIGH	Place small quantities between sheets of kitchen paper, larger quantities on a plate or microwaveproof bacon rack covered with kitchen paper. Microwave for 3½–4 minutes for 4 rashers; and 12–14 minutes for 450g/1lb, turning over once. Leave to stand for 1–2 minutes before serving.
joint	900g/2lb joint	HIGH	Remove any skin and score the fat into a diamond pattern. Sprinkle with a little brown sugar and stud with cloves if liked. Place on a microwaveproof roasting rack or upturned saucer in a dish. Microwave for 20–24 minutes, rotating the dish twice. Leave to stand, covered with foil, for 10–15 minutes before serving.

BEEF

roast joint	per 450g/1lb	HIGH then MEDIUM	Ideally place the joint on a microwaveproof roasting rack or upturned saucer inside a roasting bag. Calculate the cooking time according to weight and microwave on HIGH for the first 5 minutes then on MEDIUM for the remaining time. Turn the joint over halfway through the cooking time.

per 450g/1lb
topside or sirloin (boned and rolled)

rare	8–9 minutes
medium	11–12 minutes
well done	15–16 minutes

forerib or back rib (on the bone)

rare	7–8 minutes
medium	13–14 minutes
well done	15 minutes

forerib or back rib (boned and rolled)

rare	11–12 minutes
medium	13–14 minutes
well done	15–16 minutes

Cover the joint with foil after cooking and leave to stand for 10–15 minutes before carving.

minced beef	450g/1lb	HIGH	Place in a microwaveproof dish, cover and microwave for 10–12 minutes, breaking up and stirring twice.
hamburgers	1 x 115g/4oz 2 x 115g/4oz 3 x 115g/4oz 4 x 115g/4oz	HIGH	Ideally cook in a preheated browning dish. If this isn't possible then cook on a roasting rack and increase the times slightly. Microwave for 2½–3 minutes for 1; 3½–4 minutes for 2; 4½–5 minutes for 3; and 5–5½ minutes for 4, turning over once halfway through the cooking time. Leave to stand for 2–3 minutes before serving.
meatloaf	450g/1lb loaf	HIGH	Place your favourite 450g/1lb seasoned beef mixture in a microwaveproof loaf dish, packing in firmly and levelling the surface. Microwave for 7 minutes, allow to stand for 5 minutes, then microwave for a further 5 minutes. Leave to stand, covered with foil, for 3 minutes before serving.
steaks	2 x 225g/8oz rump, sirloin or fillet steaks 4 x 225g/8oz rump, sirloin or fillet steaks	HIGH	Cook with or without the use of a browning dish. If cooking without, then brush with a browning agent if liked prior to cooking. Place in a lightly oiled microwaveproof dish and turn over halfway through the cooking time. Microwave for 5–5½ minutes for 2 x 225g/8oz steaks; and 7½–8½ minutes for 4 x 225g/8oz steaks.

If using a browning dish then preheat first, add a little oil and brush to coat the base. Add the steaks, pressing down well. Turn the steaks over halfway through the cooking time. Microwave for 2¼–2½ minutes for 2 x 225g/8oz steaks; and 3½–4 minutes for 4 x 225g/8oz steaks. Leave to stand for 1–2 minutes before serving. |

GAMMON

braised steaks	4 x 115g/4oz steaks	HIGH	Remove the rind and scissor-snip the fat off the gammon steaks. Place in a large shallow microwaveproof dish. Add 150ml/¼ pint/⅔ cup wine, cider or fruit juice (and marinate for 1 hour if liked). Microwave for 4 minutes, rearranging once. Leave to stand, covered, for 5 minutes before serving.
raw joint	per 450g/1lb	HIGH	Place in a pierced roasting bag in a microwaveproof dish. Microwave for 12–14 minutes per 450g/1lb, turning over halfway through the cooking time. Cover with foil and leave to stand for 10 minutes before carving.

KIDNEYS

fresh lamb's, pig's or ox	115g/4oz 225g/8oz 450g/1lb	HIGH	Halve and core the kidneys. Preheat a browning dish. Add 5ml/1 tsp oil and the kidneys. Microwave for 4 minutes for 115g/4oz; 6–8 minutes for 225g/8oz; and 12–15 minutes for 450g/1lb, turning and rearranging twice. Leave to stand, covered, for 3 minutes before serving.

LAMB

roast joint	per 450g/1lb	HIGH then MEDIUM	Place the joint on a microwaveproof roasting rack or upturned saucer inside a dish and shield any thin or vulnerable areas with a little foil. Calculate the cooking time according to weight and microwave on HIGH for the first 5 minutes, then on MEDIUM for the remaining time. Turn the joint over halfway through the cooking time.

per 450g/1lb
leg joint with bone
    rare   8–10 minutes
    medium   10–12 minutes
    well done   12–14 minutes
boned leg joints
    rare   10–12 minutes
    medium   13–15 minutes
    well done   16–18 minutes
shoulder joints
    rare   7–9 minutes
    medium   9–11 minutes
    well done   11–13 minutes

chops and steaks	2 loin chops 4 loin chops 2 chump chops 4 chump chops	HIGH	Brush with a browning agent if liked, or cook in a browning dish. Microwave for 6–7 minutes for 2 loin chops; 8–9 minutes for 4 loin chops; 6–8 minutes for 2 chump chops; and 8–10 minutes for 4 chump chops, turning over halfway through the cooking time. Leave to stand for 2–3 minutes before serving.
rack	1.2kg/2–2½lb rack with 7 ribs	HIGH	Chop rack in half and place both pieces together, bones interleaved guard-of-honour style, then tie in place. Place on a microwaveproof roasting rack. Microwave for 12 minutes for rare; 13 minutes for medium; and 14½–15 minutes for well-done lamb, rotating the dish every 3 minutes. Cover with foil and leave to stand for 10 minutes before carving.

LIVER

fresh lamb's liver	450g/1lb	HIGH	Preheat a browning dish. Add 15ml/1 tbsp oil and 15g/½oz/1 tbsp butter. Add sliced, washed and dried liver, pressing down well. Microwave for 1 minute, turn over and microwave for a further 4–5 minutes, rearranging once. Leave to stand for 2 minutes before serving.

PORK

roast joint	per 450g/1lb	HIGH *or* MEDIUM	Place the joint in a microwaveproof dish on a rack if possible. Times are given for roasting on HIGH or MEDIUM. Both methods work well but the latter tends to give a crisper crackling. Turn the joint over halfway through cooking. Brown and crisp under a preheated hot grill after cooking if liked and before the standing time. Calculate the cooking time according to weight and microwave for:

per 450g/1lb
loin, leg and hand joints on bone
HIGH 8–9 minutes *or* MEDIUM 12–14 minutes
loin and leg joints (boned)
HIGH 8–10 minutes *or* MEDIUM 13–15 minutes
Cover with foil after cooking and leave to stand for 10–20 minutes before carving.

chops	2 loin chops 4 loin chops 2 chump chops 4 chump chops	HIGH	Brush with a browning agent if liked, or cook in a browning dish. Microwave for 4–5 minutes for 2 loin chops; 6–8 minutes for 4 loin chops; 8–10 minutes for 2 chump chops; and 11–13 minutes for 4 chump chops, turning over once halfway through cooking. Leave to stand for 5 minutes before serving.
pork fillet or tenderloin	350g/12oz	HIGH *then* MEDIUM	Shield the narrow, thin ends of the fillet with a little foil. Place on a microwaveproof roasting rack or upturned saucer in a dish. Microwave on HIGH for 3 minutes, then on MEDIUM for 10–15 minutes, turning over once. Leave to stand, covered with foil, for 5–10 minutes before serving.
sausages standard 50g/2oz size	2 4 8	HIGH	Prick and place on a microwaveproof roasting rack in a dish if possible. Brush with a browning agent if liked or cook in a preheated browning dish. Microwave for 2½ minutes for 2; 4 minutes for 4, and 5 minutes for 8 sausages, turning over once halfway through the cooking time. Leave to stand for 2 minutes before serving.

VEAL

roast joint	per 450g/1lb	HIGH *or* MEDIUM	Place the joint on a microwaveproof rack or upturned saucer in a dish. Times are given for cooking on HIGH or MEDIUM. Both methods work well, but the latter is ideal for less-tender cuts or large joints. Calculate the cooking time according to weight and microwave for:

per 450g/1lb
HIGH 8½–9 minutes *or* MEDIUM 11–12 minutes
Turn the joint over halfway through the cooking time. Cover with foil after cooking and leave to stand for 15–20 minutes before carving.

Beef and Mushroom Burgers.

Cooking Vegetables

ARTICHOKES globe	1 2 4	HIGH	Discard the tough, outer leaves. Snip the tops off the remaining leaves and trim the stems to the base. Wash and stand upright in a microwaveproof bowl. Pour over the water and lemon juice for 90ml/6 tbsp water and 7.5ml/1½ tsp lemon juice for 1; 120ml/4fl oz/½ cup water and 15ml/1 tbsp lemon juice for 2; and 150ml/¼ pint/⅔ cup water and 30ml/2 tbsp lemon juice for 4. Cover and microwave for 5–6 minutes for 1; 10–11 minutes for 2; and 15–18 minutes for 4, basting and rearranging twice. Leave to stand for 5 minutes before serving.
Jerusalem	450g/1lb	HIGH	Peel and cut into even-size pieces. Place in a microwaveproof bowl with 60ml/4 tbsp water or 25g/1oz/2 tbsp butter. Cover and microwave for 8–10 minutes, stirring once. Leave to stand, covered, for 3–5 minutes before serving.
ASPARAGUS fresh whole spears	450g/1lb	HIGH	Prepare and arrange in a shallow microwaveproof dish with pointed tops to the centre. Add 120ml/4fl oz/½ cup water. Cover and microwave for 12–14 minutes, rearranging the spears half way through the time but still keeping the tips to the centre of the dish.
fresh cut spears	450g/1lb	HIGH	Prepare and place in a large shallow microwaveproof dish. Add 120ml/4fl oz/½ cup water. Cover and microwave for 9–11 minutes, rearranging once. Leave to stand, covered, for 5 minutes before serving.
AUBERGINES fresh cubes	450g/1lb	HIGH	Cut unpeeled aubergine into 2cm/¾in cubes. Place in a microwaveproof bowl with 25g/1oz/2 tbsp butter. Cover and microwave for 7–10 minutes, stirring every 3 minutes. Leave to stand, covered, for 4 minutes. Season *after* cooking.
fresh whole	225g/8oz 2 x 225g/8oz	HIGH	Peel off stalks, rinse and dry. Brush with a little oil and prick. Place on kitchen paper and microwave for 3–4 minutes for 1 aubergine; 4–6 minutes for 2, turning over once. Leave to stand for 4 minutes. Scoop out flesh and use as required.
BEANS fresh green	225g/8oz whole 450g/1lb whole 225g/8oz cut 450g/1lb cut	HIGH	Place whole or cut beans in a microwaveproof bowl and add 30ml/2 tbsp water. Cover and microwave for 8–10 minutes for 225g/8oz whole beans; 15–18 minutes for 450g/1lb whole beans; 7–9 minutes for 225g/8oz cut beans; and 12–15 minutes for 450g/1lb cut beans, stirring once. Leave to stand, covered, for 2–3 minutes before serving.
fresh baby green whole or French whole	225g/8oz 450g/1lb	HIGH	Place in a microwaveproof bowl with 30ml/2 tbsp water. Cover and microwave for 7–9 minutes for 225g/8oz; 12–15 minutes for 450g/1lb, stirring 3 times. Leave to stand, covered, for 2–3 minutes, before serving.
fresh sliced runner beans	225g/8oz 450g/1lb	HIGH	Place in a microwaveproof bowl with 30ml/2 tbsp water. Cover and microwave for 7–9 minutes for 225g/8oz; 12–15 minutes for 450g/1lb, stirring 3–4 times. Leave to stand, covered, for 2–3 minutes before serving.
fresh shelled broad beans	225g/8oz 450g/1lb	HIGH	Place in a microwaveproof bowl and add the water: 75ml/5 tbsp for 225g/8oz beans; and 120ml/4fl oz/½ cup for 450g/1lb beans. Cover and microwave for 5–7 minutes for 225g/8oz; 6–10 minutes for 450g/1lb, stirring once. Leave to stand, covered, for 2–3 minutes before serving.
BEETROOT fresh	4 medium	HIGH	Wash the beetroot and pierce the skin with a fork but do not peel. Place in a shallow microwaveproof dish with 60ml/4 tbsp water. Cover loosely and microwave for 14–16 minutes, rearranging twice. Leave to stand, covered, for 5 minutes before removing skins to serve or use.

BROCCOLI

fresh spears	225g/8oz 450g/1lb	HIGH	Place spears in a large shallow microwaveproof dish with tender heads to centre of dish. Add 60ml/4 tbsp water. Cover and microwave for 4–5 minutes for 225g/8oz; 8–9 minutes for 450g/1lb, rotating the dish once. Leave to stand, covered, for 2–4 minutes before serving.
fresh pieces	225g/8oz 450g/1lb	HIGH	Cut into 2.5cm/1in pieces. Place in a microwaveproof bowl with 60ml/4 tbsp water. Cover and microwave for 4½–5 minutes for 225g/8oz; 8½–9½ minutes for 450g/1lb, stirring once. Leave to stand, covered, for 3–5 minutes before serving.

BRUSSELS SPROUTS

fresh	450g/1lb 900g/2lb	HIGH	Remove outer leaves, trim and cross-cut base. Place in a microwaveproof dish and add water: 60ml/4 tbsp for 450g/1lb; 120ml/4/fl oz/½ cup for 900g/2lb. Cover and microwave for 6–7 minutes for 450g/1lb; 12–14 minute for 900g/2lb, stirring once. Leave to stand, covered, for 3–5 minutes before serving.

CABBAGE

fresh	225g/8oz 450g/1lb	HIGH	Core and shred, and place in a large microwaveproof dish. Add water: 60ml/4 tbsp for 225g/8oz; 120ml/4/fl oz/½ cup for 450g/1lb. Cover and microwave for 7–9 minutes for 225g/8oz; 9–11 minutes for 450g/1lb, stirring once. Leave to stand, covered, for 2 minutes before serving.

CARROTS

fresh baby whole and sliced	450g/1lb whole 450g/1lb sliced	HIGH	Place in a microwaveproof dish with 60ml/4 tbsp water. Cover and microwave for 12–14 minutes for whole; 10–12 minutes for sliced. Leave to stand, covered, for 3–5 minutes before serving.

CAULIFLOWER

fresh whole	675g/1½lb	MEDIUM	Trim but leave whole, and place floret-side down in a microwaveproof dish with 250ml/8fl oz/1 cup water. Cover and microwave for 16–17 minutes, turning over once. Leave to stand for 3–5 minutes before serving.
fresh florets	225g/8oz 450g/1lb	HIGH	Place in a microwaveproof dish with water: 45ml/3 tbsp for 225g/8oz; 60ml/4 tbsp for 450g/1lb. Cover and microwave for 7–8 minutes for 225g/8oz; 10–12 minutes for 450g/1lb, stirring once. Leave to stand for 3 minutes before serving.

CELERY

fresh sliced	1 head (about 9 stalks)	HIGH	Slice into 5mm/¼in pieces and place in a shallow microwaveproof dish with 30ml/2 tbsp water and 25g/1oz/2 tbsp butter. Cover and microwave for 5–6 minutes, stirring once. Leave to stand, covered, for 3 minutes before serving.
fresh celery hearts	4 hearts	HIGH	Halve each celery heart lengthways and place in a shallow microwaveproof dish. Add 30ml/2 tbsp water and a knob of butter if liked. Cover and microwave for 4½–5 minutes, turning once. Leave to stand, covered, for 3 minutes before serving.

CHINESE CABBAGE

fresh	450g/1lb	HIGH	Slice and place in a large microwaveproof dish. Add 30–45ml/2–3 tbsp water. Cover and microwave for 6–8 minutes, stirring once. Leave to stand, covered, for 3–5 minutes. Season after cooking.

COURGETTES

fresh	225g/8oz 450g/1lb	HIGH	Top and tail, and slice thinly. Place in a microwaveproof dish with butter: 25g/1oz/2 tbsp for 225g/8oz; 40g/1½oz/3 tbsp for 450g/1lb. Cover loosely and microwave for 4–6½ minutes for 225g/8oz; 6–8 minutes for 450g/1lb, stirring once. Leave to stand, covered, for 2–3 minutes before serving.

CURLY KALE fresh	450g/1lb	HIGH	Remove the thick stalk and stems, then shred. Place in a microwaveproof bowl with 150ml/¼ pint/⅔ cup water. Cover and microwave for 15–17 minutes, stirring every 5 minutes. Leave to stand for 2 minutes before serving.
FENNEL fresh sliced	450g/1lb	HIGH	Place in a microwaveproof bowl with 45ml/3 tbsp water. Cover and microwave for 9–10 minutes, stirring once. Leave to stand, covered, for 2–3 minutes before serving.
KOHLRABI fresh sliced	450g/1lb 900g/2lb	HIGH	Trim away the root ends and stems, scrub and peel the bulb and cut into 5mm/¼in slices. Place in a microwaveproof bowl with water: 45ml/3 tbsp for 450g/1lb; and 75ml/5 tbsp for 900g/2lb. Cover and microwave for 5–6 minutes for 450g/1lb; 9–11 minutes for 900g/2lb, stirring twice. Leave to stand, covered, for 3–4 minutes. Drain to serve.
LEEKS fresh whole	450g/1lb 900g/2lb	HIGH	Trim and slice from the top of the white to the green leaves in 2–3 places. Wash thoroughly and place in a microwaveproof dish with water: 45ml/3 tbsp for 450g/1lb; and 75ml/5 tbsp for 900g/2lb. Cover and microwave for 3–5 minutes for 450g/1lb; 6–8 minutes for 900g/2lb, rearranging twice. Leave to stand, covered, for 3–5 minutes before serving.
fresh sliced	450g/1lb	HIGH	Place in a microwaveproof dish with 45ml/3 tbsp water. Cover and microwave for 8–10 minutes, stirring once. Leave to stand, covered, for 2–3 minutes before serving.
MANGETOUTS fresh	115g/4oz 225g/8oz	HIGH	Trim and place in a microwaveproof bowl with water: 15ml/1 tbsp for 115g/4oz; 30ml/2 tbsp for 225g/8oz. Cover and microwave for 3–4 minutes for 115g/4oz; and 4–5 minutes for 225g/8oz, stirring once. Leave to stand, covered, for 2 minutes before serving.
MARROW fresh	450g/1lb	HIGH	Peel, remove seeds and cut into small neat dice. Place in a microwaveproof dish without water. Cover loosely and microwave for 7–10 minutes, stirring once. Leave to stand, covered, for 2–3 minutes before serving.
MUSHROOMS fresh whole	225g/8oz 450g/1lb	HIGH	Trim and wipe mushrooms. Place in a microwaveproof dish with water or butter: 25g/1oz/2 tbsp butter or 30ml/2 tbsp water for 225g/8oz mushrooms; and 40g/1½oz/3 tbsp butter or 45ml/3 tbsp water for 450g/1lb mushrooms. Cover and microwave for 3–4 minutes for 225g/8oz; and 4–5 minutes for 450g/1lb, stirring twice. Leave to stand for 1–2 minutes before serving. Season after cooking.
fresh sliced	225g/8oz 450g/1lb	HIGH	As above but microwave for 2–3 minutes for 225g/8oz mushrooms; and 3–4 minutes for 450g/1lb mushrooms.
OKRA fresh	450g/1lb	HIGH	Top and tail, and sprinkle lightly with salt. Leave to drain for 30 minutes. Rinse and place in a microwaveproof dish with 30ml/2 tbsp water or 25g/1oz/2 tbsp butter. Cover and microwave for 8–10 minutes, stirring once. Leave to stand, covered, for 3 minutes before serving.
ONIONS fresh whole	450g/1lb or 4 medium	HIGH	Peel and place in a microwaveproof dish. Cover and microwave for 10–12 minutes, rearranging and rotating once. Leave to stand, covered, for 2 minutes before serving.
fresh sliced	450g/1lb	HIGH	Peel and cut into thin wedges or slices. Place in a microwaveproof dish with 25g/1oz/2 tbsp butter and 30ml/2 tbsp water. Cover loosely and microwave for 7–10 minutes, stirring once. Leave to stand, covered, for 5 minutes before serving.

PAK CHOI (or bok choy cabbage)	450g/1lb	HIGH		Slice stalks and leaves and place in a large microwaveproof dish. Add 30ml/ 2 tbsp water and microwave for 6–8 minutes, stirring once. Leave to stand for 3–5 minutes before serving.
PARSNIPS fresh whole	450g/1lb	HIGH		Peel and prick with a fork. Arrange in a microwaveproof dish with tapered ends to the centre. Dot with 15g/½oz/1 tbsp butter and add 45ml/3 tbsp water and 15ml/1 tbsp lemon juice. Cover and microwave for 9–12 minutes, rearranging once. Leave to stand, covered, for 3 minutes before serving.
fresh slices	450g/1lb	HIGH		Peel and slice. Place in a microwaveproof dish with 15g/½oz/1 tbsp butter, 45ml/3 tbsp water and 15ml/1 tbsp lemon juice. Cover and microwave for 9–12 minutes, stirring twice. Leave to stand, covered, for 3 minutes before serving.
PEAS fresh	115g/4oz 225g/8oz 450g/1lb	HIGH		Place shelled peas in a microwaveproof bowl with butter and water: 15g/½oz/ 1 tbsp butter and 10ml/2 tsp water for 115g/4oz peas; 25g/1oz/2 tbsp butter and 15ml/1 tbsp water for 225g/8oz peas; and 50g/2oz/4 tbsp butter and 30ml/2 tbsp water for 450g/1lb peas. Cover and microwave for 3 minutes for 115g/4oz; 4–5 minutes for 225g/8oz; and 6–8 minutes for 450g/1lb, stirring once. Leave to stand, covered, for 3–5 minutes before serving.
POTATOES mashed or creamed	900g/2lb	HIGH		Peel and cut into 1.5cm/½in cubes. Place in a microwaveproof bowl with 75ml/ 5 tbsp water. Cover and microwave for 11–13 minutes, stirring once. Leave to stand, covered, for 5 minutes. Drain and mash with butter and seasoning to taste.
new potatoes or old, peeled and quartered	450g/1lb	HIGH		Scrub and scrape new potatoes if liked. Peel and quarter old potatoes. Place in a microwaveproof dish with 60ml/4 tbsp water. Cover and microwave for 7–10 minutes for new; and 6–8 minutes for old, stirring once. Leave to stand, covered, for 5 minutes before serving.
jacket baked	175g/6oz 2 x 175g/6oz 3 x 175g/6oz 4 x 175g/6oz	HIGH		Scrub and prick the skin. Place on a double sheet of absorbent kitchen paper. Microwave for 4–6 minutes for 1; 6–8 minutes for 2; 8–12 minutes for 3; 12–15 minutes for 4, turning over once. If cooking more than 2 potatoes, arrange in a ring pattern. Leave to stand for 5 minutes, before serving.
PUMPKIN fresh	450g/1lb	HIGH		Remove the skin, seeds and membrane and cut into 2.5cm/1in cubes. Place in a microwaveproof dish with 15g/½oz/1 tbsp butter. Cover and microwave for 4–6 minutes, stirring twice. Leave to stand for 3 minutes, then season to serve plain, or mash with cream and herbs.
SPINACH fresh	450g/1lb	HIGH		Chop or shred and rinse. Place in a microwaveproof bowl without any extra water. Cover and microwave for 6–8 minutes, stirring once. Leave to stand for 2 minutes before serving. Season after cooking.
SQUASH fresh	450g/1lb	HIGH		Pierce whole squash with a knife several times. Microwave for 3–5 minutes per 450g/1lb until the flesh pierces easily with a skewer. Leave to stand for 5 minutes. Halve, scoop out the seeds and fibres and discard. Serve fresh in chunks or mash with butter.
SWEDES fresh	450g/1lb	HIGH		Peel and cut into 1cm/½in cubes. Place in a microwaveproof bowl with 15g/½oz/1 tbsp butter and 30ml/2 tbsp water. Cover and microwave for 10–12 minutes, stirring twice. Leave to stand, covered, for 4 minutes. Drain to serve.

SWEETCORN

corn on the cob, fresh husked	1 x 175g/6oz 2 x 175g/6oz 3 x 175g/6oz 4 x 175g/6oz	HIGH	Wrap individually in clear film or place in a microwaveproof dish with 60ml/4 tbsp water and cover. Place or arrange evenly in the oven and microwave for 3–4 minutes for 1; 5–6 minutes for 2; 7–8 minutes for 3; and 9–10 minutes for 4, rotating and rearranging once. Leave to stand, covered, for 3–5 minutes before serving.

SWEET POTATOES

fresh	450g/1lb, whole 450g/1lb, cubed	HIGH	If cooking whole, prick the skins and place on absorbent kitchen paper. Microwave for 7–9 minutes, turning twice. Allow to cool for handling and peel away the skins to serve. To cook cubes, place in a microwaveproof bowl with 45ml/3 tbsp water. Cover and microwave for 6–8 minutes, stirring twice. Drain and toss with butter and seasoning. Leave to stand for 2 minutes before serving.

SWISS CHARD

fresh	450g/1lb	HIGH	Remove and discard the thick stalk and shred the leaves. Place in a microwaveproof dish with 150ml/¼ pint/⅔ cup water. Cover and microwave for 5½–6½ minutes, stirring every 3 minutes. Leave to stand for 2 minutes before serving. Season after cooking.

TOMATOES

whole and halves	1 medium 4 medium 4 large (beef)	HIGH	Prick whole and/or halved tomatoes, arrange in a circle on a plate, cut-sides up. Dot with butter and season to taste. Microwave for ½ minute for 1 medium; 2–2½ minutes for 4 medium; and 3½–4 minutes for 4 large (beef) tomatoes, according to size and ripeness. Leave to stand for 1–2 minutes before serving.

TURNIPS

whole	450g/1lb	HIGH	Choose only small to medium turnips. Peel and prick with a fork. Arrange in a ring pattern in a shallow microwaveproof dish. Dot with 15g/½oz/1 tbsp butter and add 45ml/3 tbsp water. Cover and microwave for 14–16 minutes, rearranging once. Leave to stand, covered, for 3 minutes before serving.
sliced or cubed	450g/1lb	HIGH	Place slices or cubes in a microwaveproof dish with 15g/½oz/1 tbsp butter and 45ml/3 tbsp water. Cover and microwave for 11–12 minutes for slices; and 12–14 minutes for cubes. Leave to stand, covered, for 3 minutes before serving.

Broccoli and Chestnut Terrine.

Middle-Eastern Vegetable Stew.

Cooking Frozen Vegetables

ASPARAGUS
frozen whole spears	450g/1lb	HIGH	Place in a microwaveproof dish with 120ml/4fl oz/½ cup water. Cover and microwave for 9–12 minutes, rearranging once. Leave to stand for 5 minutes before serving.

BEANS
frozen green beans	225g/8oz whole 450g/1lb whole 225g/8oz cut 450g/1lb cut	HIGH	Place in a microwaveproof bowl with water, cover and microwave with 30ml/2tbsp water for 9–10 minutes for 225g/8oz whole beans; 60ml/4 tbsp water and 14–15 minutes for 450g/1lb whole beans; 30ml/2 tbsp water and 6–7 minutes for 225g/8oz cut beans; and 60ml/4 tbsp water and 10–12 minutes for 450g/1lb cut beans, stirring once. Leave to stand, covered, for 2–3 minutes before serving.
frozen baby green or French whole beans	225g/8oz 450g/1lb	HIGH	Place in a microwaveproof bowl with water, cover and microwave with 30ml/ 2 tbsp water for 8–9 minutes for 225g/8oz beans; and 60ml/4 tbsp water and 13–15 minutes for 450g/1lb beans, stirring 3 times. Leave to stand, covered, for 2–3 minutes before serving.
frozen sliced runner beans	225g/8oz 450g/1lb	HIGH	Place in a microwaveproof bowl with water, cover and microwave with 30ml/ 2 tbsp water for 6–7 minutes for 225g/8oz beans; and 60ml/4 tbsp water and 10–12 minutes for 450g/1lb beans, stirring twice. Leave to stand, covered, for 2–3 minutes before serving.
frozen shelled broad beans	225g/8oz 450g/1lb	HIGH	Place in a microwaveproof bowl with water, cover and microwave with 60ml/ 4 tbsp water for 6–7 minutes for 225g/8oz beans; and 120ml/4½fl oz/½ cup and 10–11 minutes for 450g/1lb beans, stirring twice. Leave to stand, covered, for 2–3 minutes before serving.

BROCCOLI
frozen spears	450g/1lb	HIGH	Place in a microwaveproof dish with 60ml/4 tbsp water. Cover and microwave for 13–14 minutes, stirring once. Leave to stand, covered, for 2–3 minutes before serving.

BRUSSEL SPROUTS
frozen	450g/1lb	HIGH	Place in a microwaveproof dish with 30ml/2 tbsp water. Cover and microwave for 10–11 minutes, stirring once. Leave to stand, covered, for 3–5 minutes before serving.

CABBAGE
frozen	225g/8oz 450g/1lb	HIGH	Place in a large microwaveproof dish with water, cover and microwave with 60ml/4 tbsp water for 6–8 minutes for 225g/8oz; and 120ml/4½fl oz/½ cup water and 8–10 minutes for 450g/1lb, stirring once. Leave to stand, covered, for 2 minutes before serving.

CARROTS
frozen whole and sliced	450g/1lb whole 450g/1lb sliced	HIGH	Place in a microwaveproof dish with water. Cover and microwave with 30ml/2 tbsp water for 10–12 minutes for whole carrots; and 30ml/2 tbsp water and 8–10 minutes for sliced carrots, stirring once. Leave to stand, covered, for 2–3 minutes before serving.

CAULIFLOWER
frozen florets	450g/1lb	HIGH	Place in a microwaveproof dish with 60ml/4 tbsp water. Cover and microwave for 8–9 minutes, stirring once. Leave to stand, covered, for 2–3 minutes before serving.

COURGETTES
frozen sliced	450g/1lb	HIGH	Place in a shallow microwaveproof dish with 40g/1½oz/3 tbsp butter if liked. Cover loosely and microwave for 7–8 minutes, stirring once. Leave to stand, covered, for 2–3 minutes before serving.

LEEKS
frozen sliced | 450g/1lb | HIGH | Place in a microwaveproof dish with 45ml/3 tbsp water. Cover and microwave for 11–12 minutes, stirring once. Leave to stand, covered, for 2–3 minutes before serving.

MANGETOUTS
frozen | 225g/8oz | HIGH | Place in a microwaveproof dish with 30ml/2 tbsp water. Cover and microwave for 3–4 minutes, stirring once. Leave to stand, covered, for 2–3 minutes before serving.

MIXED VEGETABLES
frozen | 225g/8oz 450g/1lb | HIGH | Place in a microwaveproof dish with water. Cover and microwave with 30ml/2 tbsp water for 4–5 minutes for 225g/8oz; and 30ml/2 tbsp water and 7–8 minutes for 450g/1lb, stirring once. Leave to stand, covered, for 2 minutes before serving.

MUSHROOMS
frozen whole button | 115g/4oz 225g/8oz | HIGH | Place in a shallow microwaveproof dish with a knob of butter. Cover and microwave for 3–4 minutes for 115g/4oz; and 5–6 minutes for 225g/8oz, stirring twice. Leave to stand, covered, for 1–2 minutes. Season to taste to serve.

PARSNIPS
frozen whole | 450g/1lb | HIGH | Arrange in a shallow microwaveproof dish with tapered ends to centre. Cover and microwave for 9–10 minutes, rearranging once. Toss in butter and seasonings to serve. Leave to stand, covered, for 2–3 minutes before serving.

PEAS
frozen | 225g/8oz 450g/1lb | HIGH | Place in a microwaveproof dish with water. Cover and microwave with 30ml/2 tbsp water for 4–6 minutes for 225g/8oz; and 60ml/4 tbsp water and 6–8 minutes for 450g/1lb, stirring once. Leave to stand, covered, for 3 minutes.

SPINACH
frozen | 275g/10oz packet | HIGH | Place in a microwaveproof dish. Cover and microwave for 7–9 minutes, stirring twice to break up during cooking. Season *after* cooking.

SWEDES
frozen cubed swede | 450g/1lb | HIGH | Place in a microwaveproof dish, cover and microwave for 8–10 minutes, stirring twice. Leave to stand, covered, for 2–3 minutes. Toss in butter and seasonings or mash with same to a purée.

SWEETCORN
frozen sweetcorn kernels | 450g/1lb | HIGH | Place in a microwaveproof dish with 60ml/4 tbsp water. Cover and microwave for 7–8 minutes, stirring once. Leave to stand, covered, for 2–3 minutes before serving.

Summer Vegetable Braise.

Mixed Mushroom Ragout.

Cooking Pasta, Pulses and Grains

BARLEY pot barley	175g/6oz	HIGH *then* MEDIUM	Toast if liked before cooking. Place in a microwaveproof dish with 1 litre/ 1¾ pints/4 cups boiling water and a pinch of salt if liked. Cover loosely and microwave on HIGH for 3 minutes, then on MEDIUM for 40 minutes. Leave to stand for 5–10 minutes before fluffing with a fork to serve
BULGUR grains	225g/8oz	HIGH *then* MEDIUM	Place in a microwaveproof dish with 550ml/18fl oz/2¼ cups boiling water and a pinch of salt if liked. Cover loosely and microwave on HIGH for 3 minutes, then on MEDIUM for 9–12 minutes. Leave to stand for 5–10 minutes before fluffing with a fork to serve.
COUSCOUS pre-cooked	350g/12oz	MEDIUM	Place in a microwaveproof dish with 250ml/8fl oz/1 cup boiling water and 50g/2oz/4 tbsp butter. Cover loosely and microwave for 15 minutes. Leave to stand for 5–10 minutes before fluffing with a fork to serve.
DRIED BEANS aduki black black-eyed borlotti broad butter cannellini flageolet haricot mung pinto red kidney soya	225g/8oz	HIGH *then* MEDIUM	Soak dried beans overnight in cold water or hasten soaking by par-cooking in the microwave. Place the dried beans in a microwaveproof bowl with boiling water to cover. Cover and microwave on HIGH for 5 minutes. Leave to stand, covered, for 1½ hours before draining to cook. Place soaked or par-cooked beans in a microwaveproof dish and cover with boiling water. Cover and microwave all beans on HIGH for 10 minutes. Reduce the power to MEDIUM and microwave aduki, black-eyed, mung and pinto beans for 10–15 minutes; and black, borlotti, broad, butter, cannellini, flageolet, haricot, red kidney and soya beans for 20–25 minutes, adding extra boiling water to cover if needed. Drain to use.
DRIED CHICK- PEAS	225g/8oz	HIGH *then* MEDIUM	Soak dried peas overnight or according to packet instructions. Place soaked peas in a microwaveproof dish and cover with boiling water. Cover and microwave on HIGH for 10 minutes, then on MEDIUM for 20–25 minutes, adding extra boiling water to cover if needed. Drain to use.
DRIED WHOLE GREEN PEAS	225g/8oz	HIGH *then* MEDIUM	Soak dried peas overnight or according to packet instructions. Place soaked peas in a microwaveproof dish and cover with boiling water. Cover and microwave on HIGH for 10 minutes, then on MEDIUM for 10–15 minutes, adding extra boiling water to cover if needed. Drain to use.
DRIED SPLIT PEAS	225g/8oz	HIGH	Soak dried peas overnight or according to packet instructions. Place soaked peas in a microwaveproof dish and cover with boiling water. Cover and microwave on HIGH for 10 minutes. Drain to use.
DRIED LENTILS	225g/8oz	HIGH	Place the lentils in a microwaveproof dish with a few seasoning vegetables such as chopped onion, celery, carrot or bouquet garni and a squeeze of lemon juice. Add 900ml/1½ pints/3¾ cups boiling water or stock. Cover and microwave for 15–25 minutes, stirring once halfway through cooking. Cook for the shorter length of time if the lentils are to be served in a salad mixture or as a meal accompaniment, the longer time if the lentils are to be puréed for use.
MILLET	225g/8oz	HIGH *then* MEDIUM	Toast if liked before cooking. Place in a microwaveproof dish with 650ml/ 22fl oz/2¾ cups boiling water and a pinch of salt, if you like. Cover loosely and microwave on HIGH for 3 minutes, then on MEDIUM for 12 minutes. Leave to stand for 5–10 minutes before fluffing with a fork to serve.

OATS grains	175g/6oz	HIGH *then* MEDIUM	Toast if liked before cooking. Place in a microwaveproof dish with 750ml/ 1¼ pints/3 cups boiling water and a pinch of salt if liked. Cover loosely and microwave on HIGH for 3 minutes, then on MEDIUM for 20–22 minutes. Leave to stand for 5–10 minutes before fluffing with a fork to serve.
PASTA fresh: egg noodles spaghetti tagliatelle ravioli	225g/8oz	HIGH	Place the pasta in a large microwaveproof dish. Cover with 750ml/ 1¼ pints/3 cups boiling water and add 5ml/1 tsp oil. Cover loosely and microwave for 2–2½ minutes for egg noodles; 4–6 minutes for spaghetti; 2–3 minutes for tagliatelle; and 6–8 minutes for ravioli, stirring once halfway through the cooking time. Leave to stand for 2 minutes before draining to serve.
dried: egg noodles spaghetti tagliatelle short-cut macaroni pasta shapes ravioli	225g/8oz	HIGH	Place the pasta in a large microwaveproof dish. Add a generous 1.2 litres/ 2 pints/5 cups of boiling water and 5ml/1 tsp oil. Cover loosely and microwave: 6 minutes for egg noodles; 10–12 minutes for spaghetti; 6 minutes for tagliatelle; 10 minutes for short-cut macaroni; 10-12 minutes for pasta shapes; and 10 minutes for ravioli, stirring once halfway through the cooking time. Leave to stand for 3–5 minutes before draining to use.
RICE long grain white	115g/4oz 225g/8oz	HIGH *then* MEDIUM	Place the rice in a large microwaveproof dish. Add boiling water: 300ml/ ½ pint/1¼ cups for 115g/4oz rice; and 550ml/18fl oz/2¼ cups for 225g/8oz rice with a pinch of salt and knob of butter if liked. Cover loosely and microwave on HIGH for 3 minutes. Stir well then re-cover and microwave on MEDIUM for 12 minutes. Leave to stand, covered, for 5 minutes before fluffing with a fork to serve.
long grain brown	115g/4oz 225g/8oz	HIGH *then* MEDIUM	Place the rice in a large microwaveproof dish. Add boiling water: 300ml/ ½ pint/1¼ cups for 115g/4oz; 550ml/18fl oz/2¼ cups for 225g/8oz rice with a pinch of salt and knob of butter if liked. Cover loosely and microwave on HIGH for 3 minutes. Stir well then re-cover and microwave on MEDIUM for 25 minutes. Leave to stand, covered, for 5 minutes before fluffing with a fork to serve.
long grain and wild rice mix	400g/14oz packet	HIGH *then* MEDIUM	Place the rice mix in a microwaveproof dish with 650ml/22fl oz/2¾ cups boiling water, a pinch of salt and knob of butter if liked. Cover loosely and microwave on HIGH for 3 minutes. Stir well, re-cover and microwave on MEDIUM for 12 minutes, stirring once. Leave to stand, covered, for 5 minutes before fluffing with a fork to serve.
RYE grains	175g/6oz	HIGH *then* MEDIUM	Soak the rye grains for 6–8 hours in cold water then drain. Place in a microwaveproof dish with 750ml/1¼ pints/3 cups boiling water. Cover loosely and microwave on HIGH for 3 minutes, then on MEDIUM for 40 minutes. Leave to stand 5–10 minutes before fluffing with a fork to serve.
WHEAT grains	175g/6oz	HIGH *then* MEDIUM	Soak wheat grains for 6–8 hours in cold water then drain. Place in a microwaveproof dish with 1 litre/1¾ pints/4 cups boiling water. Cover loosely and microwave on HIGH for 3 minutes, then on MEDIUM for 40 minutes. Leave to stand 5–10 minutes before fluffing with a fork to serve.

Cooking Fruit

APPLES poached in light syrup	450g/1lb	HIGH	Peel, core and slice apples and place in a microwaveproof bowl with 300ml/ ½ pint/1¼ cups hot sugar syrup. Cover loosely and microwave for 3 minutes, stirring once. Leave to stand, covered, for 5 minutes.
	900g/2lb	HIGH	As above, but microwave for 5–6 minutes.
stewed	450g/1lb	HIGH	Peel, core and slice apples and place in a microwaveproof bowl with 115g/4oz/ ½ cup sugar. Cover loosely and microwave for 6–8 minutes, stirring once. Leave to stand, covered, for 2–3 minutes.
baked	4 large	HIGH	Wash and remove cores from the apples and score around the middle to prevent bursting. Place in a microwaveproof dish, stuff with a little dried fruit if liked. Pour 120ml/4fl oz/½ cup water around fruit and microwave for 9–10 minutes, rearranging once. Leave to stand, covered, for 3–4 minutes before serving.
APRICOTS poached in light syrup	6–8	HIGH	Skin, halve and stone, slicing if preferred. Place in a microwaveproof bowl with 300ml/½ pint/1¼ cups hot sugar syrup. Cover loosely and microwave for 3–4 minutes, stirring once. Leave to stand, covered, for 5 minutes.
stewed	6–8	HIGH	Stone and wash. Place in a microwaveproof bowl, sprinkle with 115g/4oz/ ½ cup sugar. Cover and microwave for 6–8 minutes, stirring once. Leave to stand, covered, for 5 minutes before serving.
BANANAS baked	2 large	HIGH	Peel and halve the bananas lengthways. Place in a microwaveproof dish with a little sugar and fruit juice. Microwave for 3–4 minutes, stirring or rearranging twice.
BLACKBERRIES poached in light syrup	450g/1lb	HIGH	Hull and rinse. Place in a microwaveproof bowl with 300ml/½ pint/1¼ cups hot sugar syrup. Cover loosely and microwave for 2 minutes, stirring once. Leave to stand, covered, for 5 minutes.
BLACKCURRANTS fresh	450g/1lb	HIGH	Top and tail and place in a microwaveproof dish with 115g/4oz/½ cup sugar and 30ml/2 tbsp water. Cover loosely and microwave for 5 minutes, stirring once. Leave to stand, covered, for 5 minutes.
CHERRIES poached in light syrup	450g/1lb	HIGH	Prick and stone if preferred. Place in a microwaveproof bowl with 300ml/ ½ pint/1¼ cups of hot sugar syrup. Cover loosely and microwave for 2–3 minutes, stirring once. Leave to stand, covered, for 5 minutes.
stewed	450g/1lb	HIGH	Stone, wash and place in a microwaveproof bowl with 115g/4oz/½ cup sugar and a little grated lemon rind if liked. Cover and microwave for 4–5 minutes, stirring once. Leave to stand, covered, for 3–5 minutes.
CRANBERRIES cranberry sauce	450g/1lb	HIGH	Place the cranberries, 90ml/6 tbsp water and 350g/12oz/1¾ cups sugar in a large microwaveproof bowl. Cover with vented cling film and microwave for 18–20 minutes, stirring every 6 minutes, until pulpy.
DAMSONS poached in light syrup	450g/1lb, whole or halved	HIGH	Prick whole damsons or halve and stone if preferred. Place in a microwave-proof bowl with 300ml/½ pint/1¼ cups hot sugar syrup. Cover loosely and microwave for 3 minutes for whole damsons; 2 minutes for halves, stirring once. Leave to stand, covered, for 5 minutes.

stewed	450g/1lb	HIGH	Stone and wash. Place in a microwaveproof bowl with 115g/4oz/½ cup sugar and a little grated lemon rind if liked. Cover and microwave for 4–5 minutes, stirring once. Leave to stand, covered, for 3–5 minutes.
GOOSEBERRIES fresh	450g/1lb	HIGH	Top and tail and place in a microwaveproof bowl with 30ml/2 tbsp water. Cover and microwave for 4–6 minutes. Stir in 115g/4oz/½ cup sugar and leave to stand, covered, for 5 minutes.
GREENGAGES poached in light syrup	450g/1lb whole or halved	HIGH	Prick whole greengages or halve and stone if preferred. Place in a microwaveproof bowl with 300ml/½ pint/1¼ cups hot sugar syrup. Cover loosely and microwave for 3 minutes for whole greengages; 2 minutes for halves, stirring once. Leave to stand, covered, for 5 minutes.
stewed	450g/1lb		Stone and wash. Place in a microwaveproof bowl with 115g/4oz/½ cup sugar and a little grated lemon rind if liked. Cover and microwave for 4–5 minutes, stirring once. Leave to stand, covered, for 3–5 minutes.
NECTARINES poached in light syrup	8	HIGH	Skin and prick thoroughly. Place in a microwaveproof bowl with 300ml/½ pint/1¼ cups hot sugar syrup and a dash of lemon juice. Cover loosely and microwave for 6 minutes, stirring once. Leave to stand, covered, for 5 minutes.
stewed	4 medium	HIGH	Stone, wash and slice. Place in a microwaveproof bowl with 115g/4oz/½ cup sugar. Cover and microwave for 4–5 minutes, stirring once. Leave to stand, covered, for 5 minutes.
ORANGES poached in light syrup	4	HIGH	Peel if preferred, or scrub the skin, then finely slice. Place in a microwaveproof bowl with 300ml/½ pint/1¼ cups hot sugar syrup. Cover loosely and microwave for 3 minutes, stirring once. Leave to stand, covered, for 5 minutes.
PEACHES poached in light syrup	4 whole or sliced	HIGH	Skin and prick thoroughly or skin, stone and slice. Place in a microwaveproof bowl with 300ml/½ pint/1¼ cups hot sugar syrup. Cover loosely and microwave for 4 minutes for whole peaches; 3 minutes for slices, stirring once. Leave to stand, covered, for 5 minutes.
stewed	4 medium	HIGH	Stone, wash and slice. Place in a microwaveproof bowl with 115g/4oz/½ cup sugar. Cover and microwave for 4–5 minutes, stirring once. Leave to stand, covered, for 5 minutes.
PEARS poached in light syrup	900g/2lb whole dessert 900g/2lb whole cooking 900g/2lb halved dessert	HIGH	Peel and prick if kept whole, or halve and core. Place in a microwaveproof bowl with 300ml/½ pint/1¼ cups hot sugar syrup. Cover loosely and microwave for 5 minutes for whole dessert pears; 10 minutes for whole cooking pears: and 3 minutes for halved dessert pears, stirring once. Leave to stand, covered, for 5 minutes.
stewed	6 medium	HIGH	Peel, halve and core. Dissolve 75g/3oz/⅓ cup sugar in a little water and pour over the pears. Cover loosely and microwave for 8–10 minutes, stirring once. Leave to stand, covered, for 5 minutes.
PINEAPPLE poached in light syrup	900g/2lb	HIGH	Peel, core and cut into bite-size pieces. Place in a microwaveproof bowl with 300ml/½ pint/1¼ cups hot sugar syrup. Cover loosely and microwave for 5 minutes, stirring once. Leave to stand, covered, for 5 minutes.

PLUMS

poached in light syrup	450g/1lb whole or halved	HIGH	Prick if kept whole or halve and stone. Place in a microwaveproof bowl with 300ml/½ pint/1¼ cups hot sugar syrup. Cover loosely and microwave for 3 minutes for whole plums; 2 minutes for halved, stirring once. Leave to stand, covered, for 5 minutes.
stewed	450g/1lb	HIGH	Stone and wash. Place in a microwaveproof bowl with 115g/4oz/½ cup sugar and a little grated lemon rind if liked. Cover and microwave for 4–5 minutes, stirring once. Leave to stand, covered, for 3–5 minutes.

RASPBERRIES

poached in light syrup	450g/1lb	HIGH	Hull and rinse. Place in a microwaveproof bowl with 300ml/½ pint/1¼ cups hot sugar syrup. Cover loosely and microwave for 2 minutes, stirring once. Leave to stand, covered, for 5 minutes.

REDCURRANTS

fresh	450g/1lb	HIGH	Top and tail and place in a microwaveproof bowl with 115g/4oz/½ cup sugar and 30ml/2 tbsp water. Cover loosely and microwave for 5 minutes, stirring once. Leave to stand for 5 minutes.

RHUBARB

fresh	350g/12oz	HIGH	Cut into 2.5cm/1in lengths. Place in a microwaveproof bowl with 30ml/2 tbsp water. Cover loosely and microwave for 6–7 minutes, stirring once. Stir in 115g/4oz/½ cup sugar and 5ml/1 tsp lemon juice. Leave to stand, covered, for 2–3 minutes.
poached in light syrup	450g/1lb	HIGH	Cut into 2.5cm/1in lengths. Place in a microwaveproof bowl with 300ml/½ pint/1¼ cups hot sugar syrup. Cover loosely and microwave for 4 minutes, stirring once. Leave to stand, covered, for 5 minutes.

STRAWBERRIES

poached in light syrup	450g/1lb	HIGH	Hull and rinse. Place in a microwaveproof bowl with 300ml/½ pint/1¼ cups hot sugar syrup. Cover loosely and microwave for 2 minutes, stirring once. Leave to stand, covered, for 5 minutes.

SUGAR SYRUP

To make sugar syrup for poaching fruits: place 115g/4oz/½ cup sugar and 300ml/½ pint/1¼ cups water in a microwaveproof jug. Microwave on HIGH for 4–5 minutes, stirring 3 times. Use as required. Makes 300ml/½ pint/1¼ cups.

Plum and Walnut Crumble.

Baked Apples with Apricots.

Defrosting Fish and Shellfish

COD frozen steaks	1 x 225g/8oz 2 x 225g/8oz 4 x 225g/8oz	DEFROST	To defrost, place in a microwaveproof dish, cover and microwave for 2–2 ½ minutes for 1 steak; 3–4 minutes for 2 steaks; and 6–7 minutes for 4 steaks, turning over or rearranging once. Leave to stand, covered, for 10 minutes before using.
frozen fillets	450g/1lb	DEFROST	To defrost, place in a microwaveproof dish with the thicker portions to the outer edge. Cover and microwave for 7–8 minutes, rearranging once. Leave to stand for 5 minutes before using.
CRABMEAT frozen	225g/8oz	DEFROST	Leave in wrappings. Microwave for 4 minutes, turning over once. Leave to stand for 2 minutes, then flake to use.
FISHCAKES frozen	4 x 75g/3oz	DEFROST	To defrost, unwrap and place in a shallow microwaveproof dish. Cover and microwave for 5–6½ minutes, rearranging once. Leave to stand for 2 minutes before cooking.
HADDOCK frozen steaks	1 x 225g/8oz 2 x 225g/8oz 4 x 225g/8oz	DEFROST	To defrost, place in a microwaveproof dish, cover and microwave for 2–2½ minutes for 1 steak; 3–4 minutes for 2 steaks; and 6–7 minutes for 4 steaks, turning over or rearranging once. Leave to stand for 10 minutes before using.
frozen fillets	450g/1lb	DEFROST	To defrost, place in a microwaveproof dish with the thicker portions to the outer edge. Cover and microwave for 7–8 minutes, rearranging once. Leave to stand for 5 minutes before using.
HALIBUT frozen steaks	1 x 225g/8oz 2 x 225g/8oz 4 x 225g/8oz	DEFROST	To defrost, place in a microwaveproof dish, cover and microwave for 2–2½ minutes for 1 steak; 3–4 minutes for 2 steaks; and 6–7 minutes for 4 steaks, turning over or rearranging once. Leave to stand for 10 minutes before using.
HERRING frozen whole	per 450g/1lb	DEFROST	To defrost, place in a shallow microwaveproof dish and microwave for 5–7 minutes per 450g/1lb, turning over once. Leave to stand for 10 minutes before using.
KIPPERS frozen fillets	175g/6oz boil-in-the-bag	HIGH	To defrost *and* cook, place the frozen boil-in-the-bag on a plate and snip a couple of vents in the bag. Microwave for 5–6 minutes, turning over once. Leave to stand for 2–3 minutes before serving.
LOBSTER frozen whole cooked	per 450g/1lb	DEFROST	To defrost, place in a microwaveproof dish, cover and microwave for 12–15 minutes per 450g/1lb, giving the dish a quarter turn every 2 minutes and turning over after 6 minutes. Leave to stand for 5 minutes before serving.
MACKEREL frozen whole	per 450g/1lb	DEFROST	To defrost, place in a shallow microwaveproof dish and microwave for 5–7 minutes per 450g/1lb, turning over once. Leave to stand for 10 minutes before using.
MUSSELS frozen cooked shelled	225g/8oz	DEFROST	To defrost, spread the mussels out on a plate in a single layer. Microwave for 3½–4 minutes, stirring to rearrange once. Leave to stand for 2 minutes before using.
PLAICE frozen fillets	450g/1lb	DEFROST	To defrost, place in a microwaveproof dish with the thicker portions to the outer edge. Cover and microwave for 7–8 minutes, rearranging once. Leave to stand for 5 minutes before using.

frozen whole	1 x 275g/10oz 2 x 275g/10oz	DEFROST	To defrost, place on a plate, cover and microwave for 4–6 minutes for 1 plaice; and 10–12 minutes for 2 plaice, shielding the tail end with a little foil halfway through cooking if necessary. Leave to stand for 5 minutes before using.
PRAWNS AND SHRIMPS frozen cooked	450g/1lb	DEFROST	To defrost, place in a microwaveproof dish and microwave for 7–8 minutes, stirring twice. Leave to stand for 2–3 minutes before using.
RED OR GREY MULLET frozen whole	2 x 200–250g/7–9oz 4 x 200–250g/7–9oz	DEFROST	To defrost, place in a shallow microwaveproof dish and microwave for 9–11 minutes for 2 whole fish; and 19–21 minutes for 4 whole fish, turning or rearranging twice. Leave to stand for 5 minutes before using.
RED SNAPPER frozen whole	450–550g/1–1¼lb	MEDIUM	To defrost individually (for best results), place in a shallow microwaveproof dish, cover and microwave for 2½–3½ minutes, turning over once. Rinse in cold water then pat dry. Leave to stand for 2–3 minutes before using.
SALMON AND SALMON TROUT frozen steaks	2 x 225g/8oz 4 x 225g/8oz 4 x 175g/6oz	DEFROST	To defrost, place in a shallow microwaveproof dish, cover and microwave for 4–5 minutes for 2 x 225g/8oz steaks; 10–12 minutes for 4 x 225g/8oz steaks; and 10 minutes for 4 x 175g/6oz steaks, turning over and rearranging once. Leave to stand, covered, for 5–10 minutes before using.
frozen whole salmon or salmon trout	450g/1lb 900g/2lb 1.5kg/3–3½lb 1.75kg/4–4½lb	DEFROST	To defrost, place in a shallow microwaveproof dish, cover and microwave for 6–8 minutes for a 450g/1lb fish; 12–16 minutes for a 900g/2lb fish; 18–20 minutes for a 1.5kg/3–3½lb fish; and 22–24 minutes for a 1.75kg/4–4½lb fish, turning over and rotating the dish twice. Shield the head and tail with a little foil as necessary. Leave to stand, covered, for 5–10 minutes before using.
SCALLOPS frozen	350g/12oz packet 450g/1lb	DEFROST	To defrost, place in a microwaveproof bowl, cover and microwave for 6–8 minutes for 350g/12oz; and 7½–10 minutes for 450g/1lb, stirring and breaking apart twice. Leave to stand, covered, for 5 minutes before using.
SCAMPI frozen cooked	450g/1lb	DEFROST	To defrost, place in a shallow microwaveproof dish and microwave for 7–8 minutes, stirring twice. Leave to stand, covered, for 5 minutes before using.
SMOKED HADDOCK frozen fillets	175g/6oz boil-in-the-bag	HIGH	To defrost *and* cook, place bag on a plate and snip a couple of vent holes. Microwave for 5–6 minutes, turning over once. Leave to stand for 2–3 minutes before using.
SMOKED SALMON frozen sliced	90–115g/3–4oz packet	DEFROST	To defrost, unwrap the salmon and separate the slices. Arrange evenly on a plate and microwave for 1½–2 minutes, turning once.
SOLE frozen fillets	450g/1lb	DEFROST	To defrost, place in a microwaveproof dish with thicker portions to the outer edge. Cover and microwave for 7–8 minutes, rearranging once. Leave to stand for 5 minutes before using.
TROUT frozen whole	2 x 225–275g/8–10oz 4 x 225–275g/8–10oz	DEFROST	To defrost, place in a shallow microwaveproof dish and microwave for 9–11 minutes for 2 whole fish; and 19–21 minutes for 4 whole fish, turning or rearranging twice. Leave to stand for 5 minutes before using.
WHITING frozen fillets	450g/1lb	DEFROST	To defrost, place in a microwaveproof dish with thicker portions to the outer edge. Cover and microwave for 7–8 minutes, rearranging once. Leave to stand for 5 minutes before using.

Defrosting Poultry and Game

CHICKEN frozen quarters	2 x 225g/8oz 4 x 225g/8oz	LOW	To defrost, remove any wrappings and place in a microwaveproof dish so that the meatiest parts are to the outer edge. Microwave for 7–9 minutes for 2 x 225g/8oz quarters; and 15 minutes for 4 x 225g/8oz quarters, turning over and rearranging once. Leave to stand for 10 minutes before using.
frozen drumsticks, about 115g/4oz each	2 4 6	LOW	To defrost, remove any wrappings and place in a shallow microwaveproof dish so that the meatiest parts are to the outer edge. Microwave for 4–5 minutes for 2; 7–8 minutes for 4; and 12 minutes for 6 drumsticks, turning over and rearranging once. Leave to stand for 10 minutes before using.
frozen thighs, about 115g/4oz each	4 8	LOW	To defrost, remove any wrappings and place in a shallow microwaveproof dish so that the meatiest parts are to the outer edge. Microwave for 8 minutes for 4 thighs; and 15 minutes for 8 thighs, turning over and rearranging once. Leave to stand for 10 minutes before using.
frozen wings	450g/1lb 900g/2lb	LOW	To defrost, remove any wrappings and place in a shallow microwaveproof dish. Microwave for 8 minutes for 450g/1lb; and 15 minutes for 900g/2lb wings, turning over and rearranging twice. Leave to stand for 10 minutes before using.
frozen boneless breasts	2 x 225g/8oz 4 x 225g/8oz	LOW	To defrost, remove any wrappings and place in a shallow microwaveproof dish. Microwave for 8 minutes for 2 x 225g/8oz breasts; and 15 minutes for 4 x 225g/8oz breasts, turning over and rearranging once. Leave to stand for 10 minutes before using.
frozen whole chicken	1kg/2¼lb 1.5kg/3–3½lb 1.75kg/4–4½lb	DEFROST	To defrost, remove wrappings and place, breast-side down, on a microwaveproof rack or upturned saucer in a shallow dish. Microwave for 12–14 minutes for a 1kg/2¼lb bird; 18–22 minutes for a 1.5kg/3–3½lb bird; and 24–30 minutes for a 1.75kg/4–4½lb bird, turning over halfway through the time and shielding legs, wing tips or hot spots with foil if necessary. Leave to stand for 15 minutes before using. Remove any giblets at the end of the defrosting time.
frozen chicken livers	225g/8oz carton	DEFROST	To defrost, remove from carton and place in a microwaveproof dish. Cover and microwave for 6–8 minutes, separating livers as they soften. Leave to stand, covered, for 5 minutes before using.
DUCK frozen whole	2.25kg/5–5½lb per 450g/1lb	DEFROST	To defrost, shield the wing tips, tail end and legs with foil as necessary for half of the time. Place breast-side down in a shallow microwaveproof dish and microwave for 10 minutes; turn breast-side up and microwave for a further 15–20 minutes, rotating twice. Stand, covered, for 15 minutes before using. Alternatively, defrost for 5–6 minutes per 450g/1lb.
frozen duck portions	4 x 350–400g/ 12–14oz portions	HIGH *then* DEFROST	To defrost, place in a microwaveproof dish and microwave on HIGH for 7 minutes. Turn over, rearrange and microwave on DEFROST for 10–14 minutes. Leave to stand, covered, for 15 minutes before using.
GAME BIRDS frozen grouse, guinea fowl, partridge, pheasant, pigeon, quail and woodcock	1 x 450g/1lb 2 x 450g/1lb 1 x 900g/2lb 4 x 450g/1lb	DEFROST	To defrost, place on a plate or in a shallow microwaveproof dish, breast-side down. Cover loosely and microwave for half the recommended times: 6–7 minutes for 450g/1lb bird; 12–14 minutes for 2 x 450g/1lb birds; 12–14 minutes for 900g/2lb bird; and 24–28 minutes for 4 x 450g/1lb birds, turning breast-side up after half the time and rearranging if more than 1 bird. Allow to stand, covered, for 5–10 minutes before using.
GIBLETS frozen	1 bag from poultry bird	DEFROST	To defrost, place in a microwaveproof bowl, cover and microwave for 2–3 minutes. Use as required.

TURKEY			
frozen whole	2.75kg/6lb 4kg/9lb 5.5kg/12lb 6.8kg/15lb	MEDIUM	To defrost, place the bird breast-side down in a shallow microwaveproof dish and microwave for a quarter of the time. Turn breast-side up and cook for a further quarter of the time. Shield wing tips and legs with small pieces of foil and turn turkey over, cook for the remaining time. Microwave for 21–33 minutes for a 2.75kg/6lb bird; 32–50 minutes for a 4kg/9lb bird; 42–66 minutes for a 5.5kg/12lb bird; and 53–83 minutes for a 6.8kg/15lb bird, checking for hot spots frequently. Leave to stand, covered, for 30–45 minutes, before using.
frozen drumsticks, about 350–400g/ 12–14oz each	2 4	LOW	To defrost, place in a microwaveproof dish with the meatiest parts to the outer edge. Microwave for 12–16 minutes for 2 drumsticks; and 24–26 minutes for 4 drumsticks, turning over and rearranging once. Leave to stand, covered, for 10 minutes before using.
frozen breasts, about 225g/8oz each	2 4	LOW	To defrost, place in a microwaveproof dish. Microwave for 5–7 minutes for 2 breasts; 10–12 minutes for 4 breasts, turning over and rearranging once. Leave to stand, covered, for 10 minutes before using.

Chicken and Fruit Salad.

Defrosting Meat

BACON			
frozen rashers	225g/8oz vacuum pack	DEFROST	To defrost, place on a plate. Microwave for 2–3 minutes, turning over once.
frozen joint	450g/1lb 900g/2lb	DEFROST	To defrost, if in vacuum pack, then pierce and place on a plate. Microwave for 8 minutes for 450g/1lb joint; 15–17 minutes for 900g/2lb joint, turning over twice. Leave to stand, covered, for 20–30 minutes before using.
BEEF			
frozen uncooked joint	per 450g/1lb joints on bone per 450g/1lb boneless joints	DEFROST	To defrost, place joint on a microwaveproof roasting rack or upturned saucer in a dish. Microwave for 5–6 minutes per 450g/1lb for joints on bone; and 10 minutes per 450g/1lb for boneless joints, turning over once. Leave to stand, covered, for 30–45 minutes before using.
frozen mince	225g/8oz 450g/1lb 900g/2lb	DEFROST	To defrost, place in a microwaveproof bowl and microwave for 5 minutes for 225g/8oz; 9–10 minutes for 450g/1lb; and 17–18 minutes for 900g/2lb, breaking up twice during the cooking time. Leave to stand for 5–10 minutes before using.
frozen stewing or braising steak cubes	225g/8oz 450g/1lb	DEFROST	To defrost, place in a shallow microwaveproof dish and microwave for 5–7 minutes for 225g/8oz; 8–10 minutes for 450g/1lb, stirring twice. Leave to stand 5–10 minutes before using.
frozen hamburgers	4 x 115g/4oz	DEFROST	To defrost, place on absorbent kitchen paper and microwave for 10–12 minutes, turning over and rearranging twice. Leave to stand 2–3 minutes before using.
frozen steaks	1 x 175–225g/6–8oz 4 x 115–175g/4–6oz 2 x 225g/8oz	DEFROST	Place on a plate. Cover and microwave for 4 minutes for 1 x 175–225g/6–8oz steak, 4–6 minutes for 4 x 115–175g/4–6oz steaks; and 6–8 minutes for 2 x 225g/8oz steaks; turning over once. Leave to stand, covered, for 5–10 minutes before using.
GAMMON			
frozen uncooked joint	450g/1lb 900g/2lb	DEFROST	To defrost, place joint on a plate and microwave for 4–5 minutes for a 450g/1lb joint; and 8–10 minutes for a 900g/2lb joint. Leave to stand, covered, for 10–15 minutes before using.
frozen steaks	2 x 115g/4oz 4 x 115g/4oz	DEFROST	To defrost, place on a plate and microwave for 3–5 minutes for 2 x 115g/4oz steaks; and 7–9 minutes for 4 x 115g/4oz steaks, turning over once. Leave to stand for 5 minutes before using.
HAM			
frozen uncooked joint	450g/1lb 900g/2lb	DEFROST	To defrost, place the joint on a plate and microwave for 4–5 minutes for a 450g/1lb joint; and 8–10 minutes for a 900g/2lb joint, turning over once. Leave to stand, covered, for 10–15 minutes before using.
frozen sliced cooked	115g/4oz packet	DEFROST	To defrost, place on a plate and microwave for 3–4 minutes, turning over once. Leave to stand for 5 minutes before using.
KIDNEYS			
frozen lamb's, pig's or ox	2 lamb's 4 lamb's 2 pig's 4 pig's 225g/8oz ox 450g/1lb ox	DEFROST	To defrost, place in a microwaveproof bowl, cover and microwave for 1½–2 minutes for 2 lamb's; 4 minutes for 4 lamb's; 4 minutes for 2 pig's; 7–8 minutes for 4 pig's; 6 minutes for 225g/8oz ox; and 9–10 minutes for 450g/1lb ox kidney, rearranging 3 times. Leave to stand, covered, for 5 minutes before using.

LAMB			
frozen chops	2 x 115–175g/4–6oz loin chops 4 x 115–175g/4–6oz loin chops 2 x 115–175g/4–6oz chump chops 4 x 115–175g/4–6oz chump chops	DEFROST	To defrost, place on a microwaveproof roasting rack and microwave for 3–4 minutes for 2 x 115–175g/4–6oz loin chops; 6–8 minutes for 4 x 115–175g/4–6oz loin chops; 3–4 minutes for 2 x 115–175g/4–6oz chump chops; and 6–8 minutes for 4 x 115–175g/4–6oz chump chops, turning over and rearranging once. Leave to stand, covered, for 10 minutes before using.
frozen uncooked joint	per 450g/1lb boned and rolled joint per 450g/1lb joints on bone	DEFROST	To defrost, place joint on a microwaveproof roasting rack or upturned saucer in a dish. Microwave both types of joint for 5–6 minutes per 450g/1lb, turning over once. Leave to stand, covered, for 30–45 minutes, before using.
LIVER			
frozen slices	225g/8oz 450g/1lb	DEFROST	To defrost, spread slices on a plate. Cover and microwave for 4–5 minutes for 225g/8oz; and 8–9 minutes for 450g/1lb, turning twice. Leave to stand, covered, for 5 minutes before using.
PORK			
frozen chops	2 x 115–175g/4–6oz loin 4 x 115–175g/4–6oz loin 2 x 225g/8oz chump 2 x 225g/8oz chump	DEFROST	To defrost, place on a microwaveproof roasting rack and microwave for 3–4 minutes for 2 x 115–175g/4–6oz loin chops; 6–8 minutes for 4 x 115–175g/4–6oz loin chops; 7–9 minutes for 2 x 225g/8oz chump chops; and 14–16 minutes for 4 x 225g/8oz chump chops, turning and rearranging once. Leave to stand for 10 minutes before using.
frozen fillet or tenderloin	350g/12oz per 450g/1lb	DEFROST	To defrost, place on a microwaveproof roasting rack and microwave for 3–4 minutes for a 350g/12oz fillet or tenderloin; and 5–6 minutes per 450g/1lb, turning over once. Leave to stand for 10 minutes before using.
frozen uncooked joint	per 450g/1lb joint on bone per 450g/1lb boneless joints	DEFROST	To defrost, place joint on a microwaveproof roasting rack or upturned saucer in a dish. Microwave both types of joint for 7–8 minutes per 450g/1lb, turning over once. Leave to stand, covered, for 20–45 minutes before using.
SAUSAGEMEAT			
frozen	450g/1lb	DEFROST	To defrost, remove any wrappings and place in a shallow microwaveproof dish. Cover and microwave for 6–8 minutes, breaking up twice. Leave to stand, covered, for 4–5 minutes before using.
SAUSAGES			
frozen	4 standard 8 standard 8 chipolatas 16 chipolatas	DEFROST	To defrost separated or linked sausages, place on a plate, cover and microwave for 3–4 minutes for 4 standard; 5–6 minutes for 8 standard; 3 minutes for 8 chipolatas; and 5 minutes for 16 chipolatas, separating, turning over and rearranging twice. Leave to stand, covered, for 2–5 minutes before using.
VEAL			
frozen chops	2 4 6	DEFROST	To defrost, arrange in a microwaveproof dish so that the thicker portions are to the outer edge. Cover and microwave for 5–6 minutes for 2 chops; 8–10 minutes for 4 chops; and 12–15 minutes for 6 chops, turning and rearranging twice. Leave to stand, covered, for 5–10 minutes before using.
frozen roast	900g/2lb 1.5kg/3–3½lb 1.75kg/4–4½lb 2.25kg/5–5¼lb	DEFROST	To defrost, place in a microwaveproof dish and microwave for 16–18 minutes for a 900g/2lb joint; 24–27 minutes for a 1.5kg/3–3½lb joint; 32–36 minutes for a 1.75kg/4–4½lb joint; and 40–45 minutes for a 2.25kg/5–5¼lb joint, turning twice. Shield any thinner areas with foil as they defrost. Leave to stand, covered, for 10–20 minutes before using.

General Defrosting Chart

BISCUITS frozen	225g/8oz	DEFROST	Arrange in a circle around the edge of a plate. Microwave for 1–1½ minutes, turning over once halfway through cooking. Leave to stand for 5 minutes before serving.
BREAD frozen large white or brown sliced or uncut loaf	800g/1¾lb	DEFROST	Loosen wrapper but do not remove. Microwave for 4 minutes. Leave to stand for 5 minutes before slicing or removing ready-cut slices. Leave a further 10 minutes before serving.
frozen individual bread slices and rolls	1 slice/1 roll 2 slices/2 rolls 4 slices/4 rolls	DEFROST	Wrap loosely in kitchen paper and microwave for ¼–½ minute for 1 slice/1 roll; ½–1 minute for 2 slices/2 rolls; and 1½–2 minutes for 4 slices/4 rolls. Leave to stand for 2 minutes before serving.
frozen pitta bread	2 4	DEFROST	Place on a double thickness piece of kitchen paper and microwave for 1½–2 minutes for 2 pittas; and 2–3 minutes for 4 pittas, turning once halfway through the cooking time.
frozen crumpets	2 4	HIGH	To defrost *and* reheat. Place on a double thickness piece of kitchen paper and microwave for ½–¾ minute for 2 crumpets; 1–1½ minutes for 4 crumpets, turning once.
CAKES frozen small light fruit cake	small light fruit cake 1 slice	DEFROST	To defrost, place on a microwaveproof rack and microwave, uncovered, for 5 minutes for a whole small cake; ½–¾ minute for 1 slice, rotating twice. Leave to stand for 10 minutes before serving.
frozen Black Forest gâteau	15cm/6in gâteau	DEFROST	To defrost, place on a serving plate and microwave, uncovered, for 4–6 minutes, checking constantly. Leave to stand for 30 minutes before serving.
frozen cream sponge	15cm/6in sponge	HIGH	To defrost, place on a double thickness piece of kitchen paper and microwave for 45 seconds. Leave to stand for 10–15 minutes before serving.
frozen jam sponge	15–18cm/6–7in sponge	DEFROST	To defrost, place on a double thickness piece of kitchen paper and microwave for 3 minutes. Leave to stand for 5 minutes before serving.
frozen small sponge buns	2 4	DEFROST	To defrost, place on a rack and microwave for 1–1½ minutes for 2 buns; and 1½–2 minutes for 4 buns, checking frequently. Leave to stand for 5 minutes before serving.
frozen chocolate éclairs	2	DEFROST	To defrost, place on a double thickness sheet of kitchen paper and microwave for ¾–1 minute. Leave to stand 5–10 minutes before serving.
frozen doughnuts	2 x cream filled 2 x jam filled	DEFROST	To defrost, place on a double thickness sheet of kitchen paper and microwave for 1–1½ minutes for 2 cream-filled doughnuts; and 1½–2 minutes for 2 jam-filled doughnuts. Leave to stand 3–5 minutes before serving.
CASSEROLES frozen	2 servings 4 servings	HIGH	To defrost *and* reheat. Place in a microwaveproof dish, cover and microwave for 8–10 minutes for 2 servings; 14–16 minutes for 4 servings, breaking up and stirring twice as the casserole thaws. Leave to stand, covered, for 3–5 minutes before serving.
CHEESECAKE frozen	individual fruit-topped individual cream-topped family-size fruit-topped family-size cream-topped	DEFROST	To defrost, remove from container and place on a microwaveproof serving plate. Microwave for 1–1½ minutes for individual fruit-topped; 1–1¼ minutes for individual cream-topped; 5–6 minutes for family-size fruit-topped; and 1½–2 minutes for family-size cream-topped, rotating once and checking frequently. Leave to stand for 5–15 minutes before serving.

CREPES OR PANCAKES frozen	8	MEDIUM	To defrost, place a stack of 8 crêpes or pancakes on a plate and microwave for 1½–2 minutes, rotating once. Leave to stand for 5 minutes, then peel apart to use.
CROISSANTS frozen	2 4	DEFROST	To defrost, place on a double thickness piece of kitchen paper and microwave for ½–1 minute for 2 croissants; and 1½–2 minutes for 4 croissants.
FISH IN SAUCE frozen boil-in-the bag	1 x 170g/6oz 2 x 170g/6oz	DEFROST *or* MEDIUM	To defrost *and* cook, pierce the bag and place on a plate. Microwave for 11–12 minutes on DEFROST for 1 x 170g/6oz bag; and 10–12 minutes on MEDIUM for 2 x 170g/6oz bags. Shake gently to mix, leave to stand for 2 minutes then snip open to serve.
FLANS & QUICHES frozen unfilled cooked flans	15–18cm/6–7in	DEFROST	To defrost, place on a plate and microwave for 1–1½ minutes. Leave to stand for 5 minutes before using.
frozen filled cooked flans	10cm/4in 20cm/8in	HIGH	To defrost *and* cook, place on a plate and microwave for 1–1½ minutes for a 10cm/4in flan; and 2½–3½ minutes for a 20cm/8in flan. Leave to stand for 5 minutes before serving or using.
FRUIT CRUMBLE frozen cooked frozen uncooked	made with 900g/2lb prepared fruit and 175g/6oz crumble topping (to serve 4)	DEFROST *then* HIGH	To defrost *and* cook, microwave frozen cooked crumble for 15 minutes on DEFROST, then 5 minutes on HIGH; and frozen uncooked crumble for 15 minutes on DEFROST, then 10–14 minutes on HIGH, until cooked or reheated.
LASAGNE frozen prepared	450g/1lb	DEFROST *then* HIGH	To defrost *and* cook, remove any foil packaging and place in a microwave-proof dish. Cover and microwave on DEFROST for 8 minutes. Allow to stand for 5 minutes, then microwave on HIGH for 8–9 minutes. Brown under a preheated hot grill if liked.
ORANGE JUICE frozen concentrated	175ml/6fl oz carton	HIGH	To defrost, remove lid and place in a microwaveproof jug. Microwave for 1–1½ minutes, stirring once. Add water to dilute and serve.
PASTA frozen cooked	275g/10oz	DEFROST	To defrost *and* reheat, place in a microwaveproof dish, cover and microwave for 10 minutes, stirring twice. Leave to stand, covered, for 2–3 minutes before serving.
PASTRY frozen shortcrust and puff	200g/7oz packet 400g/14oz packet	DEFROST	Do not remove from wrappings unless unsuitable for microwave. Microwave for 2½–3 minutes for a 200g/7oz packet; and 4 minutes for a 400g/14oz packet. Leave to stand for 3 minutes before using.
PATE frozen	115g/4oz pack 200g/7oz pack 275g/10oz slice	DEFROST	Unwrap and place on a plate or leave in dish if suitable for microwave. Cover and microwave for 1 minute for 115g/4oz pack; 3–4 minutes for 200g/7oz pack; and 3–4 minutes for 275g/10oz slice, rotating 2–3 times. Leave to stand for 15–20 minutes before serving.
PIZZA frozen	30cm/12in 13cm/5in	HIGH	To defrost *and* cook. Place on a plate and microwave for 3–5 minutes for a 30cm/12in pizza; and 1½–2 minutes for a 13cm/5in pizza, rotating the dish twice.
RICE frozen cooked	225g/8oz 450g/1lb	HIGH	To defrost *and* reheat. Place in a microwaveproof dish, cover and microwave for 5–6 minutes for 225g/8oz; and 7–8 minutes for 450g/1lb, stirring twice. Leave to stand, covered, for 2 minutes before using.

SCONES frozen	2 4	DEFROST	To defrost, place on a double thickness piece of kitchen paper. Microwave for 1¼–1½ minutes for 2 scones; 3 minutes for 4 scones, rearranging once.
SOUPS frozen	300ml/½ pint/1¼ cups 600ml/1 pint/2½ cups	HIGH	To defrost *and* reheat. Place in a bowl, cover and microwave for 4–4½ minutes for 300ml/½ pint/1¼ cups; and 7–7½ minutes for 600ml/1 pint/2½ cups, breaking up and stirring 2–3 times.
STOCKS frozen	300ml/½ pint/1¼ cups 600ml/1 pint/2½ cups	HIGH	Place in a jug or bowl, microwave uncovered: 2½–3 minutes for 300ml/½ pint/1¼ cups; and 5–6 minutes for 600ml/1 pint/2½ cups, stirring and breaking up 2–3 times.
WHITE SAUCE frozen and variations (such as cheese, parsley or mustard)	300ml/½ pint/1¼ cups	HIGH	To defrost *and* reheat. Place in a microwaveproof dish and microwave for 4–5 minutes, stirring twice. Whisk to serve.
YOGURT frozen	150g/5oz carton	HIGH	To defrost, remove lid and microwave for 1 minute. Stir well and leave to stand for 1–2 minutes before serving.

Maple and Banana Teabread.

Index

Acknowledgements

For their assistance in the production of this book the
publishers would like to thank:

Panasonic Consumer Electronics
Panasonic House
Willoughby Road
Bracknell
Berks RG12 8FP

Photography by:
James Duncan
Steve Baxter
Karl Adamson
Amanda Heywood
Edward Allwright
David Jordan
David Armstrong

Prop styling for
photography:
Judy Williams
Kirsty Rawlings
Blake Minton
Madeleine Brehaut
Claire Louise Hunt

Preparation of food for
photography:
Wendy Lee
Jane Stevenson
Katherine Hawkins
Judy Williams
Christine France
Elizabeth Wolf-Cohen
Sue Maggs
Janet Brinkworth
Annie Nichols
Jenny Stacey
Elizabeth Martin

Original recipe writing:
Sarah Gates
Christine France
Maggie Pannell
Catherine Atkinson
Judy Jackson
Elizabeth Lambert-Ortiz
Janet Brinkworth
Annie Nichols
Jenny Stacey
Maxine Clark
Shirley Gill
Hilaire Walden
Elizabeth Wolf-Cohen
Sue Maggs
Manisha Kanani
Shehzad Husain
Elizabeth Martin
Carol Bowen

Microwave recipe
consultant:
Carol Bowen